**PERGAMON INTERNATIONAL LIBRARY**
of Science, Technology, Engineering and Social Studies
*The 1000-volume original paperback library in aid of education,
industrial training and the enjoyment of leisure*
Publisher: Robert Maxwell, M.C.

# THE ECONOMICS
# OF URBAN AREAS

## THE PERGAMON TEXTBOOK
## INSPECTION COPY SERVICE

An inspection copy of any book published in the Pergamon International Library will
gladly be sent to academic staff without obligation for their consideration for course
adoption or recommendation. Copies may be retained for a period of 60 days from
receipt and returned if not suitable. When a particular title is adopted or recommended
for adoption for class use and the recommendation results in a sale of 12 or more copies,
the inspection copy may be retained with our compliments. The Publishers will be
pleased to receive suggestions for revised editions and new titles to be published in this
important International Library.

# THE ECONOMICS
# OF URBAN AREAS

BY

**BRIAN GOODALL**
DEPARTMENT OF GEOGRAPHY
UNIVERSITY OF READING

**PERGAMON PRESS**
OXFORD · NEW YORK · TORONTO · SYDNEY
PARIS · FRANKFURT

| U.K. | Pergamon Press Ltd., Headington Hill Hall, Oxford OX3 0BW, England |
| U.S.A. | Pergamon Press Inc., Maxwell House, Fairview Park, Elmsford, New York 10523, U.S.A. |
| CANADA | Pergamon of Canada Ltd., 75 The East Mall, Toronto, Ontario, Canada |
| AUSTRALIA | Pergamon Press (Aust.) Pty. Ltd., P.O. Box 544, Potts Point, N.S.W. 2011, Australia |
| FRANCE | Pergamon Press SARL, 24 rue des Ecoles, 75240 Paris, Cedex 05, France |
| FEDERAL REPUBLIC OF GERMANY | Pergamon Press GmbH, 6242 Kronberg-Taunus, Pferdstrasse 1, Federal Republic of Germany |

First edition 1972

Reprinted 1974, 1978, 1979

Library of Congress Catalog Card No. 72–75677

*Printed in Great Britain by
Biddles Ltd., Guildford, Surrey*

ISBN 0 08 016892 2 hardcover

# Contents

v

## 4.   Urban Land-use Patterns

## 5.   Urban Location Decisions: (1) Businesses

## 6. Urban Location Decisions: (2) Households

## 7. Urban Growth: (1) Outward Expansion

## 12.  Government and the Urban System

# Preface

STUDENTS of urbanization and its consequences must assemble information and understand ideas from diverse fields—archaeology, building and civil engineering, demography, economics, geography, law, mathematics, politics and administration, psychology, regional science, sociology, traffic engineering, urban and regional planning, etc. This book attempts an introductory survey of one of these fields, namely economics, and emphasizes the importance of economic considerations in the functioning of urban systems. Such a general introduction demands selection and compression of material, but I hope I have at least illustrated the scope of urban economic interests. A work of this nature draws heavily on the work of others and, as an alternative to elaborate footnotes, the sources of important contributions are given in the text using the Harvard System format and are grouped together at the end of the text in alphabetical order.

An increasing general interest in the United Kingdom in urban areas and their problems has indicated the need to apply economic principles to this field. Urban growth has taken place and will continue to take place. It has been and will be accompanied by problems, many of an economic nature. Government action is necessary if urban organization is to make its fullest contribution to society's well-being. A knowledge of the economic working of the urban system as a whole and of the individual urban area will lead to a better understanding of our urban way of life and ensure that government action is as effective as possible.

It is, therefore, hoped that this book will introduce students of economics to a particular field of application of economic principles but even more that it will prove useful to all students of urbanization wishing to learn something of the economic aspects of urbanization. In that respect a prior knowledge of economics is helpful but not essential. In addition, it should enable persons whose practical work brings them, everyday, into contact with the ideas and problems discussed to see their work in a different light. Particular benefit should accrue to persons employed in or connected with the planning of urban areas and urban systems. The book will serve as a textbook in the case of students studying for certain degrees and diplomas and certain professional qualifications connected with urban studies. For example, it is suitable for students of estate management, urban and regional planning, applied economics, urban geography, land use studies, and urban studies in general as well as for students undergoing professional training in town planning, estate agency, etc., where a knowledge of urban economics and land economics is required.

Finally I wish to acknowledge colleagues who have assisted in various ways. It is, in fact, impossible to isolate specific contributions of individuals since advice and stimulus has been given over many years, most often by way of informal discussions. Thus I am alone responsible for any omissions or misinterpretations. I would, however, like to pay special thanks to the Geografisk Institut of the University of Aarhus, where I spent the academic session 1969/70, for Aarhus gave me that precious commodity time to undertake the research and begin writing. I am most grateful to Mrs Monika Wheeler for the speed and accuracy with which she has undertaken the required typing, and to Mrs Mary Petts for drawing the many diagrams. Throughout my wife has helped in numerous ways, and for her encouragement and patience I am especially thankful.

*University of Reading*                                      BRIAN GOODALL

# CHAPTER 1

# Introduction

## The Economic Dimension of Urbanization

To plan for the improvement of the urban scene whilst ignoring economic considerations would be to invite disaster. Economic resources are limited in quantity and differ in quality. Decisions to allocate these resources amongst competing uses must be taken so as to achieve the highest possible level of economic efficiency. Moreover, tomorrow must resemble today, for the cumulation of past investments far outweighs changes taking place at the present. This is not to suggest, however, that urbanization is an organic growth, determined by natural laws which cannot be controlled but only observed. Development of the urban system, that interdependent set of urban areas of varying sizes and functions, is the result of a series of decision processes. Some are formal decisions, others less so; some are conscious decisions, others not; many are private decisions, others are public ones. This complex, interdependent and never-ending stream of decisions, taken by private individuals, firms, and public organizations, has moulded and directed urban development, stimulating it at certain times and in particular places, retarding it or redirecting it at other times and other places. The state of knowledge concerning many of these processes is, however, still relatively undeveloped.

Increasingly private and public decisions turn on the spatial arrangements of the urban system. A dramatic illustration is the concentration of population and activities into metropolitan urban areas. This has intensified and brought into sharp focus previously existing problems involving resource use such as the congestion on urban roads and other local transport networks, of substandard and slum housing, the search for sources of additional water supply, the pollution of water and air, the fragmentation and lack of co-ordination in local government, as well as other quantitative and qualitative dissatisfactions with urban environments. Welfare issues and concern for the quality of life present particularly pressing and intractable problems in urban areas. An understanding of the urban process is, therefore, critical to society's ability to manage and control urban development.

Although the mechanism of urban society is largely economic, economists were amongst the last of the social scientists to recognize the urban system as a field demanding of their attention. Even so, economic efficiency is widely accepted as a socially desirable goal—materialistic as it may be people want the highest real value of output over costs from the resources available that will maximize their satisfaction. The urban system must be studied with regard to its efficiency of functioning in terms of resource use, especially as powerful forces constantly press on the urban system's ability to adapt to changing conditions. Given urbanization's economic base, the economist must be able to explain the existence, character, and function of the urban system as a whole and of the individual urban area. Such explanation and understanding should provide a basis and guide for certain policy decisions. Economic analysis will also contribute to a fuller understanding of other, less specifically economic, urban phenomena, since many of these work through the price mechanism. For example, the slum becomes more intelligible through the analysis of its economic aspects such as the labour market participation of its inhabitants, the economic motivations of slum landlords, and the returns to slum property.

Questions concerning efficiency in the use of resources abound within the urban system and the individual urban area. Certain general questions, intriguing for their intellectual character, seek to contribute an understanding of urbanization. What sizes and spatial arrangement of urban areas lead to the most efficient use of resources? What is the relationship between rapid industrialization and the expansion of the urban system? What economic principles underlie the service functions of the urban system? Is there any economic relationship between spatial patterns of invention and innovation and of urban areas? What contribution does urban growth make to national economic growth? At the level of the individual urban area there are further questions. What is its growth potential? What are the economic factors contributing to growth? To decline? Why do some urban areas grow more rapidly and at the expense of other urban areas? What forces operate in shaping intra-urban activity location patterns? What physical layout of the urban area achieves the most efficient use of resources? Is there a maximum or optimum size for an urban area?

Interesting though these and many other like questions are, there is another set of, perhaps, more urgent questions relating to present-day urban problems. Once again, efficiency of resource use is involved, and an effective solution demands that economic analysis distinguishes cause, symptoms, and consequences. What economic factors contribute to urban blight? Does the solution lie in the amount and character of urban redevelopment? Or should rehabilitation be encouraged? What are the economic disadvantages of urban sprawl? What amount and quality of urban public services should be provided? And should they be charged for? What are the economic causes and effects of traffic congestion in urban areas? What are the economic consequences of differing numbers and sizes of local government units in urban areas? What is the nature and extent of the multiplier effect of new investment? What economic basis, if any, is there for aiding an urban area whose economic base is declining? What are the economic consequences of overcrowding, excessive noise, or air pollution? Given the present state of knowledge the answers to these and many other questions are certainly not all forthcoming, but possible lines of inquiry will be suggested in many cases during the subsequent course of this book. Attention is devoted first to the questions of general economic nature since an understanding of the basic principles is essential to the analysis of problems and especially for prescription.

### The Nature of Economic Analysis

The essence of scientific investigation is to enable prediction or forecast: to be able to state definitively that under certain clearly specified conditions such and such will happen. Further, if conditions are altered in a particular way this will alter the result in a given way. To know how different results are brought about by changes in attendant conditions is the first step towards establishing control. This is a basic objective of the application of economic analysis to urban areas.

Economics as a discipline seeks explanations in terms of the behaviour of actual decision-making units. The processes of decision making, operating through the market, determine the use and allocation of scarce resources. Prices established in these markets play a crucial role in allocating resources to different uses and in determining the resultant level and distribution of income.

Any social science can approach its subject-matter from inductive or deductive poles. Induction implies generalizations based on empirical observation whilst deduction proceeds from assumed conditions, via logical reasoning, to its generalizations. Problems in undertaking controlled experiments of persons going about their everyday business and, especially, in the availability of statistics, processing techniques, and equipment, led economists to favour the deductive approach. Improvements in the latter fields have stimulated an increasing number of inductive contributions. With either approach an attempt is made to establish a body of theory which, in addition to supplying an explanatory rationale, also frequently provides a rationale for prediction. The components and variables identified by a theory are functionally related, and an understanding of the form of this relationship is vital to an appreciation of the depth of explanation in any case. Functional relationships are of three basic forms. Firstly, a cause-and-effect situation where, given certain circumstances, there is one and only one result. Secondly, a situation where the operation of chance factors produces a variety of results all of which cluster around a theoretical end result. Thirdly, a situation in which variables show a tendency to move similarly. This, of course, involves correlation but not necessarily causality as in the two previous cases. The second situation, of probabilistic causality, is increasingly relied upon in explaining urban economic decisions and patterns. The purpose of theory building and analysis is, therefore, to clarify these relationships, and the need to define clearly the exact conditions under which the generalization operates should be obvious. Within the body of theory there is a distinction between explanatory theory and normative theory. Explanatory theory tells "what is and why" but normative theory states "what ought to be". The two need not coincide. Social sciences in general have shied away from the normative element, but if the efficiency of existing situations is to be evaluated and assistance rendered in solving the problems facing society, then a positive attitude must be taken as to "what ought to be". Theoretical knowledge provides a key to understanding, indicates the type of factors to be looked for in any situation, and offers a guide to how conditions should be influenced to improve upon a situation.

Aims of decision-making units, such as profit-maximization for the individual firm and satisfaction-maximization for the individual consumer, are assumed, as well as the broader collective aims that should guide the behaviour of larger interest groups like an urban community. In order to decide whether, from an economic point, one situation or action is to be preferred to another, either a satisfaction or an efficiency criterion may be used. Both involve problems of measurement. How is satisfaction objectively measured? How do changes in the value of money affect the efficiency criterion? (Lean and Goodall, 1966, pp. 226–7; Lean, 1969, pp. 3–5). No situation should be judged allocationally superior without cognizance of its distributional effects. The most efficient use of resources is represented by the production of those goods and services that have the highest real value over costs.

## Economics in Urban Analysis

THE PRICE MECHANISM

Basic to any economic approach is the mechanism of prices and markets which is relied upon to a considerable extent to order the economy, including the urban economy. Price and allocation theory must be called upon to explain the internal functioning of parts of the urban economy. Consider, for example, the application of elementary price theory to a simplified urban accommodation market. Assume there is, in a given urban area, a fixed number of identical units of accommodation which are only available for renting and a population with known income distribution. The price of a unit of accommodation will be determined by the interaction between the inelastic supply of accommodation and the demand for that accommodation. Price will tend to an equilibrium level at which quantity demanded is equal to quantity supplied. In Fig. 1.1a this is where demand curve $D$ intersects the supply curve $S$ establishing a price $OP$ at which quantity $OX$ is both demanded and supplied. Now assume an increase in demand due, say, to an increase in the urban area's population. This is shown by a new demand curve $D_1$, and price rises from $OP$ to $OP_1$. At a price of $OP$ there would be an excess demand of $XY$, and competition between the greater number of persons for the same amount of accommodation drives price up to $OP_1$, at which quantity demanded (on $D_1$) equals

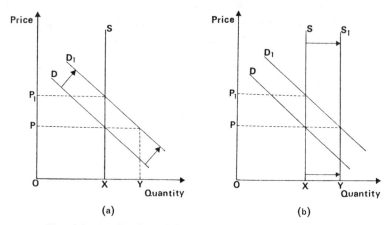

Fig. 1.1. Application of demand–supply analysis to urban accommodation.

quantity supplied. At this higher price landlords will be making extra profits. This will be an incentive to existing landlords and new landlords to build and supply more units of accommodation. This represents an increase in supply, shown in Fig. 1.1b by the movement of the supply curve from $S$ to $S_1$, and leads to a decrease in price. The adjustment to supply, *ceteris paribus*, continues to take place until the profits of landlords return to a normal level. That will be when quantity $OY$ is both demanded and supplied at price $OP$.

Therefore changes in demand, working through the price mechanism, bring about alterations in resource allocation. Resources will automatically be used in the most efficient way because producers, in striving to maximize profits, must respond to consumer demand as well as producing any given output at the lowest possible cost. The price mechanism also ensures that consumer satisfaction is maximized since it is reasonable to assume that each consumer spends his income in such a way as to maximize his satisfaction, and the profit motive sees to it that the desired goods and services are forthcoming.

Within an urban area it is the price system which plays a leading part in allocating land to particular uses, uses to certain locations, labour between urban firms, retail goods to urban consumers, and so on. The adjustment of the individual urban area to growth and change would largely take place through the operation of the principles outlined. Indeed, some students have argued that many present-day urban problems arise out of the fact that behaviour in certain cases is not subject to the discipline of price as in the case of traffic congestion (Thompson, 1965a, Introduction). However the presentation of equilibrium conditions as in the above example may imply a tendency toward the attainment of equilibrium in the real world. Equilibrium can never be attained in real life. The value of such equilibrium analysis lies in the better grasp it enables one to obtain of the laws of change and the workings of a system. The study of the urban real property market as a whole, its sub-markets, the factors influencing the demand for and supply of urban land uses and of the extent to which the operation of the price mechanism in these spheres brings about an efficient allocation of resources in urban areas, is thus an integral part of microeconomic urban analysis.

IMPERFECTIONS IN THE PRICE MECHANISM

However, the price mechanism does not function as smoothly in practice as in the theoretical situation, nor are all goods and services subject to prices. These limitations and limits must be recognized and understood. Prices yield a utilization of resources which is socially efficient only if those prices reflect the social costs and benefits involved. Social costs and benefits are here taken to include private costs and benefits. For any given action social cost will be greater than private cost only if that action gives rise to negative externalities. Similarly, social benefit may be greater than private benefit where a given action results in positive externalities. Externalities are, therefore, costs and benefits not reflected through the price mechanism to the person carrying out an action but they are represented by increased private costs and benefits to other persons. For example, in the case of traffic congestion one additional car-user will add to the delays to existing road-users, that is, increase their private costs because of lower journey speeds and increased fuel consumption. The sum of these increases in private costs equals the social cost of the journey made by the additional car-user, but the latter only pays the private costs associated with his journey. If the additional car-user had to pay the social costs of his journey as well he may consider, say, alternative means of transport, in which case resources may well be used differently. Such externality effects are very common in urban areas.

Differences between social and private costs and between social and private benefits lead to a misallocation of resources. Assuming, as is usual under conditions of pure competition, the use of marginal cost pricing, in a situation where marginal social cost is greater than marginal private cost the producer would equate price with marginal private cost in order to maximize his profits. However, equating price and marginal social cost would bring about the most efficient allocation of resources from the community's point of view. Where the typical motivation in urban land development is the hope for large profits, the developer may show little sense of social responsibility for sound community development. For example, housing estates may be constructed without a full range of ancillary facilities. In theory any productive or consumptive action causing negative externalities, as with urban car-users, should be taxed to internalize them, whilst any action yielding positive externalities, say private provision of children's playgrounds, should be subsidized accordingly. There cannot be pure competition in all sectors of the economy as this line of argument demands, for, in some cases marginal cost pricing would lead to losses, as in the provision of roads, nor can some of the externalities be internalized because of problems of isolating and evaluating the effects involved. Effective cost–benefit techniques therefore have a vital role to play in public decision taking at the urban level.

The market provides a reasonably accurate measure of consumer preferences, and thus the amount of resources consumers wish to devote to the production of their purchases in those sectors of the economy dealing with the more personal and individual goods and services. What of goods for which there are no prices? Many aspects of the urban economy are concerned with such collective goods and services as education, roads, police, and fire services. Since there is no market in which the profit motive can guide resources into the provision of collective goods it is difficult to decide upon the values society places on them and the extent to which resources should be used in their provision. Action on the part of government bodies is necessary to ensure their provision. This is an extremely important realm of operation for urban authorities because the provision of these non-profit goods is critical to the success and efficiency of private profit-making ventures.

The reallocative function of the market for resources may not proceed as smoothly as in our theoretical situation, so the supply of goods and services is slow to adjust to changes in demand. There are various hindrances to the free flow of resources between productive lines. Where skilled workers in the building trades have to serve a long apprenticeship then, *ceteris paribus*, in the absence of a reserve of unemployed such workers, the longer the time period that must elapse before supply could be increased by the amount $XY$ in Fig. 1.1b. Persons often react to competition by erecting barriers against it. The existing landlords of the earlier situation may form an organization that lays down rules of conduct which allow them to obtain a higher price for their accommodation than in the absence of such collusion. They may be able to prevent the entry of new landlords, perhaps, because they control the supply of building land or materials. If there is no collusion individual landlords may try to persuade potential tenants that their accommodation is differentiated from the rest so that they can obtain higher prices and hence extra profits. Monopoly situations thus arise and, moreover, monopoly power does not have to be absolute before its effects are noticeable. In urban areas "natural" monopoly situations are not uncommon where the level of demand in the urban area as a whole or part of an urban area is sufficient to support only one producer.

There are two further reasons why the monopoly element may be particularly relevant in urban situations. Firstly, the non-transferability of land in geographical space means that every site has a unique spatial relationship with all other sites. Here the degree of monopoly power in respect of a given site will depend on the extent to which other sites are close substitutes. Secondly, the fragmentation of ownership of urban land may prevent some land being transferred to its most efficient use. This may occur when the most efficient use requires the amalgamation of adjacent plots and some owners refuse to co-operate because they hope to take advantage of their monopoly position. To overcome such problems in the case of the transfer of land from private to public ownership for use as roads, schools, and the like may call for powers of compulsory purchase.

However well the market may work in allocating resources to their most efficient uses, the result may not accord with wise social policy. One reason may be the failure to provide collective goods which has already been referred to. Another reason concerns the distribution of income and wealth, itself the outcome of market forces, for the price mechanism leads to a maximization of satisfaction within a given distribution of income and wealth. An alternative distribution may well give a higher aggregate level of satisfaction; thus it may be necessary for the Government to redistribute income or otherwise interfere with the working of the price mechanism. In urban areas the price mechanism also has to work within a given physical framework which represents the historical cumulation of past investment decisions. The allocation of resources within this framework may not be as efficient as the pattern of resource use that would be produced in the absence of such constraints. The durability of urban buildings is important here as such an investment decision is expensive to reverse.

The price mechanism, therefore, rather obviously fails to provide anything resembling the most efficient use of resources and, indeed, a number of urban problems may well arise from the imperfections and malfunctionings of the market mechanism. However, the price mechanism does have a role to play in the urban system, and this needs to be examined in some detail. What would be the result if the price system worked perfectly? How do the various imperfections discussed alter the efficiency of operation of the urban system and the individual urban area? What role can prices perform within the urban economy and how can the framework of the market mechanism be improved to increase the efficiency of resource utilization? These are some of the questions that must eventually be answered if the maximum level of operational efficiency of urban areas is to be achieved and maximum use is to be made of the advantages of the price mechanism as an aid in determining efficient resource use.

## GROWTH AND MACRO-ECONOMICS

Both the macro and growth aspects of economics are concerned with aggregates, and especially with the national level of those aggregates. On the one hand, macro-economic theory has concentrated on explaining short-term fluctuations in total income and product and has emphasized the part played by aggregate demand in determining investment, employment, production, and, therefore, income levels. Growth analysis, on the other hand, seeks an explanation of the rate of growth of the productive base and represents a longer-term emphasis designed to show how and why the upper limit of supply changes over time. The existence of this body of theory at the national level means that economic studies of urban systems and areas, and, for that matter, regions, are freed from the start from having to explain the general state of the national economy.

Economic studies of urban systems and areas will be concerned with aggregate performance at the national level. In this respect it is important to realize the interaction between national and sub-national levels and that national policies have repercussions at the sub-national level. Therefore an individual urban area can only partially control its future course for the effectiveness with which it pursues macro and growth objectives is seriously limited by what is happening nationally. The relationship between an urban area, its region, and the rest of the nation, the variations which occur within the urban system, and the relationships between variables within urban areas, are therefore among the factors studied as having a bearing on aggregate urban performance.

At the aggregate level of analysis many urban and regional problems would appear to stem from undesirable rates of growth. Too fast a growth brings such problems as congestion of facilities and the appearance of bottlenecks in the supply of resources. To grow too slow may bring structural unemployment as new opportunities are not created quickly enough to take up all the workers displaced by declining industry. Urban governments must understand the growth process if they are to have any influence on the future course of events and, in particular, on the nature of the investment decision. The least influence can be exerted by urban government in attempting to remedy the local effects of national business cycles. Here it must rely on the national government to ensure a level of aggregate demand sufficient for the full employment of resources.

Conventional tools of economic analysis can be applied most readily in the case of static urban income analysis: to the level of income, its growth, stability, and distribution. The nature of the economic opportunities found in urban areas is vital here. The current growth rate of an urban area's income level depends, in the short run, on the rate of increase in demand for its exports. Thus an urban area specializing on the production of commodities with an income elastic demand will have brighter growth prospects than an area producing goods whose demand is income inelastic. The stability of income also depends on the nature of the products, for the demand for durables, whose purchase can be easily postponed, is less stable than the demand for non-durables. The range of economic opportunities must influence the distribution of income for the degree of inequality of incomes will reflect the industry mix. The local or urban multiplier effect will be especially important since extra income gained from increased exports may generate additional imports and, therefore, have less impact on the urban area than where local production, consequent upon increased local demand, replaced imports.

Population responds to economic opportunity. Therefore the nature of an urban area's economic opportunities is a guide to the size and character of the future population, income levels, and consumption wants. Moreover, a consideration of the structure and function of the urban economy as a whole as it fits into the larger economies of the region and the nation will be essential for any economic explanation of the internal functioning of an urban area. Analysis of aggregate urban performance complements the analysis of urban spatial organization.


LOCATION THEORY

Although traditional economics treated location as a constant, a body of theory has been developed to explain location in space in economic terms. Economic location theory, dealing particularly with manufacturing industry, focuses on the firm and the individual establishment, and lends itself to optimizing locational behaviour with minimization of transport costs and maximization of profits. Location theory determines location within a framework of general equilibrium and requires optimizing behaviour of producers and consumers throughout the system. These principles of locational choice suggest that, ideally, every location decision is a matter of balancing anticipated costs and revenues at alternative sites under differing degrees of uncertainty in order to determine the profit-maximizing location. The relative advantages of possible locations at any time reflect differentials in input and transport costs and differing opportunities in respect of scale and agglomeration economies. All costs vary over time and space, but only transport costs vary systematically with distance from a given point, and this fact underlies the regularity of theoretical spatial patterns. In practice this dependence on what is essentially a single-factor explanation, the variable cost of overcoming distance under *ceteris paribus* conditions, is a critical limitation of the theory. Moreover, the result is a static pattern and the analysis is not geared to the treatment of locational mobility and locational stability over time. Of course much can be inferred about locational transformation by resort to comparative statics, and the principles of industrial location analysis will remain a powerful tool in the analysis of short-run urban and regional change.

Location theory contributes to an understanding of the factors influencing locational decisions on an inter-urban and inter-regional scale rather than on the intra-urban level. It will indicate that one urban area is the preferred location to alternative urban areas but will rarely distinguish the preferred site in that urban area from alternatives. However, the same general principles of locational choice apply to the distribution of productive and consumptive activity within an urban area although the relative importance of the factors may be very different. Locational choice via the market in practice does not work as perfectly as in the establishment of the theoretical optimum since the imperfections of the price mechanism discussed earlier have repercussions for locational patterns. Especially difficult is the problem of co-ordination of market location decisions under conditions of imperfect knowledge. The profit-maximizing criterion may be questioned.

Decisions may be made on the basis of a satisfactory, rather than maximum level of profits. Where satisficer motives replace optimizer ones there is greater flexibility of locational choice. The relative efficiency of alternative urban land-use patterns needs to be evaluated, actual patterns explained, and future ones forecast. Location theory provides some of the keys to understanding these problems and finding solutions.

Thus it would appear that the tools of economic analysis are especially suited (1) to explaining causal as distinct from empirical relationships in urban systems, urban economies, and urban space, (2) to evaluating the relative merits of alternative courses of action affecting the urban system and urban areas on a cost–benefit basis, and (3) to providing a foundation on which policy decisions can be based.

## The Use of Economic Models

It is as well to be aware of the two senses in which models are used in economic analysis. "Model" may be used to describe either the theoretically abstract situation constructed as the basis for a deductive line of reasoning or the operational model used in the prediction of future patterns of economic behaviour. Theoretical models designed, for example, to explain the spatial distribution of economic activities usually begin with certain simplifying assumptions regarding spatial homogeneity. Whilst such general assumptions are not unacceptable in large-dimension models, at the scale of the individual urban area such assumptions can seriously detract from the usefulness of conclusions drawn from the model. The degree of abstraction may, therefore, be responsible for these models providing only partial insights into the explanation of actual patterns. In spite of divergences between theoretical models and the real world it is important to understand something about the character of the urban economy and urban structure in conditions which are theoretically optimal for the functioning of urban activities. This is especially so where the normative element reflects optimization for the community as a whole. As a consequence ways of implementing public policy may be suggested and the possible limitations of public policy in regulating and organizing the urban economy may be recognized. Thus a principal objective of developing theories, relating to urban function and spatial structure, is to contribute to techniques for forecasting and predicting, especially where an evaluation of alternative courses of public action is involved. It is here that operational models come into their own, the more so as past trends are infrequently a reliable guide to future development.

A substantial gap exists between the most precise theoretical formulations of locational behaviour, empirical investigation, and the construction of operational models. The operational model, whilst maintaining a commitment to a theory, must be an accurate representation of reality yet still contain sufficient simplification/aggregation to allow its statement in terms of mathematical structure. Such models have an impact beyond urban economics, most obviously in planning fields. In the planning process the relationships analysed via operational models can be used to mitigate trends considered to be undesirable and to speed up desirable trends. In order for his current decisions to be responsive to the future environment, the planner needs some idea of the size and shape of the future urban economy and its structure. Thus operational models, as well as assisting in the evaluation of priorities, allow the planner to anticipate public service needs and meet them in an efficient and timely manner.

Planners are interested in changing trends. Operational models, in identifying and quantifying strategic relationships, provide details of the instrumental variables that can and should be influenced by policy in order to achieve objectives. The planner's ability to change trends so that they fall in line with declared objectives depends on his understanding of the direct and indirect consequences of changes in the instrumental, or control, variables.

## Urban Policy and Planning Implications

The earlier discussion of economic analysis revealed its strengths for use in applied research. In particular the ability to evaluate alternatives can provide valuable guidance for the formulation of public policy. The difference between two analytical situations will indicate the economic gain from a given action or the economic cost of not carrying out that action. A clarification of the economic issues involved is achieved, but the choice between two prescribed courses of action implies some hierarchy of underlying values. Economic forces cannot be ignored by policy-makers since efficiency in the use of resources will be a criterion having some bearing on public decisions. In this context planning may be regarded as a system designed to improve the rationality of decisions in terms of the major objectives of society. Although policy decisions are influenced by the economic activities in an area they, in turn, shape those economic activities, and the resultant adaptation of economic forces to policy measures may bring about a more or less efficient use of resources. It would obviously be preferable if economic forces could be harnessed to help achieve policy objectives.

Economic growth, which is often assumed to be the lever through which desirable changes can be effected, does not automatically solve urban problems. It follows, therefore, that public intervention is both necessary and wise. Economic analysis contributes to policy decisions relating to both the urban economy in aggregate and internal urban structure. For example, an understanding of the factors determining functional relationships between urban areas, such as degrees of specialization and relative transport costs, enables the planner to con- sider the geographical distribution of urban areas in a region in terms of that development which will make the best use of the region's re- sources. The extent to which current investment decisions can be influenced is critical here. The planning process directly or indirectly bears on investment decisions which account for a large part of national resources. About one-eighth of the annual gross national product of the United Kingdom represents investment in additions to or improve- ments of the urban and regional infrastructure and buildings. There is a need for the rational assessment of this investment. As planning is fast becoming the major determinant of the location of this investment, the planner must understand the investment decision and its role in the processes of production and consumption because, in turn, that investment is the major determinant of the level of efficiency with which resources are used.

Policy with respect to the aggregate performance of the urban economy is still in its infancy, but there are certain pointers as to the role local government can play. National governments, by increasing their expenditures, can raise the level of demand within the nation and hence employment, but an urban or regional government cannot exert an equivalent leverage on local spending by increasing its expenditure. This is because a local government would find it difficult to run the considerable and continuing deficit that would be necessary and, more important, a large proportion of its increased spending would be dissipated throughout the national economy via the purchase of imports into the area. Therefore if it is accepted that central government economic policy, operating at the national level, has banished for ever depression and its associated mass unemployment, future problems at the urban and regional level will arise, more and more, as a result of changes affecting geographically concentrated and specialized industries. These will show as localized depressed areas and structural unemployment. This situation may accord local government a role in manpower/employment policy since structural unemployment may be tackled from the supply side. Local governments may facilitate redeployment in various ways.

Growth *per se* frequently appears as the local target. However, a better utilization of resources might be obtained by encouraging the growth of urban areas of a certain size rather than the growth of all urban areas.

The planning of the internal functioning of urban areas is important because of the extreme interdependence of urban activities. Here the critical issue appears to be the allocation and management of land so that the more general community interest may be served without too severe an infringement of private liberty. Again, the success of government efforts to guide and control land use depends on how well changes in spatial patterns of interaction and intraurban location have been anticipated. To illustrate: in the case of a new urban area a target population is necessary because of the relationship between the size of urban area and urban form. Should the population increase indefinitely there is the problem of adjusting the proportion of land used for non-profit uses, especially roads, relative to other land uses. Urban planning must be economically responsible for, as policy expands, the market will perform a declining role in allocation and organization. Planning will become more and more responsible for the efficient use of resources. Certain measures which see a more compact urban form as increasing the efficiency of resource use may well be dissipated by the powerful effects of transport improvement. Indeed, this suggests the question as to whether economic forces can be controlled and altered? The economic forces and motivations which have brought about the observed pattern of agglomeration in order to minimize transport costs and time may be so compelling that only the most rigorous and expensive forms of intervention can alter the size of urban areas. London and Paris, in particular, have had little success in curbing their growth.

In summary it can be said that the present interest in urban and regional economics has come to the fore as a result of rising policy issues—the economic growth and decline of urban areas and regions, the local impact of national policies and expenditures, urban transportation, public services and public housing, urban redevelopment, and the like. The essentially applied and constructive nature of urban economics is reflected in the economist's concern with what society can do with urban areas, i.e., to improve their efficiency of operation, rather than with what the urban environment may be doing to society. Society's goals may frequently clash, and the nature of economic analysis in studying choice between alternatives is well suited to advise here, hence its indispensable role in policy formation.

Economic forces are among the most powerful of urbanizing forces and urbanization has wrought a transformation of society. The role of economic forces in this process and their contribution to the present operation of the urban system must be appreciated and understood if society is to solve successfully the many problems of urban origin it now faces. Often an appreciation of the full impact of economic factors can best be obtained through analysis along the traditional lines of abstract models, and this technique is used in introducing such concepts as the urban land market and the size and spacing of urban areas. Once this clarification is achieved, simplifying assumptions can be removed, imperfections arising in practice can be examined, and the effect of constraints imposed by society within which economic forces operate can be worked out. In this way the economic aspects of council housing may be understood as they fit into the general urban pattern and economy or the location of a new, planned urban area can be appreciated in terms of the whole urban system. This will lead naturally on to an outline of the possible contribution of economic analysis to the future development of the urban system and individual urban areas.

# CHAPTER 2

# The Economic Basis of Urban Areas

## Urbanization as an Economic Process

The present organization of our society is especially dependent on an urban way of life. The rate of economic growth of an economically advanced nation will approximate the average rate of growth among its urban areas because of the proportion of its population living in urban areas and its economic activities which take place in urban areas. It would appear that, for at least the last two centuries, economic factors have been prime motivators of urban development. Firstly, it was industrial urbanization. Then, in the twentieth century, tertiary urbanization has become increasingly important. In each case non-economic factors have reinforced the economic stimulus. A characteristic feature of the history of development of all economically advanced societies has been the coincident growth of population, employment in non-agricultural occupations, and urban areas. Developed economies do not occur without the presence of a large population specialized in non-agricultural pursuits and living in a system of functionally inter-related urban areas. The latter constitutes a hierarchy ranging from one or more metropolitan centres at the top to many medium and small urban areas at its broad base. Indeed, in metropolitan-dominated societies the old order distinction between urban and rural is in need of revision.

The fact that the degree of urbanization rises sharply as industrialization increases provokes the question whether economic development, in the form of widespread industrialization, can ever take place without the concomitant growth of urban areas. It would appear not. Urbanism is inundating all areas of the world. The fastest rate of urban growth is in those parts of Africa, Asia, and South America where economic development is now being stimulated by industrialization.

This strength and persistence of the phenomenon of urbanization is adequate testimony to its superiority as a technique for managing the use of resources and contributing to the rate of economic growth. Urban areas are the most telling example of man's ability to fashion the physical, economic, and social world he lives and works in. Viewed from the economic standpoint, urbanization is a method of using resources to meet society's needs. Efficiency in the use of resources within an urban area and between urban areas is critical to the present and future economic health of the nation. The creation or improvement of urban areas cannot, therefore, be considered an end or goal of society but is a means to an end. It is a process—not an end product.

An economic system is also a spatial system. Neither the individual urban area nor the system of urban areas can be understood if treated in the spaceless way that economic theory examines the critical elements of the price system under conditions of perfect competition. At national and higher levels urban space is discontinuous or pointform. Why do economic activities not spread themselves evenly over geographic (physical) space? The answer will be found in terms of the effects of transport costs and the heterogeneity of space from the economic view. Urbanization is an economic process with a spatial dimension in which factors of production, firms, and localities become increasingly specialized and more differentiated from each other. Specialization provides the essential link between the technical and spatial conditions of economic progress for specialization of function is accompanied by area specialization. The process brings a territorial division of labour between urban and rural areas and differentiates between urban areas. The distribution of growth between urban areas is thus one dimension of the pattern of economic growth. Moreover, as an urban area grows in population, acquires new functions, and expands existing activities, its relationships with its hinterland and with the system of urban areas are altered, its physical territory is extended, and its internal arrangements undergo adjustments.

## An Economic Definition of "Urban"

It has been customary to define urban in terms of physical characteristics reflecting the spatial agglomeration of population and activities.

Common to such definitions are (1) a physical element which emphasizes the high density settlement of the continuous built-up area and its separation from other urban centres by a much greater area of thinly settled land, and (2) an occupational element which recognizes the concentration of employment in secondary and tertiary industries. All such definitions point to the irrelevance of the administrative or political boundary of the urban area in the definitional context. This is equally true for the urban area's economic identity although, as will be discussed in a later chapter, the existence of local political boundaries is not without economic consequences.

Urbanization as a process has been stressed in the first section, and it is not the high density settlement of spatial agglomerations *per se* that is important in this context, nor even the distinctive occupational structure. If urbanization is regarded as a process, then any definition should reflect the processual characteristics. In this case it is the economic interactions which are to be singled out as providing an identity for an urban area. Economic interaction takes place in markets and the urban area may be viewed as an economy comprising a complex of markets: a labour market, a land market, a housing market, a capital market, and markets for numerous goods and services. Each of these markets has a spatial extent. For example, in the case of labour the outer limit of the market is given by the maximum commuting range. For a specialized commodity produced in the urban area, consumers may be distributed throughout the world, whereas with certain public services the market may be limited to the area under a given political jurisdiction. The spatial extent of each of these markets is not necessarily coincident, but they overlap and interlock in such a way as to form an urban economy which may be recognized as a primary unit of employment and income generation.

## Economic Motives as Urbanizing Forces

Although other factors contribute forcibly to urbanization, a knowledge of basic economic motives is essential to the understanding of urbanization. Economic systems develop out of the need for some form of organization to ensure that demands for goods and services are satisfied by the production of the right kinds and correct quantities of supplies. The urban system is no exception. The system of urban areas has therefore evolved as an effective economic mechanism in response to the ever-changing economic needs of society in the production, distribution, and consumption of goods and services. The existence of an urban system will bring about a more efficient use of resources and, hence, higher *per capita* real incomes than a society which lacks an urban system. The individual urban area becomes a productive/ distributive shell within which particularly output but also distributive efficiency is or is not achieved. An economic rationale thus pervades the individual urban area and the hierarchical system of urban areas.

The basic economic functions performed by urban areas therefore relate to the production, distribution, and consumption of goods and services in which scarce resources, with alternative uses, are allocated among unlimited wants. It is a task of producers to supply an elaborate assortment of goods and services where they can be conveniently consumed by individuals. That convenient location, for both production and consumption, is the urban area. In fact the urban area's major advantage is being able to facilitate specialization in the production and distribution of goods and services. Urban areas therefore function as specialist production centres where secondary and tertiary industries concentrate. Moreover, in economically advanced societies where people, urban areas, and regions specialize, individuals of similar income, irrespective of their geographical location, demand basically similar baskets of goods. Urban areas provide for the several steps involved in the collection and distribution of materials and commodities so functioning as market centres or central places in the distribution system. Finally, the urban area itself constitutes an obvious market for goods, a place of mass consumption.

The economic functions of urban areas can be used to identify similarities in economic emphasis between individual urban areas and will provide the basis for a classificatory system in terms of urban economic function. However, the methodology of classification will not be pursued further because of its limited usefulness for the broader aims of urban theory.

In placing the emphasis on specialization it will be realized that the economic basis of any urban area is the export of goods and/or services. The locations of the basic economic activities supporting individual urban areas are determined exogenously to the individual urban area by relative advantage in regional, national, and international markets. In practice the system of urban areas never approaches the high order of rationality developed in theoretical studies because of the influence of the past and of non-economic factors. Nevertheless, given the natural occurrence of resources and the level of technology, the actual geographical distribution of urban areas is rational to the extent that all output is obtained at minimum cost consistent with the possible uses of the nation's limited stock of resources. An economic rationale in large measure therefore underlies the present system of urban areas.

A similar argument applies for the individual urban area. If a prime motive for the existence of an urban area is the opportunity it affords for the satisfaction of economic wants, then the main determinants of the internal form of the urban area must be factors which reflect upon its ability to perform the economic functions of production and distribution as efficiently as possible. Thus the urban area, itself viewed as an economic mechanism, comprises many smaller economic (and non-economic) mechanisms. The spatial pattern within the urban area is the collective result of a large number of independent business and household location decisions and transport choices arrived at through a process of competitive bidding. Although every individual or firm may occasionally act irrationally, the internal environment of the urban area is essentially rational with each firm or household occupying its profit or satisfaction maximizing location. Specialization is once again important, for the efficient functioning of the urban area is facilitated by specialization of land use within the urban area.

## Economic Forces in Past Urban Development

The spatial pattern of economic activity at any given time is the product of both economic and non-economic forces, and this pattern will obviously not correspond to the optimalizing assumptions of economic theory. Even so, the urban area in each major historical period has been a highly specialized phenomenon particularly adapted to the needs of the era, including the economic needs.

The clustering of population into communities is a basic form of human settlement. It arises from man's need to co-operate with his fellows in order to survive, from his gregarious instinct, from his need of a place of assembly for defensive or religious reasons, from the drive to overcome the physical obstacle of distance for human interaction, and from certain economic considerations, particularly the availability of external economies. Although the origin of urban agglomeration as a form of human settlement is obscure, it has been suggested that the urban area as a political entity came first (Boulding, 1963, p. 134) as political means were devised to channel agricultural surpluses into the hands of a ruler. Urban areas as economic entities develop only after society has developed considerably beyond the primitive struggle for existence when man finds that under certain circumstances to produce and trade is more profitable than coercion.

As surrounding countrysides set up urban areas to perform those functions that could be best performed from central positions, so pre-industrial urban areas functioned primarily as government or religious centres, secondarily as commercial centres. Market centres emerged, after goods began to move to consumers in exchange systems larger than the immediate community or social group, either as periodic fairs in systems of local trade or with the establishment of fairs along long-distance trade routes (Berry, 1967, pp. 107–11). Thus until the Industrial Revolution trade was the prime economic force in urbanization. Urban areas as central places providing, for that time, comprehensive services for their tributary areas, spread throughout productive territory. Such urban areas mostly developed out of medieval political importance and are older than urban areas whose origin is with the development of industry. The urban areas which existed were essentially small service centres for an agrarian way of life. Within the urban system factors of production were relatively unspecialized, economic functions and organizations tended to be uniform, simple, and scattered, any production of goods depended upon animate sources of power and prices were determined by haggling. Although there was a marked social differentiation in the urban population there was a minimum of specialization in urban land use. There was also little specialization between urban areas in terms of the economic functions they performed. These urban areas did not transform the societies that contained them, for the majority of the population remained rural, and the source of wealth and power remained with the land. Economic development was inhibited by the educated person's negative attitude towards business activity and work with the hands, by the lack of product standardization, and by the meagre facilities for credit and capital formation. Economic and political centres of gravity did not, therefore, shift to urban areas until the Industrial Revolution.

Where technological advance and its consequent expansion of manufacturing calls forth such a large supply of mineral and material inputs and provides such a vast and varied selection of outputs relative to the food requirements of the non-agricultural labour force, the locational ties of manufacturing and service activities to agricultural population will be broken and an industrial–urban transformation of society will take place. Such was the impact of the Industrial Revolution. Urban areas supplied the essential mechanism for the transformation of simple handicrafts into manufacturing units involving higher risks than any previously known. Thus urban areas became the decision-taking centres. In its early stages industrial development needs to be geographically polarized, as on the coalfields in the nineteenth century, because entrepreneurial ability is lacking outside such growing centres. The needs of industry determined the location of new urban areas, and existing urban areas had to adapt to the needs of industry if they were not to face relative, indeed absolute, decline.

Industrialization as an economic force in urbanization cannot be denied. Based on advantages accruing from internal economies of scale, factories assembled large labour forces and so created, virtually unaided, urban areas. Large-scale operations at one stage of production create opportunities for greater specialization at other stages through backward and forward linkages. Advantages of technical linkage coupled with high transport costs on intermediate products brought together in space these successive stages in production to form an industrial complex. This created a large urban area. The achievement of scale economies by some is a source of potential external economies that can be internalized by others. New industry, and especially small firms, are attracted by those external economies, making the urban area even larger.

Initial advantage has often been critical in urban–industrial growth. The actions of neighbouring urban areas represent a major constraint on the growth opportunities of a given urban area. If neighbouring areas attract industry on a larger scale or make an earlier start, this is a severe handicap to the given urban area's chances of growth and promotion in the urban hierarchy. Moreover, existing locations of industry are characterized by tremendous inertia and offer such a compounding of man-made advantages that they exert considerable influence on the locations of new factories. Advances in production technology usually occur in response to particular problems which arise most frequently in existing centres of industrial concentration. Invention and innovation are neither randomly distributed through time nor over space. Industrial structure or mix may be seen as the key factor in the relative growth of urban areas.

Lampard (1968) views this as a process of system transformation in the sense that the urban system can evolve new structures so as to remain stable under changing conditions. Industrial urbanization is not disequilibrating, nor does it head towards equilibrium under very specific conditions, but instead the mechanism or system adjusts itself to accommodate the changes taking place. Firstly, the adoption of innovations by individual and local specialists brings about increasing spatial differentiation in the urban system. Later, following further technical and organizational changes, reintegration of productive processes and business units may take place and the actions of adapters generalize the production throughout the system. Thus, in the long run, urban areas—as they grow larger—become more alike.

The industrial specialization of urban areas both required and facilitated the construction of an entirely new urban environment. Once the economic rationality of the industrial urban area had been established, secondary factors were called into operation. Urbanization in the nineteenth century was the stimulus for better sanitation, housing, and the like.

The advantages of specialization can only be reaped by incurring transport costs. Only through the transport system can the essential movement of persons and goods from one specialized urban area to another be maintained. The centralization of production and consumption which has been a feature of industrial development could only have occurred with parallel developments in improved methods of transport which allowed urban areas to amass raw materials from and distribute products over wide areas. The revolution in transport helped transform a relatively scattered and uniform mode of primitive activities into a highly differentiated but closely integrated system of local specialization. Urban areas, therefore, commonly develop at convenient nodal points in the transport network; at route junctions, transhipment points, and break-of-bulk points, as with the axiate spiderweb of urban area locations established during the era of rail transport. Today the major effect of transport improvements is to increase the competitive advantage of the largest urban areas.

The principal element in the nineteenth-century expansion of urban population was the great rural to urban migration as population responded to the economic opportunities offered by industry in urban areas. Indeed, urban death rates exceeded urban birth rates. The question has often been posed as to whether the pull of the industrial urban area or the push from the land was the decisive factor in the process. On the one hand, it is argued that an agricultural surplus sufficiently high to release a substantial part of the agricultural labour force is necessary to allow the concentration of persons in urban areas specialized in non-agricultural occupations. It is accepted that the agricultural surplus need not relate to the immediate region around the urban area where world transportation techniques have been mastered. On the other hand, urban development may be viewed as a main causative factor in agricultural development, providing not only the demand stimulus but frequently also the means as the technical application of urban innovations to agriculture allows food supply to more than keep pace with demand. In this case the path of economic development required a decline in the relative share of the agricultural sector, and the rural to urban migration would have occurred even with similar birth- and death-rate trends in both areas.

The traditional demographic concept of urbanization is now obsolescent since, in economically advanced societies, farm to urban migration has almost run its course, and the historical differential between urban and rural fertility rates has now been closed. The growth of urban population in the twentieth century is therefore due to the natural increase of that urban population. The population (and economic activity) movements of recent decades have become increasingly a movement from small urban areas to metropolitan areas and from the metropolitan core to the suburbs.

Growth of the individual urban area in the long run depends on the successful transition of the local economy from one export base to another. Some urban areas never respond to this challenge, being at a relative disadvantage compared to neighbouring and competing urban areas because of their isolation and the nature of their hinterland and industrial activity. As Thompson (1965a, ch. 1) points out, a scale factor is clearly at work in this process since the size an urban area has already achieved can be the critical factor in the rate and character of its future growth. A process of competition between urban areas therefore determined which urban areas survive and grow. However the relative rise and decline of urban areas as a consequence of changing locational requirements of existing and new industries is becoming a minor issue at the national level in most countries (although the fortunes of a particular urban area may still be regarded as critical by its inhabitants).

In the future, further concentration will take place within the size distribution of urban areas for two reasons: Firstly, the trend towards larger manufacturing plants provides medium-sized urban areas with a relative advantage since smaller urban areas have inadequate supplies of labour and the superior quality and array of business services in the large urban area are less necessary for the success of the self-sufficient large plant. Secondly, there comes a time when tertiary activities supplant manufacturing as the principal component in urban size growth, and as servicing becomes the major labour-demanding activity the major urban growth will shift from centres of production to centres of massive consumption and decision taking. Economic activities tend to be located with reference to metropolises. Therefore in the twentieth century it has been the very largest urban areas that, in general, have been growing most rapidly. Increasing mobility of industry and population, and in particular the increase in commuting range, have favoured large urban areas. Moreover, the top hierarchical nature of many tertiary activities has meant their presence in only a few major urban areas. Accompanying the greater concentration into large urban areas there is a redistribution of people and activities within the metropolitan region as the more equal spread of national income allows more people to take advantage of the possibilities.

Even when one accepts qualifications on the economic rationality of the urban system, empirical evidence affirms the continuing vitality of geographical concentrations of secondary and tertiary industries in expanding economies and shows that the geographical distribution of urban areas is more regular than random. These same basic tendencies in all cases, irrespective of geographical location, suggest that there are powerful economic advantages to the urban organization of society. What are these economic advantages of urbanization?

## Economic Advantages of Urbanization

For the producer, urban areas offer a unique set of scale, localization, and urbanization economies as well as factor-supply advantages. For the consumer there is the chance to earn a higher income and to choose from a greater variety of jobs and commodities. Such factors also imply that every economic activity cannot be present in every urban area: most certainly agglomeration on a large scale will be limited to a few large urban areas. Each urban area serves a variety of purposes and meets an array of needs, but no two urban areas are alike in all respects because, in order to compete, urban areas must specialize. Specialization depends on the extent of the market, and to secure a large market an urban area must export goods and services. The specialized urban area cannot be self-sufficient and will require substantial imports of other goods and services. The urban economy is thus an open economy. The growth of an urban area depends on the corresponding growth of its specialized export industries. In this sense it will be found that the discussion of relative urban size cannot be divorced from the discussion of urbanization's economic advantages because those advantages operate with varying force at different urban sizes. If each urban area is viewed as an agglomeration of mutually dependent producers and consumers, then economic forces go a considerable way towards explaining the existence and character of the urban system. The economic advantages of the urban system for the efficient use of resources can be examined under the headings of specialization, complementarity of activities, urbanization economies, factor supply, and consumption advantages.

SPECIALIZATION

The organization of the urban system is based on specialization in two respects. Firstly, there is specialization of function between urban areas. Particular activities are associated with individual urban areas, as in the case of industrial towns, holiday resorts, educational centres, garrison towns, or dormitory settlements. Secondly, there is specialization of function within the urban area whereby inhabitants concentrate on particular occupations, and other factors of production are similarly devoted to single uses.

An increase in specialization brings a decrease in costs of and/or an increase in revenues from producing goods and services. More and cheaper or better quality goods can be produced from a given amount of resources. Even where each urban area represented a closed economy, specialization would bring about an increase in the quantity and quality of goods and services produced. For instance, in the case of labour, where a person specializes on a particular task he will acquire more knowledge and greater skill regarding the performance of that task. His dexterity increases, and constant familiarity with the restricted range of operations enhances the likelihood of his being able to overcome problems as they arise and facilitates the development of new techniques and machines to aid in the task. The job will be done more quickly and cheaply because of savings in time and in expense in not having to provide such a wide variety of materials and tools. The limited range of operations involved in a specialized task make it easier and quicker for new workers to learn. Such advantages apply where labour is homogeneous. Moreover, where the supply of labour is heterogeneous, specialization allows individual workers to concentrate on those tasks where their relative advantage is greatest.

In an urban area the increased output of better quality goods is not only the result of specialization on the production of particular goods and services but also of the increase in the degree of specialization that takes place when population is clustered into urban areas. This is because specialization in one line frequently creates opportunities for specialization elsewhere. One specialist may find other specialists come into being either to use his products or to supply him with necessary tools and materials. In an urban area these other specialists are near at hand; thus specialists can more easily tap the services of or render services to other specialists. Resources are therefore used with greater efficiency as the increased output from the given supply of resources testifies.

By allowing specialization, urban areas facilitate production on a large scale. Large-scale production, in turn, allows the adoption of more specialist practices as the production process becomes further subdivided. Not only production but its associated administrative functions become subdivided as specialized departments for sales, purchases, personnel, and development are created. On the production side there may be technical advantages accruing from the ability to use indivisible units of capital equipment whose use at lower levels of output would be inefficient because they stand idle most of the time. Large-scale production means that the minimum output for the efficient functioning of such machines is exceeded. Large plants may also be able to link processes which would have to be carried out separately in small plants. Similar advantages apply to managerial, marketing, and financial actions. Together such internal economies of scale mean lower per unit production costs which, given transport costs, allow the specialized urban area to sell its commodity for a given price at a greater distance from that urban area than in the case of a less specialized urban area with higher per unit production costs.

The corollary of a high level of specialization is the need for exchange. There is a greater measure of interdependence, both direct and indirect. The specialized urban area cannot be self-sufficient and has to import foodstuffs, raw materials, and other manufactures it does not produce for itself. The more specialized an urban area becomes the more it must import to provide for the great variety of goods and services demanded by its inhabitants and the more it must export to pay for these extra imports. Specialized urban areas therefore depend on other urban areas to provide a non-local demand for their exports and to supply the necessary imports they require. Similar arguments apply to persons within urban areas, for persons only specialize on the production of a given commodity where they can exhange their surplus output for their other requirements. In a money-using economy it is the effective demand for a specialized commodity which determines how much the specialist has available to spend on his other requirements. Effective demand gives the extent of the market, and this governs the degree of specialization. For example, where a commodity is demanded by only 4 persons in every 1000, and it requires the demand of 1000 persons to keep a specialist fully occupied in supplying that good and providing that specialist with what he considers an adequate income, it will require an urban area of 250,000 persons before a person specializes wholly in the production of that commodity. If only 1 person in 1000 demanded that commodity, then, conditions of supply remaining the same, an urban area of one million persons would be needed to attract a person into full-time specialization in that line. Therefore the smaller the demand for a given commodity relative to a given number of persons, the larger will the size of urban areas have to be before a person specializes in supplying that commodity. The smaller the urban area the more restricted the number of activities present in which specialization has taken place.

The relationship between specialization and the extent of the market is reflected in the fact that some economic activities can only be supported in urban areas of certain minimal size. Studies (Florence, 1955, 1964; Ogburn and Duncan, 1964) have shown that in urban areas of around 10,000 population, convenience goods retailing and minor consumer services such as branch banks commonly exist. Between 25,000 and 200,000 retailing of durables, general professional services including commercial printing, photocopying, telephone answering and sign-painting, construction, brewing, and bottling are some of the activities likely to develop. Between 200,000 and 800,000, department stores, newspaper publishing, wholesaling, specialized professional, and public services will be added. Over 800,000, book and periodical publishing, business and financial services, retailing of luxury goods, design, special entertainment, and manufacture of highly specialized commodities such as medical and scientific instruments and art materials come into being.

The above reasoning has shown the degree of specialization to be dependent on the extent of the market. Exchange is facilitated by the close integration of the persons involved. The larger the number of persons who are accessible to each other the larger the number of possible contacts and, therefore, the larger the market. In an urban area of given population size, with a closed economy, the degree of specialization depends on the density of population and the ease of movement within the urban area. If two urban areas are identical in all respects except population density, then the urban area with the higher population density will exhibit greater specialization of activities. Where only internal transport systems differ between the two urban areas, that urban area with the more efficient transport system will show the greatest degree of specialization in its activities. If economic efficiency, in terms of the highest total real output from resources available, is taken to be a desirable goal, it would appear, *a priori*, that the larger the urban area the greater the real income per inhabitant.

Urban areas are not isolated, self-contained systems, and an additional factor contributes to the degree of specialization, namely the ease of movement of persons and goods between urban areas. Where population is scattered over a wide area and inter-urban transport is poorly developed, the degree of specialization within and between urban areas is less than where inter-urban transport is well developed. In that the urban economy is an open one, the importance of transport must be acknowledged. Those urban areas which possess good transport access to other areas will have a relative advantage over urban areas with poorer transport facilities. They will grow to a larger size, although, at any given time, the decreasing costs associated with specialized large-scale production within such urban areas are subject to diminishing returns and there will come a point where they are offset by rising transport costs to distant market areas. However, an urban area specializing in the production of a commodity can compete effectively with another less specialized urban area which is nearer to the market. The technical innovations that yielded lower per unit production costs are reinforced by the effects of transport improvements. A general improvement in transport will increase the size of the market that may be tapped from a given location and therefore increase the amount of specialization and exchange that can take place. Moreover, the spatial lengthening of production raises the threshold requirement of some industries by increasing the minimum optimum scales of operation, and this favours the growth of already efficient producing centres over inefficient and non-producing urban areas. Population follows economic opportunity and is attracted to urban areas with the greatest relative advantage, i.e. those with the greatest market potential. This increases the number of persons in the urban area and provides further opportunity for specialization and exchange. The increase in population and density of settlement will stimulate technological and transport innovations. In this way one factor reinforces others in urban growth.

## COMPLEMENTARITY OR EXTERNAL ECONOMIES

Specialization and interdependence go hand in hand but do not demand that the related activities be spatially closely linked. However, in certain cases, interdependent specialisms come together in space and form more integrated local sequences. Such activities are complementary to each other and find it advantageous to be in close proximity, which is facilitated by location in an urban area as this reduces operational imperfections and friction of space. These specialized activities may be complementary in either of two senses. Firstly, they need to use the products or services of and be in close communication with these other specialized activities in order to function efficiently. Secondly, together with other specialized activities they provide a more complete range of goods and services.

Complementarity and specialization are functionally linked, for it has been shown that as the size of market increases firms are likely to develop producing more specialized goods and services than previously. The discussion of specialization emphasized the benefits from scale economies realizable within the individual producing firm, but the action of that firm in undertaking production on a large scale may create opportunities for other specialized, and complementary, firms to come into being. These opportunities, if developed by complementary firms, represent, on the one hand, external economies of scale for the original firm, and, on the other hand, economies that can be internalized in the case of the complementary firm which is called into being. Urban areas provide many opportunities for such external economies to be internalized by the creation of complementary firms, and it is suggested that such external economies increase functionally rather than arithmetically with urban growth since specialization, and hence complementarity, depend on the size of the market.

Activities which cluster into mutually supporting complexes within an urban area are based on input–output linkages, complementary labour demands, technological interactions, and certain common market characteristics. The linkages between firms may be vertical, horizontal, diagonal, or complementary. In the vertical case firms are sequentially linked in the productive process as with the firms in London's East End furniture trade which specialize on a particular process, such as sawmills, carvers, turners, and french polishers. With horizontal linkage, firms operate at the same stage(s) of the production process but produce different outputs as with the chair-makers, dining-table-makers and cabinet-makers of the furniture industry or the major clearing banks, the London offices of Scottish, Irish, and overseas banks, merchant banks, and discount houses in the financial core of the City of London. Diagonal linkage occurs where a firm supplies a product or service to firms in several industries. For example, cleaning, towel, and maintenance service which may be offered to both manufacturing and office firms or the consultancy and staff services offered to the office community in the City. Complementary linkage is more indirect and is most likely to occur where firms have complementary rather than competitive labour demands.

To what extent are these external economies, which arise from situations independent of the resources of the individual firms involved, spatially immobile? Although certain external economy benefits may not be irrevocably tied to a given location, in other cases the effect of access to external economies diminishes rapidly with increasing distance. It may be possible to tap the advantages of access to the large, local pool of skilled labour created by the demands of like firms at any location within commuting range, but where the quick dissemination of information is essential to risk minimization face-to-face contact is necessary and this is best facilitated by locations in close proximity. The advantages of external economy situations are particularly helpful to small firms.

Advantages of complementarity through external scale economies increase with increasing urban size. Bigger and tighter-knit complexes of secondary and tertiary industry imply larger but fewer urban areas.

URBANIZATION ECONOMIES

Diverse types of economic activities also find an advantage from locating in the same urban area. It would appear that, up to a point, these economies of urban concentration increase with growth, for the whole urban area gains in efficiency as its size increases. Large urban areas have a clear-cut advantage in their cheaper and more flexible transport systems which give better hinterland connections and more frequent services; in the amount of rentable space that becomes available; in the range and sophistication of the auxiliary and business services offered; and in their superior research, development, education, and training facilities. Moreover, the scope of the urban public economy increases in breadth and depth with increasing urban size. There may be considerable internal economies available in the provision of certain public services, such as sewage disposal and refuse collection, so that public utility systems are also cheaper and more flexible. Hence the principle of specialization and the profitable introduction of indivisible factor units applies equally to the public sector.

The massing of reserves possible in urban areas means that individual firms need not keep large stocks of materials and equipment but can operate on a hand-to-mouth basis, for supplies are available at short notice when needed. The multiplicity of interaction among the large number of persons employed in secondary and tertiary industries in urban areas quickens the rate of technological invention and innovation, encourages the adoption of more efficient managerial and financial techniques, and increases the speed of dissemination of ideas and diffusion of skills. Large urban areas amass customers and therefore constitute an obvious market for goods which offers advantages for producers of mass-consumption goods. Such urbanization economies are captured by private firms and individuals as lower costs in going about their business and a more efficient use of resources is achieved.

Thus, once established, an urban area acquires advantages which serve to attract additional economic activity. Economic activity is forever changing, some activities will be declining, others expanding. If the above reasoning applied to all urban areas then, via a process of circular and cumulative causation, each urban area would expand indefinitely within the limits of its resource base. Where urban areas are in competition for the large market areas that allow maximum specialization only a limited number can attain very large size. The most conspicuous factor determining which urban areas achieve such size may well be initial advantage. The eleven leading industrial urban areas of the United States had been singled out by 1910, and of the twenty-five largest urban areas in that country in 1910 only six had been relegated by the 1950s (Lampard, 1968; Pred, 1966, ch. 2). Of the fourteen major urban areas in England outside of London, as recognized by Smailes in 1944, thirteen still held that rank in the late 1960s (Smith, 1968). Continuing growth depends on an urban area's ability to substitute new or expanding activities for declining ones. Ghost towns are the extreme indication that this is not always possible. Successful substitution in turn depends on the urban area's acquired advantages—the size and skill range of its labour force, the variety of its services, the extent of its markets, etc.—and the more developed these are the more favourable conditions for substitution. Once again, size is important. The larger the urban area the more diversified its industrial structure, manufacturing and office, and the strength of its available economies and linkages makes it difficult for firms involved to consider relocation. This is reinforced by the impact of consumer-oriented activities, the amount of immobile capital which exists in the urban area, and power politics.

FACTOR SUPPLY ADVANTAGES

The longer the time period the more important are supply considerations, and urban areas offer attractive locations for many economic activities because factors of production are more generally available there. These factor supply advantages are probably most marked in the cases of labour and entrepreneurship.

The significance of labour as a locational factor increases as the average size of plant increases and as technological advance demands less in the way of previous training and experience. The size of the labour pool in urban areas is such that firms requiring a supply of either all types of labour or a particular skill find it more readily available there than elsewhere. Depending on age structure, urban areas may have a larger proportion of population in the working age groups than non-urban areas: they certainly have higher activity rates because of the higher proportion of single and married women who are available for work. To illustrate an urban area's supply advantage in respect of skilled labour, assume that a firm requires fifty highly specialized workers and that only 1 person in 500 can perform the particular job because of the special training and aptitude necessary. This firm will have to locate where it is easily accessible to 25,000 persons. Such special skills are, however, not evenly distributed over the geographic population but tend to be relatively more concentrated in the larger urban areas. Urban areas attract not only the more but also the less capable persons, so the supply of semi- and unskilled labour is greatest in urban areas, especially the supply of female labour. Therefore industries which use labour intensively, such as tertiary activities, find urban locations essential to their success. The greater the competition for labour and the more labour of a particular type that is needed, the more critical it is for a firm to locate in an urban area.

The urban labour market's advantage of greater elasticity is one that increases with the size of urban area. The greater inelasticity of the labour market in small urban areas reflects in higher labour costs per unit output. In large urban areas firms are able to expand without having to raise wage levels or provide special transport. Even so, higher wages are paid in larger urban areas, and this serves to encourage immigration, the labour supply adjusting to the demand, as well as promoting the growth of consumer-oriented industry. There can be marked differentials in wage rates within an urban area although it is to be expected that the larger the urban area the greater the interpersonal variation due to differences in education, skill, and attitude because of the wider variety of persons attracted. Wage differentials between urban areas of similar size may exist because of differences in such factors as the degree of unionization and local attitudes to innovation.

The availability of capital funds has rarely been a factor retarding economic growth in advanced societies because capital funds are mobile and the supply of credit responds quite readily to demand. This is not to say that the availability of capital funds was not critical to successful innovation at an earlier stage of development. Today, however, although the supply of funds in the short-run may be curtailed by government action, in the long-run the necessary supply is forthcoming. Even where the capital market is largely organized on a national or regional level, certain local aspects may still be important. A small firm wishing to innovate will find it impossible to raise funds on the national market and will have to rely on purely local sources to obtain the necessary funds. In so far as small firms can still grow into large firms, the availability of local capital to small firms in an urban area may influence the rate of urban growth a decade later. The larger the urban area the greater is the supply of funds, usually at lower rates of interest as financial institutions in competitive situations work on the insurance principle of making money on the average customer and the dissemination of information regarding investment opportunities is more efficient. In contrast to capital funds, existing real capital is often highly immobile, but certain types, real property for example, may be more easily disposed of the larger the urban area.

Land as a factor of production includes not only the space on which economic activities are performed but also raw materials. Land is heterogeneous and there are sure to be differences in the natural occurrence of raw materials at urban locations and in the characteristics of land available for urban development, e.g. differences in the proportion of flat land. Such differences will be reflected in the relative advantages of urban areas in the performance of their various activities. To a large extent, at greater or lesser cost, supplies of materials and sites are responsive to demand. Materials are transportable so the supply to any given urban area could be altered in the short run. Land for urban use, although fixed in amount at the centre of an urban area, increases in amount as the radius or urban development extends. A doubling of the radius of development quadruples the developed area; a trebling of the radius brings a ninefold increase in the developed area. Thus the supply of potential urban space increases more than proportionately with increasing distance from the centre.

In an open economic system entrepreneurship lies at the heart of urban development. Development proceeds through the direct and indirect effects of innovation and is, therefore, a reflection of entrepreneurs' willingness to take risks. Risk or uncertainty has a spatial dimension, and entrepreneurs often show a strong preference for places where present and anticipated risks appear lowest. These will be urban areas, especially the larger areas. The frequency of innovation in any urban area is a function of the supply of inventions and capital funds and the demand for innovations and information respecting technical advance. Demand for innovations is greatest in those urban areas where growth of specialization multiplies interactivity linkages and creates technological disequilibrium between the stages of the production process. Such an urban area will also be the place with the greatest accumulation of know-how in the activities concerned. Thus the larger the urban area the greater the frequency of innovation. Of course entrepreneurs differ in their willingness to innovate, the aggressiveness of their policies, and in their ability to survive downswings in demand. Entrepreneurial availability contributes to urban growth and development in another way for Thompson (1965a, ch 1) comments that an entrepreneurial genius is more likely to be always available in an urban area of 500,000 than in an urban area one-tenth that size. This would allow the larger urban area to give birth to new activities at critical stages in its growth. Moreover, the entrepreneurial genius, if born in the smaller urban area, is likely to migrate to the larger.

ECONOMIC ADVANTAGES TO THE CONSUMER OF
LIVING IN URBAN AREAS

By living in an urban area an individual gains access to a wider range of employment opportunities and a greater variety of goods and services. It is much easier to rise in economic status within the span of a lifetime within an urban area than outside of it. Specialization of activities within urban areas makes it more likely that a person can find a job for which his abilities best suit him and allows producers to pay higher wages at the same time as enjoying increased profit margins. If a person wished to become a probation officer, then, assuming only 1 person in 100 is on probation and that a probation officer can look after 200 probationers, the population within travelling distance of the probation office must be 20,000 before it is economic to create a position for a full-time probation officer. Changing jobs is also easier in urban areas since there is a greater chance of finding alternative employment which needs the same skills and offers the same reward without having to move home. The superior range of goods and services available in urban areas is also a function of specialization. Besides the wider choice of goods there are better medical, educational, entertainment, and other cultural facilities.

Both the range of job opportunities and the diversity of goods and services increase with increasing urban size. Large urban areas raise the real income of their inhabitants compared to smaller ones by extending the effective range of consumer choice. Goods imported into smaller urban areas can be efficiently produced with consequent savings in transport costs, and goods, especially luxury ones, which are not available in smaller areas, are offered for sale. Increasing urban size expands the local market and pulls successive economic activities across the threshold of profitable local production. Cost-of-living differences between urban areas of varying size are obscure, especially because of the problem of evaluating the highly specific facilities of large urban areas, such as symphony orchestras. Small urban areas must, however, bear higher transport costs on imports, i.e. pay higher delivered prices for these goods.

The economic advantages of the urban way of life are compelling ones and appear to favour increasing urban size. More and more the large urban area or metropolis is becoming the focus of economic organization. It may be quite possible for a group of smaller towns to pursue a collective existence, as with the Piedmont industrial crescent (Chapin and Weiss, 1962) or the urban areas which form the nucleus of the East Midlands Economic Planning Region. The urban system is not static for growth, and decline of individual urban areas will alter their relative spatial positions and the economic structure of an urban area will react on the quantity and quality of resources available in that area. Overall, given the free enterprise system which operated throughout the nineteenth and early twentieth centuries and the degree of freedom it accorded individuals and firms, it would appear that the largest urban areas have the greatest economic advantages. However, as will be seen later and in particular in Chapter 12, there are important qualifications regarding the operation of that system.

### Interaction of Economic and Non-economic Forces

Neither the individual urban area nor the urban system as a whole can be regarded as solely economic mechanisms. The urban way of life means that urban areas may also be viewed as social unities. Urban areas have a political identity and represent a psychological and physical setting. The urban system and pattern is thus the result of a complex interplay of physical, economic, behavioural, and technical factors. An understanding of the role of economic factors is essential to the full understanding of urbanization and the functioning of urban areas, but it must be remembered that economic explanations on their own are not enough. Although the emphasis throughout this book is on the economic dimension the constant interaction of economic and non-economic factors must be borne in mind. Such interaction may modify the operation of an economic system whilst, in their turn, non-economic factors may be shaped by economic forces. A few examples will illustrate the nature of the interactions.

Whatever the reasons for persons and activities clustering in urban areas in the first instance, economic and non-economic forces will then reinforce each other. An urban area's original purpose may have been to provide a good defensive site, a seat of the royal court or government, or a religious centre, but once established certain economic activities will be attracted to that urban area. Where economic factors provided the underlying reason for the establishment of an urban area it may prove attractive to certain social organizations which, in bringing more persons to the area, open up further avenues for economic development. Economic and non-economic forces appear to be mutually reinforcing.

The economic concept of specialization applies not only to economic production but to activities in general. Social organizations will reap benefits from specialization and these may again be related to size of urban area. The variety of clubs, charities, and other social organizations catering for individual interests are more numerous and cover a wider range of special interests, the unusual as well as the popular, the larger is the urban area. Only the most important religious denominations can attempt to provide a specialized place of worship in each small urban area, but as size of urban area increases so many more deviant denominations can support specialized places of worship. Such arrangements are only to be expected since social activities, like economic ones, are expressions of human interaction and the costs of overcoming physical distance must work as shapers of that interaction. Indeed, many of the behavioural processes in urban areas either have an economic dimension or at least work themselves out through the market mechanism.

Population changes are not so much a cause as a symbol of a complex combination of forces. Economic factors may have been a prime motivator of the fall in the birth rate in the depression years of the 1930s, but other population changes reflect other factors. Due to health conditions, death rates exceeded birth rates in early nineteenth-century urban areas. This would have had long-run consequences for the supply of urban labour if net immigration had not more than offset the excess of deaths over births. Population movements, resulting from religious or political persecution, can have very favourable effects for the recipient areas as the refugees may establish new industries in the urban areas where they settle.

Reference was made earlier in the chapter to interaction between technological factors, economic motivations, and urban growth. Urban areas frequently experience situations which foster technological advance, not only within single industries but also in transport and public services. The profitable introduction of an invention at one stage of the production process can create problems of operation at previous or subsequent stages, and attention is then focused on finding a solution to those problems. In this way technological advance and economic motivation interacted to produce the factory system and the joint stock organization that contributed so much to the industrial growth of nineteenth-century urban areas. The demands of these early industrial urban areas for labour created problems of dense living and intra-urban transport and stimulated improvements in sewerage and water-supply systems and transport innovations such as early morning workmen's tickets on the railways. On a more local level, physical conditions, building technology, and the profit motive interacted, so that in the process of urban expansion sites with any development handicap—such as excessive slope, unstable subsoil, or liability to flood—were avoided. Further urban growth, and especially advances in building technology, e.g. raft construction or pile foundationing, make it profitable to develop such sites.

Political factors are especially important today. The choice of an urban area, whether existing or new, as the location for the national or regional capital gives an immediate boost to the area's employment opportunities. Economic activities needing close and frequent contact with government offices will be drawn to that urban area which will also influence future developments in the transport network. A new urban area may be created to house the national government as with Brasilia and Canberra. The political function may be shifted between urban areas with consequent effects on the fortunes of urban areas as the history of the capital function in many American states bears witness. Public authorities are responsible for a very large proportion of annual fixed investment, and their decisions in this field, on the construction of new motorways, international airports, and the like, exert a tremendous influence on private economic location decisions. Government policies may be deliberately framed to aid depressed urban economies, as with the aid available in the United Kingdom under the 1960 Local Employment Act when aid was given on an employment exchange basis. Where small fishing ports and holiday resorts qualified for aid there was an implied value judgement that such areas could be made economically viable. At the local level the pattern of expansion and redevelopment in individual urban areas can be influenced by regulations and standards laid down by local politicians acting on advice from their planners.

Finally, one must recognize the operation of random elements in the system, for actions are not always rational. Decisions are often made in relative ignorance of the full facts. Even in the economic realm of entrepreneurs making calculated locational decisions on the basis of full facts, some make viable choices and others, through faulty reasoning, are unsuccessful. Of other entrepreneurs who choose locations on the basis of inadequate information, some are successful and others not so. In the case of the latter successful entrepreneurs their location may not be the one that yields maximum profits but adequate profits for the entrepreneur concerned. In this way random elements appear in an overall, apparently rational, pattern.

The existence of these other factors must be recognized in an analysis of urban areas, for economic forces do not operate in a vacuum. Other factors provide limits within which economic forces must operate, and these limits may facilitate or retard the operation of economic forces. However, it is often desirable to analyse the effect of economic factors in isolation as this allows the full directional impact of the economic forces to be examined. This method is used frequently in subsequent chapters. In the final analysis the economic factors must be combined with the non-economic ones; thus the attempt must be made to show how economic activities adapt to the limits imposed by other factors and how economic motivations still attempt to bring about the most efficient use of resources within those limitations.

## Economic Problems of Urban Growth and Organization

The emphasis on the economic advantages of urbanization should not be taken to mean that the urban area, as it was and as it now is, always functions smoothly or indeed represents the optimum form of urban organization. Overwhelming though these economic advantages may be, it is possible for the urban mechanism to misfunction, in which case resources will be used in other than the most efficient way. There are certain growing pains, consequent upon the rapidity of growth of and degree of concentration in urban areas, which are reflected in problems of adjusting the existing urban area and urban system to changing conditions. The unimpeded operation of the price mechanism is, itself, subject to imperfections, and is also unable to bring about all the necessary adjustments. Malfunctionings of an economic nature involve economic costs, and these must be set against the economic benefits derivable from urban organization. Numerous though the problems of an economic nature are, only a few examples will be referred to at this stage.

The fate of the economy of an individual urban area is frequently dictated by factors outside the control of the area. For example, the greater an urban area's relative advantage, compared to other areas, in the production of a good the larger the proportion of regional, national, and even international demand satisfied by plants located in that urban area and, therefore, the larger the proportion of that urban area's resources employed in that industry. What are the growth prospects for this urban area? How stable are its export industry's earnings? A secular drop in demand for the products of its export industry will give rise to serious structural unemployment since adjustment to the new situation is not instantaneous. Generally, the more specialized is an urban area's industry the faster its growth rate, but the more diversified its industrial structure the more stable its growth rate. Not all urban areas can have a share of the stable industries; thus the urban area's share of unstable industries is an important factor from the long-term income generating view of its inhabitants. In relation to urban size small urban areas tend to have either stable or unstable industries, whereas the largest urban areas, have a mix of stable and unstable.

Economic factors appear to favour increasing size of urban area, but absolute size, from an economic point of view, may be a brake on growth. After a certain size there are increased costs of operating and living in urban areas because of congestion of facilities, especially public transport and roads, increasing journey lengths associated with the larger built-up area, and the increased costs of public services due, perhaps, to managerial diseconomies. The size at which these cost increases become apparent is a function of urban technology. If the same level of benefit could be achieved but at a lower level of cost, then a more efficient use of resources is possible.

The increased costs are principally in the form of external diseconomies since the individual or firm does not have to bear the full costs of an action because the costs reflected through the price mechanism to the individual or firm concerned represent only part of the cost involved, the remainder being borne as higher private costs by the public at large. Thus benefits and costs cannot be confronted in a single private accounting unit. The present level of these external diseconomies is reflected in society's concern, which suggests that these diseconomies can no longer be ignored. Attempts must be made to internalize these diseconomies so that private units are aware of the full costs to society of their actions.

Problems of an economic nature also arise from interaction between economic and non-economic factors. With urban growth bringing an expansion in the built-up area the individual urban area may become politically fragmented, since local government boundaries are slow to adjust, and this may result in economic fragmentation in the supply of public services, often at the expense of internal scale economies, and in delay in improvements to public services. The nature of the limits within which economic forces have to work may increase the economic cost of performing everyday tasks. For example, restrictions on the density of development near the urban centre force the use of more distant sites, make longer journeys necessary, and entail the use of more resources for transportation. Whether this was acceptable or not would depend on the change in economic benefits. If the same level of benefit was being derived at a greater resource cost, such controls would not be justified from an economic point of view.

There are many other problems of an economic nature or with an economic dimension, ranging from the effect of major transport improvements on the urban system as a whole to problems of slums, blighted areas, and income inequalities within a single urban area. However, the increasing importance of urbanization in all parts of the world suggests that the overall advantages outweigh the disadvantages. As long as maladjustments and misfunctionings accompany urbanization, then society is not gaining the maximum possible benefit from the urban way of life, and resources are being drained from other forms of capital formation and production. An understanding of the economic functioning of the system is essential for successful prescription.

# CHAPTER 3

# The Urban Real Property Market

## Nature and Function of the Urban Real Property Market

The use of land and buildings within an individual urban area represents the cumulative effect of a multitude of decisions and actions taken by households, institutions, corporate interests, and government. The result of these unco-ordinated decisions is not chaos. There is an underlying rationale and order due to the effectiveness of market price as a means of resource allocation, in this particular case working via the market in urban real property. In our society the mechanism is mainly one of transactions between owners of real property and those who wish to rent or purchase space and buildings for use as dwellings and business premises. This market for urban land and buildings is an expression of rational behaviour, for both space and location are economic commodities subject to supply and demand forces, whilst profit and satisfaction-maximization serve as guides to private behaviour. Land and building uses are, therefore, responsive to changes in costs and in demand. The process of interplay between the many demands and supplies is one of competitive bidding. Any generally accepted bidding process will bring about a market solution. Emphasis here is placed on the process of price or value determination in the urban real property market rather than on the nature of the values themselves or on the resultant distribution of activities in urban space. The nature of urban land and property values will be briefly discussed, however, towards the end of this chapter, and the spatial pattern of uses resulting from the operation of the market forms the subject matter of subsequent chapters.

In the case of urban areas it is desirable to refer to the real property market rather than, simply, the land market. With few exceptions, such as surface car-parking, it is necessary to erect a building on an urban site before an income can be derived from the site. The income from the site when so improved (or real property) represents a joint income to land and building which, in practice, it is often difficult to separate into component parts. Moreover, in any market period transactions involving changes in ownership or use of existing buildings, with a view to their continued use, are more numerous than ones involving raw land. The latter are confined to deals involving agricultural land or redevelopment sites. The demand for land for development is derived from the demand for buildings needed by potential or existing urban activities. Thus agricultural land on the suburban fringe is needed for conversion to urban use and redevelopment land in central areas for alternative, more intensive uses. Sooner or later this once raw land may appear on the market as real property, i.e. land plus buildings. Since many people demanding urban property make no distinction between land and buildings but make what might be termed a "package purchase", this aspect of the market will be treated as representative. The market in raw land may then be viewed as a sub-market along with sub-markets in other partial interests in real property.

Therefore three goods—land, buildings, and location—are usually traded in the urban real property market, but there is only one transaction and one price in any particular case. This makes the measurement of performance in the property market more difficult than in most other markets. Within any urban area the price mechanism, operating in the real property market, performs several allocational roles. Besides deciding which of the competing users obtain available real property, the price mechanism will also determine the proportion of owner-occupied compared to rented property, for both users and investors will be competing in the market. In addition the amount of resources allocated to the repair and maintenance of existing improvements and buildings and the amount of resources devoted to new buildings will be determined. Attention is focused on the allocational role, but it must be remembered that any pricing solution has not only an allocational side but also a distributional one. In this case the distribution of income from urban real property ownership will be determined.

### Motivations of Property-users and Investors

The durability of real property allows ownership and right of use to be separated. Persons will pay a rent for the right to use a property and the owner will receive that periodic rent payment for assigning the right to use to another person. The owner is then treating the property as an investment. Thus investment and occupation interests are always possible in a particular real property, for, with any property there are the alternatives of owning and using, owning but not using, and using but not owning. Both users and investors may, therefore, appear in the market in the roles of buyer or seller. Why do some users rent and others own the real property they occupy? Of course, where a user is going to rent real property it is necessary for someone else to hold that property as an investment. Why do some owners let and others occupy and use the real property they own? In general the decision of both potential users and investors is based on the consideration of alternatives, although the alternatives of purchasing and renting may not be found in all parts of the urban real property market. Should real property only be available for purchase this is because the alternative is not sufficiently attractive to potential investors and users. This would happen if the rent users were willing to pay was not high enough to persuade someone to hold the property as an investment or where the purchase price obtainable was so high that investors would not forgo that sum for the rent potential users were willing to pay.

A potential property-user must decide (a) whether to rent or purchase real property and (b) on the amount and location of the real property required. These are, in effect, simultaneous decisions because the action of the potential users in both cases is determined by the desire to maximize profits or satisfaction. When selling, users or investors seek to obtain the maximum revenue from the sale of their interest.

A user will purchase real property if he estimates that he will get greater profit or satisfaction by purchasing than by paying a rent investors would be prepared to accept and using the money saved elsewhere. Where the potential user borrows funds to finance his purchase he will compare the interest payable on the loan with the rent he would have to pay. Certain factors, such as greater security of tenure or prospect of capital gain, may induce the user to pay a rate of interest higher than the rent. In the case of users purchasing real property, potential investors must believe that they can obtain greater returns or profit from investing an equivalent sum to the purchase price in an alternative of comparable risk than from the rent which the user would be prepared to pay. Where the user decides that he will gain greater profit or satisfaction from renting real property, then the rent offered must be high enough for the investor to consider that he receives a higher return from purchasing or holding real property than from purchasing an alternative investment. Viewed another way, the purchase price the potential user would be willing to pay is not high enough relative to the rent offered to attract the property away from the investor.

A potential property investor is faced with the decision whether to let the real property or use it himself. Where the investor-owner decides to use the property himself it is, in effect, the same type of decision as that already discussed, where a user decides to purchase property. Usually, therefore, the decision for the potential investor is one of choosing between alternative investments both within and outside the urban real property market.

It should be emphasized that the investment aspect is present in every decision to purchase or rent real property, even though this may not always be apparent. With most types of real property the alternatives are available at existing prices since some investors will be prepared to hold property and some users will prefer to purchase property at those prices. These situations can mutually co-exist because competitors (users and investors) hold a variety of expectations about the future and a variety of opinions regarding rates of compensation.

With regard to the amount and location of real property sought, every user has the ability to derive some profit or satisfaction from every real property. The profit or satisfaction level will be measured by the price or rent-paying ability: the greater the profit or satisfaction the greater the price or rent a user will offer. Users need an evaluation function by which to appraise the relative merits of real properties. User requirements for space and location are determined by both the internal and external functioning of the activity, the former determining the quantity and quality of real property needed and the latter the location. Thus the demand price or rent depends on the relationship between the characteristics of the activity and the characteristics of the real property and its location relative to other uses. The same user will therefore offer different prices or rents for different real properties because of the varying suitability of properties and locations for his activity. For the same reason different uses will offer different prices or rents for the same real property.

## The Determination of Real Property Prices

A SIMPLIFIED URBAN REAL PROPERTY MARKET

In any urban area the real property market will comprise a series of sub-markets of varying degrees of complexity and overlap. A sub-market may be created because of significant locational differences between real properties being bought and sold as in the case of accommodation where suburban housing may be treated separately from central housing. Sub-markets also arise from differences in type of real properties; thus shop properties will be distinguished from industrial premises. A further reason is found in the existence of different interests in a real property, in particular, the distinction between occupational and investment interests. There is considerable variation between sub-markets as to the number of transactions in any period, the number of and role played by intermediaries between buyer and seller, and the incidence of legislation and other restraints which serve to confuse the element common to all sub-markets, i.e. the process by which prices or values are determined. Therefore, in order to clarify the processes involved in the determination of values, a simplified version of the urban real property market will be used here. It is necessary to make the following assumptions:

(1) There are a given number of buyers and sellers with perfect knowledge of market conditions.
(2) That real property units are homogeneous and that the number

of sales is sufficient to establish a continuous market through time.

(3) Real property is bought and sold by free contract and the transaction is unhampered by legal or social constraints, nor is there any government action such as property taxation or subsidization to influence prices.

(4) Any person will engage in a transaction that yields him gain.

(5) There are no conveyancing or removal costs.

(6) The distribution of income and consumer preferences are given.

(7) Capital funds can be borrowed as necessary and according to income.

(8) That all real property interests are unencumbered freeholds, i.e. the complete unit available for owner occupation.

## CEILING AND FLOOR PRICES

The market price of urban real property reflects economic decisions on the part of buyers and sellers with respect to its future productivity as assessed by its anticipated net income in various uses. The potential buyer has to place a value to himself, at the present time, on the ownership and/or use of each unit of real property in which he is interested. For any given unit of real property there is a maximum or ceiling price which a particular buyer will be prepared to pay for that interest. Investment and occupational interests in real property must be distinguished in order to understand the determinants of a person's ceiling price for a real property.

For the investor it is the income he expects to receive, usually in the form of rent, over the future. The investor must discount each increment of future income at the appropriate rate of interest which is determined, theoretically, by the amount of money he requires at dates in the future to persuade him to give up a given present sum. Personal rates of discount vary because of differences in personal preferences, in present income and capital position compared to expected income and capital, and in assessment of risks attaching to an investment. However a common influence will be the yield obtainable on alternative investments with similar characteristics. In the case of occupational interests the income or satisfaction derived from use is again a determining factor, but here, especially in the case of houses, substitute real properties must be considered and the ceiling price of a person for a given property will reflect the price at which any substitute property can be bought. In both cases these ceiling price valuations are subjective and different potential buyers will arrive at different prices for the same real property. The potential buyer's subjective valuation thus places a maximum or ceiling price on what he is prepared to pay in the last resort. Obviously he will be better off if he can obtain the property at a lower price than his ceiling figure.

In a similar way potential sellers make subjective valuations of their real properties and these fix the minimum or floor prices on the values of those properties. This minimum value will be influenced by the present value of the income or satisfaction the seller is enjoying, by the selling prices of comparable properties and, in the case of an occupier, by the cost of equivalent reinstatement. Again, sellers' subjective valuations, even of comparable real properties, are likely to differ.

MARKET PRICE

Real property will be bought and sold as long as one or more potential buyers have ceiling prices above the floor prices of the potential sellers of the relevant property. Where no potential buyers have ceiling prices exceeding sellers' floor prices no transactions will take place. Where there is only one potential buyer of a real property with a ceiling price higher than the seller's subjective valuation or floor price the market price will be fixed somewhere between the buyer's ceiling price and the seller's floor price by bargaining. These two prices place limits on the possible movement of market price. The stronger the seller's bargaining position the closer market price to the buyer's ceiling price and the weaker his position the closer market price to his floor price. With several potential buyers of a real property, under the assumption of perfect knowledge, the seller will be aware of all the buyers' offers and buyers aware of each other's offers so that market price will be fixed somewhere between the highest and second highest ceiling prices of the buyers involved. Competition between potential buyers for the property will force the value up to this level.

In the case of a single potential buyer whose ceiling price is high enough and several potential sellers of real property then, under the assumption of homogeneous units of real property, as the buyer is indifferent between properties, the potential seller who makes the sale will be the one with the lowest floor price. Market price will be fixed between the lowest and second lowest of the seller's floor prices. Should there be two such potential buyers, market price will be fixed by the potential seller with the second lowest floor price since competition between the buyers for the lowest seller's property forces price up to this level where competition between the two sellers for available buyers prevents price going higher.

The same line of reasoning applies where there are many buyers and sellers. Assume there are ten potential house-sellers, each with minimum or floor prices fixed by their subjective valuations, arranged in ascending order as follows: £4000, £4100, £4200, £4300, £4400, £4500, £4600, £4700, £4800, and £4900. Also assume ten potential house-buyers whose subjective valuations set their maximum or ceiling prices of £3900, £4000, £4100, £4200, £4300, £4400, £4500, £4600, £4700, and £4800. Comparing these figures there are nine instances where a buyer's ceiling price matches a seller's floor price but there will not be nine transactions. Every seller will be trying to get the highest price for his property and every buyer will try to buy at the lowest price. Under the assumptive conditions, market price—as can be seen from Table 3.1—is fixed at £4400. At £3900 there are ten buyers but no seller, so competition between potential buyers drives price up. At £4000 there will be one potential seller and the potential buyer whose ceiling price was £3900 will have dropped out. Again, competition between buyers in a situation of excess demand forces price up and, in the process, eliminates further potential buyers but brings in more potential sellers until the number of buyers equals the number of sellers. This is at a market price of £4400. At any price higher than £4400 there is a situation of excess supply as sellers outnumber buyers and competition between potential sellers will bring price down. The five buyers will be those with ceiling prices equal to or higher than market price and the five sellers will be those whose floor prices are equal to or lower than market price.

Thus market price is determined collectively by the subjective ceiling and floor prices of all prospective buyers and sellers. Market price does not alter the subjective maximum of a buyer or the subjective minimum of a seller as such, although it does alter the price a buyer has to pay or a seller receives.

The situation used to explain the determination of property prices results in an equilibrium price since the number of units purchased at that price equals the number offered for sale. This need not be a market-clearing solution in the sense that a particular real property remains

TABLE 3.1. DETERMINATION OF MARKET PRICE

| *Buyers' ceiling prices* | *No. of buyers* | *Sellers' floor prices* | *No. of sellers* |
|---|---|---|---|
| (£) | | (£) | |
| 3900 | 10 | | 0 |
| 4000 | 9 | 4000 | 1 |
| 4100 | 8 | 4100 | 2 |
| 4200 | 7 | 4200 | 3 |
| 4300 | 6 | 4300 | 4 |
| 4400 | 5 | 4400 | 5 |
| 4500 | 4 | 4500 | 6 |
| 4600 | 3 | 4600 | 7 |
| 4700 | 2 | 4700 | 8 |
| 4800 | 1 | 4800 | 9 |
| | 0 | 4900 | 10 |

unsold because of a too high floor price asked by its owner. The fact that his property remains unsold may bring about an adjustment in the owner's floor price in a subsequent market period. Under the system of competitive bidding outlined an unequivocal market-clearing solution can be reached so long as no one potential buyer offers the highest price for two or more properties. The assumption of homogeneous real property units may be relaxed.

The ten houses differ in location, also in size; hence each of the ten potential house-purchasers has to place a maximum or ceiling price on each of the ten houses available. Assume that, at present, each of the ten potential house-purchasers live in one of the ten houses and that his floor price for selling is determined by his subjective valuation of the property's worth and that it also represents the ceiling price he would pay for that residence. Thus he would be prepared to move if someone offered a higher price than this floor level since it is assumed that everyone will engage in a transaction which yields gain.

A matrix of these ceiling prices is presented in Fig. 3.1. House-purchasers have been ranked according to income, A having the

| House \ Household | 1 | 2 | 3 | 4 | 5 | 6 | 7 | 8 | 9 | 10 |
|---|---|---|---|---|---|---|---|---|---|---|
| A | 950 | 1100 | 2000 | 1000 | 1450 | 850 | 1500 | 750 | 800 | 1600 |
| B | 1000 | 1200 | 1800 | 950 | 1400 | 1000 | 1300 | 700 | 650 | 1800 |
| C | 900 | 1100 | 1600 | 850 | 1100 | 950 | 1600 | 650 | 700 | 1700 |
| D | 1000 | 950 | 1600 | 850 | 1500 | 750 | 1400 | 650 | 750 | 1600 |
| E | 950 | 1300 | 1500 | 750 | 1400 | 750 | 1300 | 600 | 700 | 1400 |
| F | 1200 | 1200 | 1300 | 900 | 1200 | 800 | 1000 | 600 | 650 | 1200 |
| G | 1100 | 1200 | 1300 | 1200 | 1250 | 950 | 1200 | 550 | 800 | 1300 |
| H | 1000 | 1050 | 1300 | 900 | 1200 | 1100 | 1000 | 700 | 750 | 1200 |
| I | 1000 | 950 | 850 | 750 | 950 | 1000 | 900 | 750 | 900 | 1100 |
| J | 850 | 750 | 1000 | 700 | 1000 | 950 | 750 | 800 | 800 | 1100 |
| Seller's Floor Price | 1000 | 1300 | 1000 | 900 | 1100 | 750 | 1000 | 550 | 800 | 1800 |

House occupied at Start ⌈1000⌉    House occupied at End ⌈2000⌉

FIG. 3.1. Matrix of ceiling prices (£) for given housing market conditions.

highest income and J the lowest. Each row in the matrix shows the ceiling prices of a given potential purchaser for each of the ten houses, including the house in which he is at present living. Each column shows the ceiling prices that each of the ten purchasers would pay for the house in question. The matrix can be used to show the adjustments that take place in a given market period. The house occupied by a potential purchaser at the beginning of the period is indicated by stippled shading and the house that purchaser occupies at the end of the period by line shading. Thus at the beginning of the period house number 3 was occupied by J who set a floor price of £1000 on his house. As column three of the matrix shows, eight households have higher ceiling prices than this for house number 3, and competition between these potential purchasers allows A to buy the house since his is the highest ceiling price. The market price of house 3 will be somewhere between A's ceiling price of £2000 and the next highest ceiling price B's, of £1800. A sells the house he occupied at the beginning of the period to I, the only potential buyer to have a ceiling price above A's floor price, although two others, G and J, have ceiling prices equal to the floor price. Other houses similarly change hands, with the exception of houses 2 and 10 where E and B stay put because there are no ceiling prices as high as the floor prices they place on their houses.

Thus the situation at the end of the relevant market period is a market-clearing solution and an equilibrium situation since no users of real property can be made better off by changing their combination of property and location and no owner can increase his revenue by changing the price of his property. An essential point to be grasped from the market solution where location is considered is that the price of any real property is related to the price of other real properties. Should one household offer the highest price for two or more properties, the solution will depend on bilateral bargaining between the potential purchaser and the several property owners with the next highest ceiling price for each real property providing a floor to each owner's bargaining position.

Each market period clearing solution would be examined by property owners for guides to profitable investments in real property improvements. As improvements come onto the market so the improved real properties will be revalued by potential buyers. The matrix of ceiling prices would be altered and a new solution in the making. Property owners' expectations of profit from improvements may or may not be realized. Frequently, in response to market signals, property developers flood the market with a particular type of improvement in the next period. Competition between owners would, in fact, drive the price of this type of property improvement down in the market-clearing solution. The passage of time will also bring changes in the number and type of households seeking accommodation, including changes in the requirements of existing households. As long as some households are moving the pattern of access and contiguity changes for all. The market solution is, therefore, the outcome of optimum-seeking households, each bidding for its best combination of two variables—quantity of space and location *vis-à-vis* all other units—and competitive bidding ensures that each real property is occupied, in the long run, by its highest and best use.

## Some Practical Market Complications

The efficiency with which the urban real property market in practice establishes similar prices for properties with the same amenity, risk, and prospective income characteristics is dependent on the type of real property under examination, its market structure, and the effectiveness of the methods of market communication. The larger the number of buyers and sellers and the greater the homogeneity of real property the more transactions that will take place at market price. This would probably be true for the market in suburban owner-occupied housing, but in many other cases, such as vacant sites in central areas or first-class shop property, the deals involve a non-standardized commodity of high unit value, and there is not a continuous market in which price is firmly established. Variations in the degree of market organization and the considerable time ordinarily needed to effect property deals also have a bearing on price determination. The urban real property market is more complex than the model situations but, although complications and imperfections arise in practice, the principles of price determination discussed in the above situations still hold true. However, a consideration of the complications is required for a full understanding of the operation of the urban real property market. In particular the nature of the commodity, imperfections of knowledge, market organization, frequency of transactions, and the slowness of response to changes in demand will be examined.

NATURE OF THE COMMODITY

So far it has been assumed that the commodity, real property, is a single interest comprising either undeveloped land or land together with the buildings and other site improvements thereon. The subjects of real property transactions are not the land and buildings themselves but interests in or rights over land. For example, where a shopkeeper purchases the lease of a shop he is buying the right to use the premises supplied by his landlord, subject to certain conditions that may be laid down in the agreement, in return for which he agrees to pay a specified rent. Similarly, anyone purchasing the freehold of that shop subject to the sitting tenant whose lease, assume, expires in 1980 cannot do as he pleases with the shop, for he takes over the obligations incurred by his predecessor in title. What he, in fact, purchases is the right to receive the rent payable by the tenant until 1980, the right to gain possession in 1980, and then use the shop as he pleases, as well as incurring landlord's obligations regarding repairs and other outgoings up to 1980. Thus there may be more than one marketable interest in the same parcel of real property. The basic reason for the multiplicity of interests in real property is that different persons place different subjective values on those interests because persons vary in their assessment of the future, their asset preferences, and the amount of capital they own or can borrow.

As an alternative to holding the unencumbered freehold, where the freeholder is the owner of the interest free from any sub-interest, the freeholder may choose to create one of the two major forms of leasehold interest. Occupation lease refers to the situation where the landlord provides land and buildings as in the case of the shop referred to above. In this case the tenant normally pays a rack rent which is a rent approximating to the full rental value of the land and buildings together. Bargaining may not be confined to the rent but also be extended to the period of the lease and other conditions contained therein. With a building lease, which is usually of 99 years' duration, the freeholder grants the lease of the land on condition that a building is erected. At the end of the lease both land and building reverts to the landlord. In theory it was argued that the building would be at the end of its economic life when the lease expired and would be demolished and replaced by the tenant or his successor in title. Frequently the building's economic life was not co-terminus with the expiration of the lease, in which case the landlord was entitled to let the building at a rack rent. The principle assumed in the drawing up of such leasehold agreements was that the parties involved were of equal bargaining power, but this is true only under conditions of perfect competition. In practice landlords are able to dictate terms (McDonald, 1969).

The rent reserved under such a building lease—the ground rent—need not represent the full value of the land since the lease may be granted for a capital sum in addition to rent. In this case the ground rent would be lower, and the nominal ground rent is known as a peppercorn rent. The optimum combination of rent and capital payment will depend on discount rates and tenant's status. Where the tenant discounts future income at a higher rate than the landlord he will be prepared to offer an increase in rent which will more than compensate the landlord for a reduction in capital payment. Where the tenant is financially sound, the landlord will accept a smaller increase in rent for a given reduction in capital payment than where the tenant's financial position is less sound. This is a reason why multiple stores may obtain some properties even though their rental bid was not the highest. Tax factors may complicate matters further, for where rents are tax-deductible expenses but not the capital payments, the prospective tenant will prefer rent payments to any capital payment.

Further interests are possible. Leaseholders may sub-let. Freeholders may have borrowed money by way of mortgages on the security of their property. Investment interests in real property are not essentially different from stocks and shares from the point of view of investors except that they are less liquid and require more management. The market mechanism normally operates to equate the benefit-yields among comparable investments (Lean and Goodall, 1966, pp. 40–46).

Under what circumstances will several interests in a parcel of real property be created? Whenever a person discounts the income from an interest which could be created at a lower rate than the person who owns the right to create the interest it is profitable to create the interest in question. As the owner of an unencumbered freehold can always split it up, its price cannot fall far short of the sum of the prices of the most profitable combination of interests he can create. The unification of several interests in a real property under one ownership will take place when the value of the encumbered interest plus the value of the sub-interests is less than the price that would be paid for the unencumbered freehold. This would occur whenever a potential purchaser is prepared to accept a lower yield overall on the present incomes from the various interests than the present owners of those interests require. Of course there may be many instances where the unification of interests is impeded, as when legislation confers security of tenure on sitting tenants beyond the terms of their present leases, and the prices of those interests will not reflect the advantages to be derived from unification. This would also make it the more difficult for the market to adjust to changing conditions.

The urban real property market will, therefore, determine the division between owner-occupied and rented property. In the case of housing, for example, assuming rents remained constant, the capital values of both types of housing would tend to a common level, otherwise some house-occupiers and some investors holding rented property will find an advantage in switching housing types or assets. Assuming in Fig. 3.2 that $XY$ represents the stock of houses, then $OO$ shows the number of houses that would be owner-occupied at each level of capital values. When capital values are low, the greater the number of households who are potential owner-occupiers, whilst at high capital values a smaller number of persons will want to be owner-occupiers. $RR$ shows the number of houses held for investment and, therefore, available for renting. Given the level of rents, at low capital values, a large proportion of the stock could be sold as investments, and the higher the capital value the smaller the proportion of stock investors are willing to hold. As the whole stock must be held for investment or owner-occupation an equilibrium would be reached at a capital value of $XP$ $(= YP)$ when $XZ$ houses are rented and $ZY$ are owner-occupied.

## IMPERFECT KNOWLEDGE

Prices of individual interests in real property may deviate from the common or market level because buyers and sellers lack perfect knowledge. A higher level of calculation and communication than exists in real markets has been assumed so far. A potential buyer is likely to view a number of properties before making a purchase, and a potential seller will test the offers of a number of buyers before making a sale. However, few persons investigate the full range of alternatives

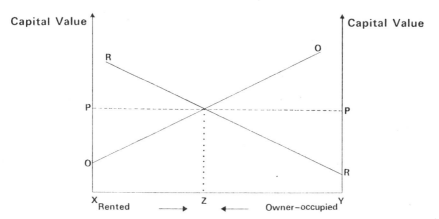

FIG. 3.2. Division of housing stock between renting and owner-occupation.

and none do so frequently. Where a potential buyer lacks information or is forced to buy quickly he is much more likely to pay a price which is higher than the general market level. It can be suggested that such a buyer has a high ceiling price because he is discounting future income at a relatively low rate. The potential seller who lacks information or makes a sale in a hurry because of a need for immediate cash will receive a price lower than the general market level. His floor price is low because he is discounting future income at a relatively high rate. Where a potential seller purchased his interest during boom conditions he may hold tenaciously to his interest for a price that will recover his expenditure despite changing conditions. In another case where the original owner of an interest dies, his heirs may regard it as a windfall and sell the interest for whatever price they can get.

Few occupiers move from one real property to another simply to gain a reduction in rent or make a capital gain as the model assumed they would. Switching of occupation interests is nowhere near as frequent as in the model. This is a stabilizing force in the market since, *ceteris paribus*, a person prefers his existing real property to an alternative, for in adapting his activities to the characteristics of the property and location and vice versa, he will have made an investment which is seldom recoverable in the market. Moreover, the search for alternatives can be tedious, transaction or conveyancing costs are high, and a move itself expensive. In the case of householders most persons move for a particular reason—a change of job or an increase in family size for instance—and they tend to decide what they can afford without any specific calculation of present values. They then choose the most suitable house available within that price range. Ceiling prices in these circumstances for any particular property depend on the prices at which alternatives are available. Potential buyers of similar income will tend to consider the same alternatives; therefore the spread in ceiling prices will not be great. Moreover, the price accepted by the seller will reflect what he can obtain from other purchasers, the asking prices of other similar properties up for sale, and, where known, realized prices of others recently sold. In most cases buyers, and especially sellers, rely on professional advice in the matter of prices. This is an attempt to overcome imperfect knowledge, and in a sub-market such as owner-occupied housing, price is determinate within fairly narrow limits for the expert. In other cases, such as offices in a medium-sized urban area, the market may be neither so large nor as well organized and price variations more common.

Imperfection of knowledge is especially important in the sub-market for developable land, and herein lies the opportunity for speculative profit. Thus land in substantially the same locations may be bought and sold at different prices according to the experience or lack of experience of the buyer (Hoyt, 1933). The chance for profit from buying and holding fringe or suburban land in an undeveloped state arises because an individual's anticipations are more astute than the majority's or from an error in the consensus of opinion. If perfect knowledge were available as to the timing of future conversion, the value of that time, holding costs, and discount rates, everyone would agree as to the present worth of suburban land and there would be no opportunity for speculative gain because all future values would be fully and accurately discounted to the present. Given a free market in such land speculative demand may bid up the level of prices in the short run, but when that land is eventually released for development supply will be greater and long-run prices lower. Correct speculation levels out price fluctuations but incorrect speculation will exacerbate price movements.

## MARKET STRUCTURES

Real properties are not standardized units compared to other commodities and this adds enormously to the complexity of demand and supply analysis as the matrix model of ceiling prices hinted. The real property market is strongly influenced by ownership and legal factors and restraints, for virtually every real property is subject to different controls and agreements. Indeed, legal and social constraints are major factors in the compartmentalization of transactions into submarkets. The method of conducting transactions is one of offer and counter-offer, the only exception being occasional auctions. In these circumstances a buyer's offer price is a closely guarded secret, and the floor to the owner's bargaining position is not as stable as if he were fully aware of the range of offer prices. Auctions are often used only where there is uncertainty as to the value of real property which is not continuously available or in the case of sales by special bodies such as trustees. In some instances transactions may be sheltered from the market process, as with deals between government authorities, divisions of a corporation, or members of a family.

Only a very small proportion of real properties of any type are on the market at any one time. All households and economic activities do not appear as active participants in every market period as the model assumed. For example, real property leases do not fall in simultaneously everywhere. Where there are few sales involving a particular type of real property and where buyers and sellers are not well informed relative skill in bargaining plays an important part in determining prices. The economic forces discussed then influence only the broader features of the situation. For example, in the market for development rights in suburban land there are few buyers and sellers at any one time, and it would appear that a major factor in the development or non-development of land is the character of the landholder himself. Transactions are veiled in secrecy, tracts vary in size and character. In the short run, institutional factors such as estate holdings and trustee owners affect the marketability of tracts of land. The landowner may thus either facilitate or hinder the process of land conversion depending on his decision to hold or sell land. He may greatly simplify the process if he assumes the roles of developer and property seller. Some present owners may have ample capital for which they seek investment outlets, others can have a pressing need for capital they can raise by the sale of their land. Some owners may be optimistic about future increases in the value of their land, others are more cautious.

Although the reliance of most potential buyers and sellers on professional advice in the valuing, surveying and conveyancing of interests contributes to the overcoming of imperfections of knowledge, it can lead to monopoly power. The degree of monopoly power in the hands of middlemen such as estate agents, mortage institutions, law firms, and contractors varies with type of property.

MARKET RESPONSE

In urban areas, because of the durability and immobility of real property, change is slow and costly. A consequence of durability is that the short-run supply of real property is fixed and the time taken to construct new properties means that the yearly flow of new building has only a minor quantitative effect. This despite the fact that new building tends to supplement rather than replace existing buildings. Rents and prices therefore respond only slowly to changes in demand conditions. One further reason may be that change is difficult to perceive. Certainly potential sellers do not lower floor prices until a considerable time has elapsed. Coupled with the fact that only a small proportion of property interests comes onto the market in any one year, this means that movement towards equilibrium is very slow. For example, if there are 105 offices in a central business district all let on 21-year leases, then, with the expiration of leases spread evenly over time only five leases would come up for renewal in any one year. Consequently rents could be above equilibrium for several years.

In Fig. 3.3 it is assumed that there are $XY$ identical offices suitable for letting to only two types of office-user—solicitors and accountants.

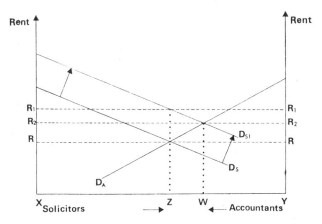

FIG. 3.3. Division of urban office market between accountants and solicitors.

Given an equilibrium starting situation where the demand curve of solicitors $D_S$ intersects the demand curve of accountants $D_A$, $XZ$ offices will be occupied by solicitors and $ZY$ by accountants at an equilibrium rent of $XR$ ($= YR$). Downward-sloping demand curves reflect the variety of expectations of potential office-users and the fact that an increase in the number of competitors will, *ceteris paribus*, reduce income and hence rent-paying ability. Then assume an increase in demand for solicitors' offices shown by the new demand curve $D_{S1}$. The new equilibrium position would require $XW$ solicitors' offices and only $WY$ accountants' offices. If few leases were available for renewal and the market was competitive, new rents would lie around $XR_1$, and only as accountants' leases expire and their offices are taken over by solicitors will rents fall to the new equilibrium of $XR_2$. In this respect, as the situation is likely to have changed before equilibrium is restored, it would appear that the level of rents (or prices) is explained less in terms of equilibrium analysis than by reference to the lack of equilibrium (Turvey, 1957). The process would work faster if some accountants assigned their leases to solicitors at a profit. The value of an office to the marginal accountant is only $XR$ but he can sell this for a sum equal to the present value of $XR_1$ minus $XR$ times the number of years of unexpired lease. The construction of new offices, if profitable, would help, but this also takes considerable time, as would the conversion of other property, but this may also be subject to unexpired leases.

GOVERNMENT INFLUENCE

Various government measures will influence, even interfere with, the market allocation of real properties. The principles behind government intervention will be fully discussed in Chapter 12. Here the role(s) of government in the property market may be illustrated by a few examples.

Government measures may influence demand and supply. In the case of demand some measures increase demand by raising the offer prices of existing prospective purchasers and encouraging new purchasers into the market. For example, being able to offset mortgage interest payments against tax liability will raise a purchaser's offer price compared to his offer price in the absence of such a concession. Subsidized interest rates under option mortgage schemes, 100 per cent mortgages from local authorities and availability of government funds for the purchase of older properties, will all increase demand. Demand will decrease and offer prices will be lowered if any of these concessions are withdrawn or reduced. The imposition of or an increase in taxes borne by property purchasers and occupiers would also decrease demand. Stamp duty on property deals, any property taxes, and even rates may have this effect.

The supply of real property is equally subject to influence by government measures. Landlord–tenant legislation will alter the balance of power between landlord and tenant, usually in favour of the latter. For example, Part 1 of the 1927 Landlord and Tenant Act conceded that a business tenant might be entitled to a new lease after his contractual tenancy had ended. The procedure was simplified and made more certain by the 1954 Act. Sitting tenants have, therefore, been granted a measure of security, and this slows down the rate at which existing properties come on to the market. It may also depress the level of rents of such properties. This is noticed even more in the case of residential property where security of tenure may be coupled with rent control. Supply has been effectively decreased for new occupiers, and adjustments are made in other parts of the property market. Alternatively, estate duty may function to increase the supply of real property being offered for sale in any time period. The break-up of a private landed estate is likely where all or part of the land has to be sold in order to meet the estate duty payable. Perhaps the most significant changes in supply conditions, especially of building land, follow from planning controls: the amount and location of available supply will depend upon the planning principles applied in each case.

The market allocation of real property will therefore reflect changes in demand and supply induced by government measures. Leasehold enfranchisement will, in the long run, lead to an increase in the proportion of real property which is owner-occupied. Improvement grants will alter the allocation of resources as between rehabilitation and new buildng.

Government measures have contrasting objectives regarding the way in which the market works. On the one hand, the recommendations of the Monopolies Commission, following an investigation of professional practices, were designed to improve competitiveness within the property market. On the other hand, the market mechanism may be largely displaced, as with the provision of council housing where supply and levels of rent are related to need, not effective demand. Furthermore, government actions in other spheres have repercussions for the real property market. For example, the Capital Issues Committee control after 1945 led some firms to raise capital by means of a leaseback transaction. A firm could raise capital without CIC sanction by selling its interest in real property on condition that it retained the use of the property. The controls had also closed some investment outlets, therefore investors were willing to experiment with new forms of investment (Lean and Goodall, 1966, pp. 75–76). The result was a change in the relative importance of the types of property interest being traded.

These illustrations, and many others, indicate the complexity of the real property market in practice, but they do not materially alter the underlying principles by which prices are determined in that market.

## Real Property Development

Most demands for change will be accommodated within the existing stock of real property by changes in the location of activities or the amount of space they consume or both. Such changes are possible within the existing stock because most buildings are suitable for many different uses. Only when demand reaches a certain level will there be an economic justification for the modification of a building to suit it more closely to its new function. Less frequently is there an economic basis sufficient to warrant demolition and replacement of existing buildings. Development is, however, a dynamic process bringing adjustments to meet changing conditions. In practice development is seldom carried out by the person who will use the newly developed real property.

The process, by which additions and alterations to the stock of real properties are made, takes place via the price mechanism. Where a person estimates that a particular site has a more profitable use than its existing one he will offer the owner or owners of the interests in that land a price greater than their valuations based on existing use. Such development will involve the destruction of some interests and the creation of others. This in itself is not development, for development takes place when there is capital expenditure on additions to and alterations to the physical structure on the land. Such development can be defined as a set of cost–revenue relationships. The profit from any of these actions is a function of the cost of that action relative to the value of the real property created. The rationale of development therefore depends on the developer's estimate of income to be expected from the new structure compared to the costs of constructing the new structure plus the costs of extinguishing existing interests in that land. In the case of redevelopment, costs must include the costs of demolition of the existing building as well as the value of the original development lost. Other costs that must be considered as part of the costs of development are "ripening costs" where the developer acquires interests well in advance of development and "period of development costs" associated with the fact that the developer makes outlays before receiving any returns. Both depend on interest rates.

Thus the basic questions a developer must answer in respect of any proposed development concern his optimum capital expenditure and the price he is willing to pay to acquire the present interests in the land. The developer will have in mind the minimum net return he requires to persuade him that it is profitable to undertake a particular development. This return will be based on returns from alternative ventures and the risks involved therein compared to the risks attaching to the particular development. The marginal net return required is likely to rise as capital expenditure increases to compensate for the higher risks involved. The marginal net return expected from the development will eventually fall with increased capital expenditure because (a) the capital sum required to produce a given increase in revenue will rise, for after a point building costs increase with increasing height, and (b) rents or prices per unit of accommodation tend to fall as the amount of accommodation provided on a given site increases. As seen in Fig. 3.4, the optimum capital expenditure on a given development will be where the marginal net return required *LM*, is equal to the marginal net return expected *EF*, which is at *B*, indicating an optimum capital expenditure of *OA*. The developer who proposes the highest capital expenditure overall may not be the developer who obtains the site since this will depend on the residual left over to purchase the interest after all other development costs have been considered. The sum to purchase the interests will depend on the anticipated income from the developed property, capital expenditure other than the purchase of these interests, and the return expected by the developer on his capital expenditure.

Thus the developer knows that if he increases the accommodation or size of building on a site he will increase the income to be expected as well as incurring increased capital expenditure. Income will, how-

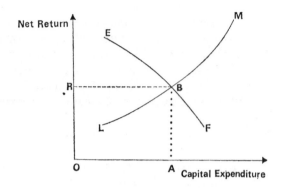

Fɪɢ. 3.4. Determination of the optimum capital expenditure on a development.

ever, increase at a diminishing rate because lower rents or prices per unit will have to be charged where larger amounts of accommodation are provided on the same site. Therefore, increased capital expenditure will increase income and, up to a point, the sum the developer will pay to acquire the interests. Figure 3.5 shows how the sum to

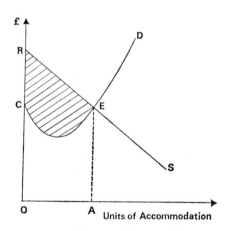

Fɪɢ. 3.5. Determination of the sum to purchase existing interests in a real property.

acquire existing interests in the site is determined. The income or revenue from the sale of each successive unit of accommodation is represented by the downward-sloping line *RS*, and all costs of development, excepting cost of interests in the land, involved in providing each successive unit of accommodation, by the curve *CD*. It is assumed that curve *CD* will decline at first because of certain economies in building as more units are provided, but eventually the cost of developing additional units must rise because building costs rise as extra storeys are added, and higher risks mean the developer requires a higher return. The optimum number of units of accommodation that should be provided on this site will be *OA*. Beyond *OA* an additional unit of accommodation will cost more to develop than the revenue it will bring in. Up to *OA* each additional unit of accommodation will bring in a revenue in excess of the costs of developing it. The sum of these surpluses represents the maximum sum of money available for the purchase of the existing interests in the land. The total income from this particular development will be given by area *OAER* and costs of development, excluding costs of interests in the land, by area *OAEC*. Therefore the maximum amount for the purchase of the existing interests is the shaded area *RCE*. If the developer can obtain these interests for less than *RCE*, he will enjoy super-normal profits. So, as the demand for the use of a site increases, it pays to provide more accommodation on that site and this, as shown, will, up to a point, increase the sum the developer is prepared to pay for the site.

Thus the greater the intensity of development the higher the sum the developer is prepared to pay to obtain existing interests. For example, if there are two sites and difference in location confers a relative accessibility advantage on one of the sites, then the more accessible site will be developed more intensively. If in Fig. 3.6 the line *TS* represents the income per unit of accommodation provided on the most accessible site compared to *RE* in the case of the less accessible site, then, assuming the same other development costs in the two cases, the developer will be prepared to pay *TSC* for the most accessible site compared to *REC* for the less accessible. The shaded area *TSER* represents the extra sum the developer is prepared to pay for the more accessible site, on which he would provide *AD* additional units of accommodation. Thus the greater the demand the greater the intensity of development of land.

Figure 3.6 also shows that a reduction in building costs or a fall in interest rates, by lowering other development costs, increases the sum available for the purchase of the existing interests and the number of

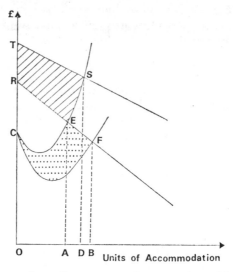

Fig. 3.6. Comparison of sums to purchase two sites with differing accessibility characteristics and the effect of a change in development costs.

units of accommodation provided. Where other development costs fall, curve *CE* moves to position *CF*, then, in the case of the less accessible site, the amount available to purchase the interests rises by the stippled area *CEF* to a total of *RCF* and the amount of accommodation provided on the less accessible site rises by *AB* units. By providing more accommodation one is in effect substituting building for land and the relative costs of land and building will determine how far this substitution takes place. Where land is cheap it will not take much building before it will pay to acquire more land to provide more accommodation, whereas if land is expensive a large amount of building is needed before building costs rise to a level where it pays to acquire more land to increase accommodation.

## The Nature of Urban Land and Property Values

The foundation of much present-day land value theory remains Ricardian rent theory which was developed to explain differential prices paid for agricultural land. This theory argued that the most productive agricultural land would be worked first and that competition between farmers would ensure that the full advantage of its greater inherent fertility would go to landlords in the form of rent. This was a payment, pure and simple, for the special characteristic, in this case fertility, of land. Early economists thus developed the analytical idea of a demand-determined surplus element in a resource's earnings. In the case of natural resources and land which have no cost of production and hence zero supply prices (the same amount of land would be available even if it earned nothing), the entire earnings represent an economic surplus or economic rent.

This line of reasoning can be easily extended to urban areas where the ability of a parcel of land to earn economic rent is due, not so much to its physical characteristics, but to accessibility advantages. Within an urban area there will be a greater demand for the more accessible sites and competition between uses will see to it that landowners gain full advantage of their site's accessibility advantages in the form of economic rent. In practice, economic rent may be defined as a surplus over and above opportunity cost which is given, in the case of an urban site, by the sum that would be earned in its next best alternative use.

The important points to be deduced from this line of reasoning are, firstly, that land values depend on land use (not vice versa), and, secondly, the value of the land is treated separately from the value of the improvements to that land. Improvements represent capital, and as such have a cost of production. In the long run, additional improvements will only be undertaken and existing improvements maintained if income accruing to those improvements covers their cost: whereas, in the case of land, it will be available whatever the income. The prices or values discussed so far in this chapter have been real property values, i.e. prices paid for all the interests in a parcel of land including improvements. In the majority of real property transactions in urban areas, both land and improvements are involved. Such is basically the distinction between the economist's conception of land as a natural resource and the legal concept of interests in land.

What importance attaches to the distinction between land and building value, especially where an attempt is made to divide the market value of an existing improved real property into land and building elements?'Frequently the investor or user regards the income from an existing improved real property as a single sum or joint income from land and building. No distinction is attempted. Certainly there will be occasions when land value is isolated but this will only be in those cases where development of vacant land or redevelopment of existing properties takes place. In both these cases a site value can be determined which represents the value of the site cleared of buildings and any other improvements. This will equal the present value of the stream of net annual incomes that can be earned by investing in the improvements necessary to put the land to its optimum use. The optimum or highest and best use is defined as that present use and programme of future use of a parcel of land which produces the highest present land value (Babcock, 1932). The value of the land is certainly an important consideration in any decision to develop or redevelop a site, since the maximum sum the developer is prepared to pay to obtain or unify the existing interests reflects his valuation of the "land". Note that the land value in this case applies to a particular point in time when a new structure is about to be erected on the site, and represents a sum that developers actually pay.

What of existing buildings? Each existing building will have a market value and, assuming an unencumbered freehold, that market value or selling price would represent a joint land and building value. The existing building may or may not represent the highest and best use of the site. This is less likely the longer the time that has elapsed since the building was erected. As was shown earlier a developer could assess the present value of anticipated income from a building representing the highest and best use of a site and estimate the costs of developing the site with such a building. The difference between the two being the maximum sum the developer would pay for the site or existing interests in that land. If this sum is greater than the market value of the existing building by more than the cost of demolition, then it will be profitable to demolish that building. From this it might be suggested that the market value of the existing building can be divided into site value (reflecting what would be the highest and best use) and a residual value which equals the building's value. If the residual is negative, redevelopment would take place; if it is positive, it indicates the sum that would have to be paid to compensate owners of existing interests for the removal of the building. It is in no sense a market value (Turvey, 1957) since no developer would offer such an amount. Thus it is the sum the developer is willing to pay for existing interests which gives a site value to be compared with the market value of the existing real property in order to arrive at a decision.

Let $V$ equal the market value of the existing real property, $V^1$ the market value of the highest and best-use building, $C$ the costs of developing that highest and best-use building, $S$ the site value of the highest and best-use building, and $D$ the cost of demolishing the existing building. Then the above propositions are:

$$S = V^1 - C, \tag{3.1}$$

and if
$$S > V + D, \tag{3.2}$$

a new building representing the highest and best use will be brought into being. The apparent division

$$V = S + (V - S) \tag{3.3}$$

has no meaning since $(V - S)$ is not the value of the existing building and is not relevant to the decision to redevelop.

An alternative line of reasoning has been used to isolate the site-value element of an existing real property. It may be argued that the existing building has a replacement or reproduction cost. Subtracting the reproduction cost from the market value of the existing real property will give the site value as a residual. If $R$ equals reproduction cost then it is suggested that

$$\text{site value} = V - R. \tag{3.4}$$

Reproduction cost may be irrelevant as when the existing building does not represent the highest and best use. Nor would any developer offer $(V - R)$ because it does not represent $S$, the site value of the highest and best use. Thus the division of the market value of an existing real property into land and building elements appears meaningless. The division is significant only at the point of time when development or redevelopment takes place, i.e. where

$$V^1 - C = V - R, \tag{3.5}$$

which requires

$$V^1 = V \tag{3.6}$$

and

$$C = R, \tag{3.7}$$

and then the calculations are unnecessary because $S$ can be found from the developer's calculation of the sum he is prepared to pay for the existing interests in a real property.

It has been argued that the value of land may appreciate over time, whereas the value of physical improvements depreciates with age (Bourne, 1967; Gottmann, 1961). From this it can be argued that, for any individual real property, payment for land increases as a proportion of total market value of that real property. This presupposes that market value can be subdivided. It can be contended that land appreciates in value because of generally increasing demands for land at particular locations within urban areas and this would be reflected in the increased sums that developers are prepared to pay for existing interests in given real properties. This effect can also be noted in the behaviour of prices paid for freehold ground rents when the reversionary interest begins to influence the value (Lean and Goodall, 1966). Certainly, buildings depreciate with use, otherwise buildings would never be redeveloped on the basis of the developer's calculations.

The value of any improved real property depends on the character and size of building and upon the suitability of the location. For every site there will be, theoretically, both an optimum use and an optimum building which together represent the highest and best use of that site at a given time. That optimum situation would give a maximum value for a real property on that site. The fact that the actual value of the existing real property falls short of this could be due to the fact that the present use is not the highest and best one and/or the design of the building falls short of the optimum.

Aggregate and individual real property values, and hence urban land values, depend on the present value of the future stream of net expected income or benefit. This present value reflects forces influencing gross income, costs, and capitalization rate. Income depends on use, investors' expectations, the competitive pull of the urban area, the nature and supply of urban public services, and changes in population, etc. Costs will be influenced by development costs, operating expenses, interest charges, and taxes. The capitalization rate, although depending primarily on interest rates, will also reflect factors such as the prospect of capital gain. In practice urban real property values in the form of capitalized future net returns provide one method of assessing such values. This capitalization of income method has its origins in time preference and interest theory. However, earlier discussion has revealed alternative methods. Real property values may be estimated by comparison with similar properties. This method is based on the economic law of substitution that shows, in competitive markets, that equal prices are established for commodities of equal status. The efficiency of the urban real property market in this respect has already been commented on. Another method is to consider replacement cost. It can be argued that replacement cost represents a ceiling on market values since the purchaser will pay no more for an interest than the price of obtaining a new version. The replacement cost method is the basis of insurance and mortgage valuations. The idea is based on long-run equilibrium price which, under conditions of pure competition, tends to equal average costs of production of representative firms. Perhaps reproduction, rather than replacement, is a better description since original materials may not be any longer available. The degree of imperfection in the urban real property market will determine the possibility of coincidence between these three methods of assessing real property value. The greater the imperfection the greater the range of values obtaining at any time.

# CHAPTER 4

# Urban Land-use Patterns

## Land-use Patterns in Urban Areas

As urbanization is largely an economic phenomenon it follows that
the internal organization of urban areas reflects economic forces
which facilitate the functioning of the economic sub-systems involved.
A rational pattern of land use develops within any urban area which
mirrors the differing requirements of the various economic activities
and classes of residence. An essential order underlies what, at first
sight, may appear to be a haphazard arrangement of land uses. Within
urban areas people and goods need to move about quickly, cheaply,
and comfortably, often at the same time, and to and from the same
places. Where the profit motive conditions the use of urban land, the
variety of behavioural patterns in the real property market tends to
produce, in the aggregate, economically motivated land use patterns.
On occasions these purely economic actions may be modified by and
in the public interest.

Part of the problem of finding market solutions consists of finding
individual locations. An urban area contains a great variety of interdependent activities and, given the general framework and level of
knowledge prevailing, the choice of location is normally a rational
decision made after the assessment of the relative advantages of
various locations for the performance of the activity in question.

Specialization is a characteristic of urban land-use patterns. Both
within and between urban areas there is more variation in the spatial
distribution of land use between different land-use categories than
within the same category. Via a process of competition, in any urban
area, large or small, activities seek out and segregate themselves in
that part of the urban area in which their optimum conditions are to

80

be found and by virtue of which they are usually able to exclude all other uses. In the case of a competitive economy there is a close limit to the disadvantages acceptable to an activity and the possible advantages of an alternative location that may be forgone. Therefore, in the long run, an activity tends to locate where it enjoys its greatest relative advantage, in which case land is used for its highest and best use. The spatial differentiation of land uses increases with increasing size of urban area reflecting that specialization of activities becomes more commonplace and complex and complementary linkages more numerous.

However, the land-use pattern in an urban area at any particular time represents the cumulative effect of a myriad of decisions and actions by various individuals and organizations. The pattern has been built up over a considerable period of time in response to repeatedly changing demands. Present spatial structure, therefore, details the current state of mutual adjustment.

Two basic factors condition urban land use. Firstly is the importance of non-profit uses of land, in particular roads and other access space. In the development of an urban area, land is automatically divided between land developed for use by persons responding to the profit motive and land which is used for non-profit purposes. The complex of land-use decisions appears to involve priming actions and secondary actions since the development of land for private profit uses is consequent upon certain priming actions, such as the provision of new roads and public utilities. The latter precondition and establish a broad framework for the mass of secondary activities that follow and make up most of the observed pattern. Thus the profitable use of private land is extremely dependent on and complemented by the non-profit uses. Such a rationale places a premium on analysing how and why priming actions occur and how they influence secondary actions.

Secondly, urban land-use patterns are fundamentally influenced by the economic base of the urban area. An economic explanation of urban land-use patterns must involve a consideration of the structure and functioning of the urban economy as it fits into the broader economy of the region and the nation. The nature of the urban economy conditions the use of existing real properties and the amount and type of land development that takes place. The position any urban area occupies in the hierarchy of the urban system will determine the presence or absence of certain economic activities with obvious repercussions for its land-use pattern. Urban function bears on location patterns in that different activities have different locational requirements. All functions will not be found in every urban area thus leading to differences in the proportion of land use in various categories between urban areas. Within an urban area its major economic activities may find their locations quite rigorously determined, and this influences locations chosen by competitive and complementary activities.

## Locational Decisions within an Urban Area

In urban areas persons are preoccupied with contacts. All economic actions of businesses and households involve contacts with other persons. Very often these contacts represent regularized exchanges of goods, services, or information. Resources must be used to allow two or more persons to meet in the exchange of goods and information so that costs of overcoming physical distance will always act to shape these contacts. Generally the cost of movement rises with increasing distance whereas the benefit derived is independent of the distance involved. Persons, therefore, generally seek to avoid unnecessary expenditure of time and effort on movement since the resources involved have an opportunity cost. The shorter the time and the less the effort involved in making contacts, the more time and resources there are to devote to other purposes. In explicit response to this, most businesses and households locate physically close to the other businesses and households with which they deal. Urban areas are themselves an illustration of the resultant focal pattern.

Within an urban area the transportation system plays a crucial role, for there is a functional relationship between that system and the urban land-use pattern. All contacts require some physical movement, if not of persons, of goods or information, and in a particular urban area the capacities of the facilities provided will, in part, determine the levels of contact or interaction possible. Thus transportation, communications, and other public facilities allow contacts to be maintained even though activities are located at some distance from each other. Within the urban area the availability of such facilities forms a network which strongly influences an activity's locational choice.

The study of urban land use may be approached from two basic points of view. Attention may be focused on the urban site and the forces which determine the use to which that site will be put. Alternatively, urban activities can be analysed from the viewpoint of the behaviour of the decision unit in choosing a location. The basic question in the first case is how to use a particular parcel of urban land and, in the second, where to locate a particular urban activity. Emphasis is here placed on the latter approach.

LOCATION CRITERIA

Urban land-use patterns are the result of individuals each bidding for their best combination of two variables—location and quantity of space. The basic principle governing the location of all private economic activity is profit-maximization. This applies equally to the use of land for residential purposes since housing for owner-occupation or renting would only be provided on a site where it represented the most profitable course of action to the landowner. Alternative criteria, such as minimization of aggregate transport costs or minimization of costs of production, are inadequate in so far as they consider only limited factors bearing on profit levels. If the factors ignored by these criteria were constant and independent of location, then profit-maximization positions would coincide with cost-minimization locations but demand may vary with location and the greater revenue obtained at a particular site may more than offset the higher cost incurred there. Attempts to explain spatial structure in cost-minimization terms have, therefore, been superseded by attempts which balance costs and benefits. Thus transport and/or production costs will be minimized where that course of action leads to higher profits than any alternative action, but transport inputs will be substituted for other inputs and vice versa where such action brings the highest returns. Substitution, where the location decision is involved, is not a simple matter. For example, accessibility or physical proximity can act as a substitute for transport, but both have to be paid for. Where access costs are high an activity may choose not only to alter its location, but also the amount of space consumed at a location. There is interaction between an activity's characteristics, accessibility, transport inputs, location, quantity of space, and other inputs. Therefore the net balance of pulls exerted on each activity is a major factor in the spatial arrangement of land uses. Each activity tends to that location where the forces of anticipated contacts are in equilibrium, i.e. the site where an activity enjoys its greatest relative advantage. For individual firms this is the location at which profits are maximized, and for individual households the location which maximizes satisfaction. In every case this is reflected by their being able to offer the highest price for the location in question, which ensures that land is put to its most profitable use.

LOCATION FACTORS

Activities seek that location, size, and shape of site that maximizes profits or satisfaction. The space and location requirements of urban activities will be determined by their internal and external functions (Rannells, 1956, ch. 4; Wingo, 1961, p. 16). The quantity, quality, and shape of space needed by each activity is conditioned by its internal functioning. In the case of business firms this will reflect certain technological and scale factors such as the layout of the production line, the minimum scale of operation, and the need for display, selling, storage, and loading space. Quantity of space will depend on intensity of use. Where a given volume of work is spread over day and night shifts, less space will be required than where it is carried out in a single shift. Less space is needed where children share a bedroom than where each child has its own bedroom. Operating costs of all businesses depend partially on size and shape of site since the latter influence the ease of handling materials and products, maintenance arrangements, or space for daylighting. Volume of business, especially in the case of retailing, may also partially depend on size and shape of site. Similar reasoning applies to households where size of site reflects consumer preferences in respect of space for privacy and quality of dwelling.

The spatial behaviour of an activity is a matter of relating these internal considerations to the general urban economic environment in an optimum way. Since the purpose of urban concentration is to facilitate contacts, then the most important class of location factor involves advantages of physical proximity, i.e. the access quality of location. The locational requirements of an activity depend on the number and nature of its external contacts. Every parcel of land has two economic characteristics of interest, a natural endowment, and a quality of location. The economic role of natural endowment is limited in the case of urban land to those geographical and geological features which affect the usefulness of the site or condition the expenditure necessary to bring it into a particular use. In urban areas the quality of location is the dominant factor, especially for business use of land. For business, location largely determines volume of sales' turnover, most especially in the case of retailing, as well as influencing operating costs in terms of distance from material sources, transport terminals, warehouses, and customers. The relative advantage of the location may also reflect the prestige status of the area and opportunities to benefit from external economies. Households similarly evaluate access advantages of locations. Here access to commercial, industrial, and other land uses is important as well as the quality of the surrounding neighbourhood. Therefore relative access advantages of location appear as the major determinant of urban land-use patterns.

## ACCESSIBILITY

Accessibility evaluates the ease with which contacts may be made, as between producer and material supplier, producer and wholesaler, wholesaler and retailer, retailer and consumer, etc., in terms of the net economic benefits derivable from using a given site. Contacts may be made in the form of communications via letter or telephone as well as by movements of persons and goods. Accessibility, for both businesses and households, bears on both the benefits derived and the costs of operating from a given site. The more accessible the site used the greater the benefits and/or the lower the costs. For example, accessibility determines a business's cost of assembling inputs and distributing products as well as influencing total revenue by conditioning the number of customers purchasing the firm's good or service. The time and effort costs of making contacts is essentially an opportunity cost, for businesses and households could be doing other things. Distance involved in contacts is always relative and is evaluated by persons in terms of their previous experiences.

Within an urban area accessibility is a relative quality accruing to each site by virtue of its relationship to the urban transport system. This functional relationship with transportation led to the contention that the costs of overcoming the friction of space comprised two elements—a site rental and a transport cost. The site rental was envisaged as the charge a landowner could levy for savings in transport costs arising from the use of his site, i.e. for the accessibility advantages of the site (Haig, 1926, pp. 402–34). Transport costs and site rentals were complementary. As already indicated, accessibility influences the volume of business conducted, the revenue obtained, and, hence, the rent or price a potential user is willing to pay for a site. In the case of retail uses, costs may be virtually the same for various locations, but revenue can differ enormously.

If equal importance is attached to access from a given site to every other urban site, then, given the transportation system, there will be a position of greatest accessibility within the urban area corresponding to the focal point of the transportation system. Around this position is a basically concentric pattern of declining accessibility with increasing distance from the position of greatest accessibility but with attenuations along major routeways. This position of maximum overall access usually refers to customer access and represents the place at which the urban population could assemble with the least expenditure of time and effort. This is not necessarily the point of least total miles of travel. Outside of the point of greatest accessibility, other positions of local accessibility occur at minor foci in the transportation system, and the basic concentric pattern of access, centripetal movement of persons, and centrifugal movement of goods is replicated in each part of the urban area although on a smaller scale than for the urban area as a whole.

Activities differ in the degree to which they can take advantage of the locational qualities of the position of greatest accessibility. Indeed, potential users differ considerably in their access needs. Most important for urban land-use patterns are those access links for which costs are high and increase rapidly with distance within the intra-urban range. These are, basically, contacts which involve movement of persons. Therefore activities requiring personal contacts tend to cluster in areas with superior mass transit facilities or heavy pedestrian traffic. Activities handling goods in bulk tend to locate adjacent to heavy transportation facilities. In general, goods-handling requires more space, both inside and outside buildings, than activities dealing with persons and, therefore, in that it uses space less intensively, goods-handling can reap less benefit from the position of greatest accessibility. Moreover, as access linkages become more difficult, greater stocks of materials and products must be held with a consequent need for more space. The differential access advantages possessed by some sites mean that the application of labour and capital to those sites yields higher returns than elsewhere and the demand for such accessible sites will be greater than for less accessible ones. As accessibility increases, transport cost savings and/or sales revenue rise, so that activities which derive the greatest benefits from occupying accessible locations will have the largest surpluses available to bid for such sites. The more important is access to an activity the smaller the range of sites it has to choose from.

The nature of the contacts necessitated in the course of an activity's functioning determine the accessibility requirements demanded of possible sites (Lean and Goodall, 1966, pp. 136–8). A producer's dealings with his customers may be on a face-to-face basis, over the telephone, via letter, or some intermediary. Compare a department store where the customer has to visit the store and comes face-to-face with a sales assistant with a mail-order store whose basic contact with customers is through the postal service supplemented, perhaps, by local field agents. Access to customers is important in both cases, but is more critical for the department store which is, therefore, more likely to occupy a site in the area of greatest accessibility. The department store relies on customers coming to what is, in effect, the producer's location, whereas in other cases, such as insurance agents and travelling salesmen, the producer or his agent goes to the customer's location. The greater the reliance on the assembly of customers at a location, the more critical the need to locate in the position of greatest accessibility. The number of contacts to be made, their frequency, regularity, and urgency must also be considered. For example, in the case of retailing, the larger the number of regular customers making non-postponable purchases at frequent intervals, the more critical is immediate accessibility.

Accessibility is similarly important for a business's contacts with its factor inputs. Considerations of type of contact; movement of factors or of producer; amount, frequency, and speed of contact are repeated for all factor requirements. Whether access to customers or to factors is the stronger for any business, depends on the relative importance of distribution and assembly costs compared to revenue possibilities. The firm dependent on access to a particular factor input may well seek a different site from the firm demanding access to final consumers. Access to customers and scale of operation are interlinked. Any consumer serving activity that can attain economies of scale without having to serve the entire urban area from a single plant, will increase its accessibility by dispersing to points of local accessibility.

It can be concluded from the various facets of accessibility that access to customers and factors will be of varying degrees of importance to business users of sites. Hence demand for sites is highly differentiated. The more important is accessibility to a given business the more restricted its choice of site because the possibility of substituting a site with poor access qualities for one with good accessibility is extremely limited. The demand of such users for sites is likely to be more inelastic than the demand of potential users with a wider range of substitution possibilities.

Households' choice of residential location also takes accessibility into account, for it is one factor influencing the level of satisfaction enjoyed by a household from the use of a residence at a given location. Members of a household seek access to job opportunities, shops, schools, hospitals, worshipping, and entertainment facilities, and the homes of relatives and friends. Travelling represents a disutility for household members, and such disutility can be minimized by locating at a site offering relative accessibility advantages. However, persons are willing to travel different distances for different purposes, and the more employment opportunities and other everyday facilities are dispersed throughout the urban area the less the premium households place on locations close to the position of greatest accessibility. Moreover, certain amenity factors influence a household's choice of residential site. Space, quiet, privacy, and fresh air add to the satisfaction derived by the household, but these qualities can usually be obtained only at less accessible sites near the edge of the urban area. Consumer preferences will determine the extent to which any household is willing to accept travel disutilities in order to gain greater amenity. It would appear that less accessibility is purchased by households as their income increases. Thus accessibility behaves as an inferior good, and more amenity is substituted for access with increasing income.

Therefore the demand for sites in an urban area reflects the degree to which any business or household is dependent on and can benefit from accessibility. This determines the rent or price they will pay for a site with the desired access qualities.

COMPLEMENTARITY

Complementary linkages tend to pull closely related activities into proximate locations. This interdependence of activities is reflected in the fact that once certain sites in an area are developed for a particular use, this largely determines the highest and best use of the remaining sites. Where a given site is surrounded by offices it is likely to be used for a commercial building since erection in the midst of an existing concentration will capitalize on the advantages of an already successful concentration. Should the available site be too small for a block of offices, it will be worth far less per square foot than the average for the area. The advantages of complementarity result in the clustering within urban areas of like uses. Each residential area tends to be populated by households of similar income occupying houses of similar standard. This is especially so the higher a household's income, since it is seen as a means of maintaining property values. Such residential segregation has repercussions for other urban land uses because people with similar incomes have similar consumption patterns and retail activities catering to the needs of a particular income group locate so as to be accessible to that group. For example, milliners, furriers, and other high fashion shops locate in response to high income groups. Surplus stores and second-hand clothes dealers are found near the lowest income groups. In this way movement of customers is minimized. Such retail uses form complementary clusters as persons use various means of transport to reach a complementary group, but once there, they walk. A group of shops are complementary in terms of attracting customers in the sense that together they provide a more complete range of goods and services. Department stores locate next door to each other to stimulate sales through comparison shopping. In one respect the department store appears to have internalized, by horizontal integration, the advantages gained by the clustering of many smaller, independent shops.

Unlike uses also cluster where integrated local sequences arise from efforts to reduce space frictions and operational imperfections. These uses are complementary in terms of cutting costs. One firm may use the by-product of another as a factor input, or firms may perform separate stages in the production of a good or require the specialist services of other activities. Where the site, or more usually the building, cannot be subdivided to provide a particular user with a sufficiently small site/building, that user may combine with others and together they can obtain a more accessible site than where each acted independently. This represents complementary use of the same real property as where retailing occupies the basement and ground floor and offices the upper floors.

Wherever a use demands a special location in an area, it must pay extra to keep out other users and such payment often arises where proximity to other businesses is needed. The number and size of complementary clusters is a function of the size of the urban area and the level of accessibility. For example, the greater the degree of accessibility, the more opportunities there are for specialist activities to come into being and the greater the likelihood of complementary clusters developing.

## INCOMPATIBILITY

In other cases the decision to locate a particular activity in an area causes other activities to seek alternate locations because the spatial proximity of any pair of land uses may be so incompatible that they seek locations protected from each other. This is due to the effect on the operation of one or both activities either in terms of a reduction in revenue/satisfaction or an increase in costs. Most obvious is the effect of the so-called obnoxious group of industries, such as oil refineries, tanneries, abbattoirs, glue, paint, and linoleum factories. Residences and factories demanding high standards of hygiene, such as food processing and pharmaceuticals, will seek locations away from obnoxious industry. On a different scale, shops prefer not to be located next to banks or cinemas because the latter's opening hours are shorter or different and their display space negligible. Competitive uses may also be considered incompatible where they are retail units selling items of an everyday or convenience nature in which comparison is unimportant. Such retail units seek locations protected from their competitors so that they may cash in on the effort needed to go to the next nearest store.

## Determination of Urban Land-use Patterns

The pattern of land use in any urban area is a reflection of the competition for sites between various uses operating through the price system. The above discussion has shown the demand for sites to be highly differentiated because the earning capacity of some firms is highly dependent on their being able to occupy particular locations. Such firms are those most reliant upon accessibility and/or complementarity and they will be prepared to pay more, relative to alternative sites, for positions with the desired characteristics than other users. Their demand for such sites tends to be relatively inelastic although the spatial extent of the market and the elasticity of demand for the final product must be considered. For example, a firm whose market comprises and is confined to the whole urban area may well face a relatively inelastic demand for its product because substitution possibilities are limited. Therefore this firm's demand for a site in the position of greatest accessibility will be relatively inelastic and its demand will become increasingly inelastic with small increases in distance from that position. A firm supplying only a small proportion of the national market for a final product where consumer demand is elastic will have a relatively elastic demand even for sites near the urban periphery.

The supply of urban sites is equally differentiated, again, by virtue of location. At any given time the supply of sites in any urban area is fixed within relatively narrow limits by (1) physical factors, such as relief, (2) the areal network of public utility services, and (3) the spatial technology of its transportation system. In accessibility terms sites adjacent to main roads or railway stations have a relative access advantage over sites more distant from such facilities. Sites in and around the focus of the intra-urban transportation system have the greatest relative advantage. Indeed, the access advantage of this focus is the key factor in urban land-use patterns.

Space and location are economic commodities subject to supply and demand forces. The urban real property market requires of each site or real property its highest and best use and this is largely determined by competition between potential users for available properties. The price paid by the successful bidder is the price necessary to keep out alternative uses, i.e. high enough to compete the site away from them. In theory all activities compete for all sites whereas in practice effective competition for the less accessible sites is restricted since certain uses would find the increased costs or lower revenue prohibitive to their operation. Where competition occurs, it may be between similar uses as with two department stores competing for the position of greatest accessibility or between different uses as when industry and residence compete for a riverfront location. The order of precedence of activities is worked out by competitive bidding. For example, in Fig. 4.1, assuming a uni-centred urban area, the downward sloping lines represent respective offer prices of potential users, based on their ability to benefit from the centre's advantages, at various distances from $O$, the position of greatest accessibility. Thus at $O$ retail use, which is most dependent on general accessibility, can compete sites away from all other users. As the offer price curve of retail use falls off more steeply than that of offices or residences, reflecting the increasing disadvantage of less accessible sites for retailing, then, at any distance greater than $OX$ away from the position of greatest accessibility, offices will be able to compete sites away from retail. Similarly beyond $OY$ the offer price of residence is greater than that of offices and residence will

occupy land out to the margin of the urban area where the offer price
of agriculture will be greater than that of residence.

The pattern of land use and the aggregate level of prices is determined by supply and demand forces, while the spatial pattern of uses
and values reflects, in particular, the differential access advantages
through the effect on the productivity of each site. The predominant
situation in practice is that activities requiring particular locations

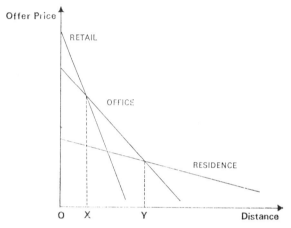

FIG. 4.1. Offer prices of retail, office, and residential uses with
distance from urban centre.

have to adjust to the existing real properties whether or not the latter
are suitable. This may reflect back on earning capacity.

Such reasoning applies to all urban areas. It is to be expected that
the same or similar activities in different urban areas will make comparable gains from occupying and using sites in equivalent positions
within each urban area. If the user of a given location in one urban
area can make large enough gains in that position to enable him to
compete the site away from other potential users, then it is likely that
another person carrying out the same activity in another urban area
will be able to make similar gains and compete a comparable position
away from other users in that area. Thus similar patterns of land use
are likely to emerge in all urban areas.

## Principles Governing Urban Layout

The similarity of land-use patterns in different urban areas supports the assertion that there are certain general principles which govern urban layouts. Guiding motives for firms, i.e. profit-maximization, and households, satisfaction-maximization, have been mentioned, and these hold true under all forms of competition although only under the assumptive conditions of perfect competition are they compatible with maximum efficiency in the use of resources from the community's point of view. In monopoly situations profit-maximization may lead to a misallocation of resources because firms are equating marginal revenue with marginal cost below price. In effect each case must be treated on its merits (or demerits). In that perfect competition can never exist in practice and monopoly situations are frequent in the spatial system, a straightforward and simple criterion may not be forthcoming. However, several attempts to suggest one have been made.

In one case (Haig, 1926) the role of transport was seen as critical. If all activities and consumers were in the same place, no resources or effort need be devoted to overcoming physical distance. Alternatively, if transportation were instantaneous and costless, urban activities could spread themselves over all usable space. Thus Haig argued that the theoretically perfect site for any activity was that which yielded the required access characteristics at the lowest costs of space friction. Friction costs comprised transport costs and site rents. These were complementary since site rent was viewed as a charge levied by landowners for the annual savings in transport costs made possible by the use of sites, compared to the highest cost location in use. The layout of urban areas under conditions of perfect competition would therefore be determined by the principle of minimization of costs of friction. This line of reasoning was developed to show (Ratcliffe, 1949, pp. 371–3) that the perfect land market would produce that pattern of land use in an urban area which resulted in minimum aggregate land values as well as lowest aggregate transport costs. Payment for location is something more than a payment for savings in transport costs, especially where final product demand varies substantially with location, as in retailing, or where amenity value influences the payment, as in the case of residence. Moreover, increased spending on transport will be substituted for other expenditures where such a course of action gives rise to greater profits or satisfaction. In so far as friction costs are only one factor bearing on the level of profitability or satisfaction, such a criterion would lead to a sub-optimal position.

An alternative line of reasoning suggests that the theoretically best pattern of land use is one where land values in an urban area are maximized (Garrison *et al.*, 1959; Lean and Goodall, 1966, p. 247; Margolis, 1968). This is based on the idea that landowners seek to maximize returns from land and the rent or price of land is a charge based on the profit or satisfaction derived from the use of a site. The greater the profit or satisfaction a user obtains from the use of a site, the more he is willing to pay for it. This profit/satisfaction may not be transferable to other sites. Thus where the friction of distance was minimized, rents/prices would be maximized because the surplus remaining after other costs had been met would be greater than, *ceteris paribus*, where friction costs were higher. Hence the ceiling prices of potential users would be higher and competition between users would raise price to a level between the highest and second highest ceiling prices. However, problems arise in practice with land value criteria because of complications (1) due to monopoly values, and (2) in separating land and building values, i.e. the value of land in use (as opposed to the acquisition value of land). Lean (1969, p. 85) suggests, therefore, that the total value of real properties be used as a measure of layout efficiency, but this accounts for only the second problem.

## Generalized Pattern of Urban Land Use

The land-use pattern of any urban area is not an exact reflection of the immediate and current space requirements but rather a reflection of the cumulative needs over a period of time which has arisen from the differing requirements of the various uses with regard to the accessibility and complementarity advantages of sites. Urban areas never attain an equilibrium pattern of land use; thus comparative static analysis cannot explain urban layout (Turvey, 1957, p. 34). However, the price mechanism always operates, in practice, within a restricted framework (Goodall, 1970) and competition within that framework will result in a market solution. Although equilibrium may never be attained because determining conditions are insufficiently stable in relation to the durability of buildings, the price system will bring a solution to the short-run allocational problem of the use of the fixed number of real properties. Thus the urban land-use pattern, at any time, comprises two elements—the buildings and other facilities built up in the long run and the activities presently using those buildings. The principle of specialization applies to both the pattern of buildings and the pattern of activities.

Taking as given the position of greatest accessibility, as determined by the transport system, it is found that land uses may be concentrically arranged about this position since certain functions are related to distance from this position. Superimposed on any concentric pattern are (1) an axial pattern reflecting major transport routes and a sectoral division of land uses, and (2) local concentrations or nuclei outside the position of greatest accessibility. The diversity of activities in any urban area is partly a function of population size. Up to a point the larger the population the larger is the internal market for locally supplied goods and, therefore, the greater the variety of facilities and specialization of land use.

The location of many activities in an urban area is quite rigorously determined as when natural factors narrow choice of site, as for a municipal airport, or where access to regional and national markets dictates direct access to inter-urban transport terminals. Access linkages and agglomerative factors produce other specialist elements in the pattern (Hoover, 1968). The distribution of activities supplying retail goods and services reflects not only aggregate demand but also supply characteristics, such as indivisibility. High-order retail uses pay top prices for sites in the position of greatest accessibility. This forms a skeleton about which other land uses are arranged according to ability to pay. In general, residence is considered as an urban-filling activity dependent primarily on basic industrial–commercial location, although residence is followed by low-order retail uses. The similarities in urban land-use patterns and the fact that distance from the position of greatest accessibility is still the most meaningful measure of urban structure, allow the general pattern of land uses to be considered under the headings of the central business district, the zone of transition, the suburbs, and the rural–urban fringe. Such a well-differentiated pattern will have emerged in urban areas of 10,000 population.

## The Central Business District

The central business district develops around the focus of intra-urban transportation facilities and is, therefore, the position of greatest accessibility to the whole urban area. Located there are high-order activities characterized by unique accessibility requirements to the maximum number of people, i.e. activities able to make the greatest net gain from the accessibility advantages. Competition for the very restricted supply of sites is great, giving rise to peak land values and fully built-on sites. Use intensity is also reflected in the tallest multi-storied buildings in the urban area, for the skyscraper is an economic way of providing access in the urban centre for activities not requiring street display space. All activities tend to assemble people especially for work, consequently daytime population far exceeds resident population. An intricate web of complementary linkages has developed, for activities use each other's products or services, or together extend the range of goods and services offered, or need close communication to function efficiently.

In horizontal plan the central business district may be irregularly shaped and, depending on the transportation system, need not be in the physical centre of the urban area. Its areal size increases as the urban area grows but not proportionately, thus the spatial concentration of various activities is inversely related to urban size. The smaller the urban area, the greater the proportionate concentration of these activities in the central business district. Even in the largest urban areas this suggests a limited scale for the central business district, and beyond the point where further benefits from division into specialist subcores is negligible, additional business districts may be established elsewhere.

Activities demanding access to the whole urban population, as a source of customers or workers, compete for central business district sites. In general, retail uses, because dependent on customer attraction, outbid competitors for the most strategic sites. Such retailing is a primary central activity and the department stores, variety chain stores, and specialist shops form a compact group, the 100 per cent district, where virtually no other use occupies ground-floor space. These stores sell shopping and/or speciality goods for which the customer is prepared to travel some distance in order to compare commodities. Corner sites, because of display advantages, will be the highest valued sites, with department stores often occupying a complete block. Surrounding the department stores are the variety chain stores, shops selling women's clothing, and, on smaller sites, specialist shops, such as jewellers, booksellers, and furriers, who often make use of arcade-type entrances to maximize display frontage. Shops requiring extensive internal display space relative to turnover, e.g. furniture stores, are found on the fringe because their bids are less competitive. Interspersed among the shops may be establishments offering consumer services—banks, restaurants, and ticket agencies. Where shops occupy only the ground floor, upper floors may be used by offices and professional services having similar accessibility requirements such as employment agencies, solicitors, accountants, and dentists.

Retailing may also be accessory to other primary central activities, so that when the central business district divides into sub-cores, convenience retailing to serve the working population will be found scattered throughout the area. Besides retailing, the other major sub-core comprises offices. These offices are involved in executive and policy-making decisions in commerce, industry, and government, and are not dependent on the general buying public but need a central location in order to obtain necessary supplies of labour. They are especially reliant upon complementarity. Although some services are internal to an office, typing for instance, many are external and require frequent face-to-face contact between members of individual offices. In the City of London the clearing banks, discount houses, merchant banks, and offices of overseas, Irish, and Scottish banks cluster around the Bank of England and the Stock Exchange because of the need for close contact with the central bank, the use of town clearing, the need for frequent and quick exchange of documents, and their participation in the various sections of the financial market

(Dunning, 1969). Offices use space more intensively than even retailing, and in largest urban areas offices may occupy the highest valued sites.

Public administration is also a prominent central use. Although shielded from market operations its accessibility requirements in many cases demand a central location. Hotels catering for visitors may cluster around passenger transport terminals. Entertainment facilities are most probably scattered amongst the shops, having similar access requirements, and size of urban area will determine whether they come together in a "bright-lights" district. Many activities presently located in the central business district are there because of access linkages/requirements that disappeared long ago. This is true for many central churches. The boundary of the central business district is indistinct but characterized by less intensive uses like car parking and warehousing.

## The Zone of Transition

Surrounding the central business district is a zone which was built up largely during the nineteenth century when transport lines were inflexible and there were few restrictions on density and type of building. Today this area possesses neither the locational advantages of the centre nor conditions generally attractive for residence. Real property owners, however, expect the central business district to expand into the zone, and this contributes to relatively high land values. The zone has undergone and is undergoing change. Few of the existing buildings were purpose-built for their present occupiers having been converted from residential use. Different parts of the zone are differentially affected by this change (Griffin and Preston, 1966). Change is most prominent where non-residential uses are invading the better quality residential areas. Such residences are converted for use as offices by local government and charitable institutions or for private educational concerns, maternity and nursing homes and the like. Here there will be some new office and flat building, giving a mixture of new and old buildings. Elsewhere in the zone, piecemeal conversion brings slower change as residence is replaced by light manufacturing and wholesaling and even lower quality residence.

Areas of stability correspond to incumbent uses which have successfully resisted invasion, most often, heavy industry or slums. There is a great variety of land use taking the zone as a whole, but like activities cluster. Thus wholesaling with stocks, private and commercial storage, and produce markets are found in close association with transport terminals and industrial establishments; commercial ribbons are located along major roads crossing the area; parking, car sales and service, are also grouped; and residences of similar type are found together.

The business activities have essential links either with the central retail-office core or the rest of the urban area. For example, warehousing of retail stocks needs access to the central shops or shops scattered throughout the outer urban area as well as adequate transport facilities. The zone acts as a nursery for small specialist firms who depend on the many industrial and commercial services available in urban areas. They are often marginal firms, uncertain as to their future, attracted by cheap premises but needing access to skilled labour. Most contribute a high "value added" during processing since few raw materials are used and products are of high value in relation to weight and bulk. Small clothing firms may produce goods for sale in central shops; printing firms serve the needs of the office community. Highly specialized firms, such as dental technicians, serve the whole urban area, whilst precision engineers may have an even wider market.

The area contains the oldest residences still used as such. Residence can compete only if high density, and this takes two contrasting forms. Luxury apartments in select residential quarters represent either old high-class districts which have resisted the infiltration of incompatible uses or the result of urban redevelopment. Elsewhere accommodation for the lowest income groups comprises either purpose-built structures provided by private enterprise or local authorities or higher quality residences converted to a more intensive use as original residents moved out and the houses slid down the social scale. Thus the present state of affairs in the zone of transition depends on the process of change, which will be discussed more fully in Chapter 7.

## The Suburban Area

The suburban area is occupied by urban-filling activities or activities dependent on access to other urban areas for markets. Residence occupies by far the largest part of this area and has been developed at moderate densities to provide households with a reasonably spacious and amenable environment not too far removed from job opportunities and central facilities and with ready access to local shops, schools, churches, and the like. Desirable neighbourhoods are homogeneous, and segregation is an economic commodity that households will pay for, so, although overall there is considerable variety in suburban housing, on any one street or estate, houses are likely to be highly standardized.

Suburban shops, catering especially for everyday needs, are located in positions of local accessibility from where they can best serve residential areas. An exception is the continuous commercial use found along major radial roads. Two contrasting patterns of retailing are thus evident. The nature of shops and services along a commercial ribbon depends (1) on the importance of the routeway which influences the attraction of traffic-serving activities, e.g. filling stations, cafés, and car-accessory shops, and (2) on the degree to which it also serves as the core of a residential area which draws convenience-type shops such as supermarkets, laundrettes, and hairdressers. The greater is residential segregation by socio-economic class the larger is the proportion of local shopping trips that can be satisfied by nucleated shopping centres—the second element in the pattern. These serve the different classes from positions providing the required local access—such as the intersection of a radial and a ring road. Nucleated centres differ considerably in size and in variety of activities present. In London suburbs, these centres may include department stores, variety chain stores, specialist shops, and public utility offices. In smaller centres a collection of shops—grocer, greengrocer, hardware store, dispensing chemist, etc.—serving only everyday needs is more likely. The internal structure of these centres reflects ability to pay for and benefit from the position of local accessibility (Garner, 1966). At the lowest level, in the older residential suburbs, the general corner shop occupies a position of local accessibility in respect of surrounding streets.

Suburban manufacturing has a lineal pattern and is primarily concerned with the production of goods for distribution beyond the immediate urban area. Not wanting access to a single market, such industry, therefore, needs access to adequate inter-urban transportation facilities. Even in suburban areas, industry finds benefits from clustering. Ring and radial roads are favoured by light industry and inter-urban rail facilities are preferred by heavier industry. Industry can effectively compete for adequate space for horizontal factory layouts and for accessory activities (parking, future expansion) in the suburban area. Industry regarded as incompatible by other urban and industrial uses is also likely to find a sufficiently isolated site in the suburban area. The suburban land-use picture is completed by other extensive land uses such as parks, allotments and playing fields, which are effectively squeezed out of more accessible locations by higher order uses.

### The Rural–Urban Fringe

Urban influence extends well beyond the continuous built-up area to include, at least, the area from which daily commuters are drawn. The single-family homes of such commuters mix with rural uses of land in the rural–urban fringe. Such commuters enjoy high incomes and the relative importance of commuting costs is less for them than for lower income groups; thus accessibility behaves as an inferior good. Since the value of land may reflect the possibilities of urban development, agricultural land must be farmed intensively if agriculture is to compete with residence. Very particular types of agriculture, directly adapted to market demand and supply forces, such as horticultural specialities, will be found (Gottmann, 1961, p. 226, and ch. 6). A correlation between part-time farming and urban opportunities is also to be expected where adjustments of farming operations permit the combination of farm and off-farm employment (Parker and Davies, 1962).

### Correlates of Urban Land-use Patterns

The economic efficiency of urban areas reflects not only in specialization of activities and land-use patterns but also in patterns of land values and use intensity. Land values are highest in the position of greatest accessibility where demand for sites is greatest and the supply most restricted and the greatest benefits are realizable. Advantages of complementarity result in the division of the central business district into sub-cores, each with its own peak value. Whether the highest land values are in the retail or office sub-core depends on the size and function of the urban area. Accessibility considerations thus tend to centralize land values in a directional sense (Horwood and Boyce, 1959; Seyfried, 1963), and values fall increasingly away from the position of peak land values as accessibility and complementarity advantages decline. For Topeka (Knos, 1962) land values were found to vary inversely with the reciprocal of distance from the central business district (and not simply inversely as had been hypothesized). The smaller the urban area, the greater is the proportion of total urban land values represented by the central business district. For Chicago the central area declined from 56 per cent of the total land value in 1836 to only 20 per cent in 1928 (Hoyt, 1933).

Outside the central business district, positions of local accessibility have higher land values than surrounding areas. These generally correspond to nucleated suburban shopping centres and suburban railway stations (Hayes, 1957). Major radial routes are followed by ridges of higher land values. Knos's Topeka study showed that land values varied inversely with the reciprocal of distance from a radial road, whilst Hayes's work in Chicago showed suburban railways running along an area of high residential values although the actual railway line ran in a trough of lower values about half a mile wide (Fig. 4.2). Residential land values are depressed near industry (Muth, 1965; Daly, 1967) as it would appear that access advantages are more than offset by unfavourable neighbourhood effects. Local shops, high ground, parks, beaches, and lakes have a favourable effect on residential land values (Brigham, 1965; Yeates, 1965; Daly, 1967), and appear to be of increasing importance. Differences in residential land values can also reflect racial or national groups. Where such groups accept a lower standard of living and are of lower economic status, there is likely to be greater physical depreciation of properties, greater rent arrears, and tenant instability which leads to the capitalization of the rent at a higher rate and, therefore, lower capital values and land values. The more employment opportunities are dispersed and the less the premium placed on locations near to the urban centre, the flatter the value gradient; indeed, land values in certain peripheral residential areas may be higher than nearer the centre as Yeates found for parts of Chicago.

Intensity of land use is also correlated with patterns of land use and land values since the greater the accessibility of land, the more profitable it is to provide additional accommodation, i.e. to use the site

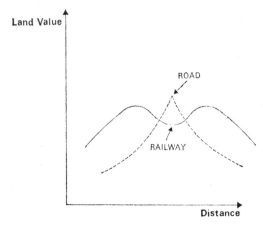

Fig. 4.2. Comparative effect of radial road and rail routes on land values.

more intensively. This is not always the case for retail productivity is very much a function of ground floor selling space rather than total floor space. In all other cases, activities making the most intensive use of sites are able to compete those sites away from less intensive uses. The greatest intensity of use is found in the position of greatest accessibility and complementarity but, in accordance with the law of diminishing returns, there are limits to the intensity with which the best sites may be used. Increased intensity eventually raises costs and a point is reached where this more than offsets benefits and forces the use of less-accessible sites. These will be less intensively developed with small peaks of greater intensity associated with positions of local accessibility.

Attempts to measure intensity of use have largely been confined to residential population density gradients. If persons respond similarly to access considerations and have the same leeway in space consumption, then densities will be highest in the central business district and will decline with increasing distance from the centre depending on the time and money costs of transport and the trade-off between spaciousness of sites and journey to the centre. Population density falls off as a negative exponential function of increasing distance from the central business district (Clark, 1951), although the steepness of decline varies considerably between urban areas. Generally, the larger the urban area, the flatter is the slope. However, Muth (1965) found that the exponential formula as a regression equation accounted for only half the observed variations in population density in south Chicago.

### Differences in Land-use Patterns Between Urban Areas

Emphasis has been focused on the economic forces producing similarities in patterns between urban areas, but striking differences also occur. Differences in overall patterns are due to variations in the framework within which these economic forces operate. Thus differences in pattern illustrate that the price system working within varying frameworks will produce different results and do not undermine the contention that the principles determining land use are the same for all areas. No two urban areas have the same background conditions or framework. Therefore, no two urban areas have identical land-use patterns. The framework will comprise physical conditions of terrain, climate and geological structure, consumer preferences and institutional considerations involving the legal qualities of land, the general availability of transport, and the provision of land uses not subject to pricing.

The economic base of an urban area has obvious repercussions for land use. A holiday resort is likely to have a smaller proportion of land devoted to manufacturing and a much higher proportion to hotels, boarding houses, and entertainment than an industrial urban area. Function has repercussions for internal organization, and this in turn influences overall shape. Shape reflects back on internal organization.

The central business district is more fully developed, and there are fewer other business districts the more compact and equal the development of an urban area in all directions. Where development is unequal, shopping provision is lower in the central business district, there are more shops per head, and more non-central shopping centres.

Physical factors have important consequences for the costs of urban construction, operation, and maintenance. Flat land promotes urban efficiency. The presence of water bodies or varying degrees of slope add to the cost of providing and maintaining the urban infrastructure and to urban running costs without commensurate additions to benefits. In an urban area athwart a river with limited crossing points, access will be more difficult than in a similar-sized urban area not on a river. Indeed, transport routes, which determine accessibility characteristics, are themselves very much influenced by relief and water bodies. An urban area athwart a through route will be more, elongated in overall shape than an urban area which is a junction for routes from all points of the compass. Linear urban areas also develop in narrow, steep-sided valleys, as in South Wales, because marginal costs of urban expansion are less in the up- and down-valley directions than for expansion up the valley sides. Where an urban area is located on a plain at the foot of a range of mountains, an asymmetrical pattern is likely since costs are lower and access is easier on the plain. Sites, such as elevated ground, which are more expensive to develop may have an amenity value which attracts high-income residence. Similarly, proximity to natural water bodies and even artificial ones (Burby, 1967) is a sought-after residential amenity. However, industry may require such water bodies for cooling or effluent disposal purposes.

Local climatic conditions can be significant. Prevailing winds carry industrial smoke in certain directions creating a "black belt" to be avoided by all who can afford to live elsewhere. Local variations in susceptibility to fog will influence the siting of municipal airports and even residences. The liability of areas to flood, the unsuitability of geological conditions for building, and similar factors also influence the pattern and intensity of land use because they determine the cost of bringing a site into a specified use. Thus economic factors bring

each site into its highest and best use within these physical limits.
Other major determinants of the framework within which economic
factors work are institutional (Goodall, 1970). For example, the wishes
of a former landowner may limit the future highest and best use of a
site as when a landowner provides an area of land to be used in per-
petuity as allotments or a park. The existence of a park will influence
the highest and best use of surrounding sites. Besides past legal decisions, government legislation in respect of land use is especially important. Laws passed in earlier times limiting the height of buildings
in the central business district, as in Amsterdam, leads to a greater
horizontal spread of the central business district than in the absence
of such regulation. Density controls may well recast population density patterns from what would otherwise have been produced. Other
laws, granting security of tenure to existing occupiers, may perpetuate
a use in an outmoded location. In particular the movement of private
land to its highest and best use must take place within the constraint
of existing publicly owned land and publicly provided facilities. The
network of roads, railways, and public utility services, the location of
schools, hospitals, and the like must be taken as given. Access to such
publicly operated transport and utility services is a major determinant
of private highest and best uses.

Further factors bringing differences in land-use patterns between
urban areas are consumer preferences, variations in individual judgements, inertia, and municipal boundaries. Consumer preferences for
single-family detached houses are more consuming of land than other
preference patterns. In the short-run poor judgement may mean land
is not used for its highest and best use, but varying degrees of profit
taking permit such uses to continue. Sunk costs may also tie uses to
particular sites long after the original advantages of those sites have
disappeared. Thus all sites within urban areas are never in their
highest and best uses at one and the same time and this in itself would
lead to differences in pattern.

## Land-use Planning

Land-use planning will have important consequences for intra-
urban location patterns. Such planning attempts to encourage a

rational pattern of land use based on community objectives rather than on individual profit- and satisfaction-maximizing ones. Differences in the extent of planning coverage between urban areas, probably most marked at an inter-nation level, may contribute to an understanding of differences in urban land-use patterns. Indeed, it is within the bounds of possibility that planning may bring about overall patterns which are markedly different from the familiar market ones. However, given a core of planning principles, similarities between urban areas would still be noted. Over time, changes in underlying planning principles may be a further factor explaining differences in urban land-use patterns. For example, a comparison of any first-generation British new town with Cumbernauld would reveal significant differences in land-use patterns because the neighbourhood concept was not applied in the latter case.

Land-use patterns produced by urban planning have much in common with those inspired by economic forces. Indeed, economic principles cannot be ignored in planning. For example, planners have given formal recognition to the principle of specialization since they have applied it to land use when grouping like and complementary activities, as in the development of suburban industrial estates, shopping and civic centres and in phasing out non-conforming uses from residential areas. Specialization of urban land use thus remains a feature.

Of course, the specialized land-use patterns of a planned environment could be very different from those evolved via the market mechanism. In fact similarities are more common than differences which attests to the relative efficiency of the market mechanism. However, differences may be noted. For example, by means of zoning and density controls planners may encourage the development of multi-storey blocks of flats at the suburban fringe. If this development is on a sufficient scale the exponential decrease of residential population density with increasing distance from the urban centre will be disturbed and a marked upward kink will appear corresponding to the high-density flat development.

Specialization may have non-economic disadvantages. In this case, planners, being guided by wider motives than purely economic ones, seek to encourage less specialized patterns of land use. Thus the planners' concern over the central business district becoming a "dead heart" may lead to solutions such as that in Rotterdam where an increased residential element is encouraged on redevelopment. However, the planner should be aware of economic forces in order to work with them in order to achieve his aims. This theme will be developed in Chapter 12.

## Theories of Urban Structure

Four general theories—the concentric, axial, sector, and multiple nuclei—have been suggested in explanation of actual urban land-use patterns. All are based, primarily, on empirical observations. The first three of the theories are also put forward as dynamic models and will be referred to again in Chapter 7 when urban change is discussed. All these theories reflect the economic principle of specialization as applied to urban land use although they lend themselves equally to interpretation in use intensity and land-value terms. Certain implicit assumptions are common to all, such as heterogeneity of the urban population, a commercial–industrial economic base, a system of private land ownership, economic competition for sites, and a uni-centred urban area, although the latter is less marked in the case of the multiple nuclei theory.

### THE CONCENTRIC THEORY

Empirical studies in Chicago gave rise to the hypothesis that the urban land-use pattern could be represented by a series of concentric zones, each specialized in a particular use, centred on the central business district (Burgess, 1925). Through competitive bidding in the urban real property market land uses are sorted out according to their ability to benefit from and therefore pay for proximity to the position of greatest accessibility. Similar activities are likely to be found at similar distances from the central business district. Five zones of relatively homogeneous land use were recognized; the central business district itself, the transition zone, a zone of low-income housing, followed by one of middle-income housing, and, finally, a commuting zone, as shown in Fig. 4.3a.

Accepting this idea as a broad generalization of urban structure it

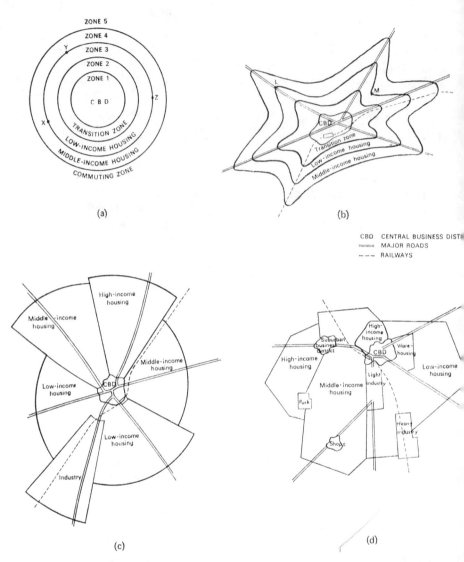

CBD  CENTRAL BUSINESS DIST⊪
≡≡≡  MAJOR ROADS
---  RAILWAYS

(a)

(b)

(c)

(d)

FIG. 4.3. Comparison of land-use patterns produced by concentric, axial, sector, and multiple nuclei theories of urban structure.

should be noted that, from an economic viewpoint, perfect regularity of concentric zoning would only arise where a central location was the major objective of all land uses and where sites at any given distance from the centre were equally accessible, irrespective of direction from the central business district. For example, in Fig. 4.3a, sites $X$, $Y$, and $Z$ are equally accessible, in all terms, from the centre. Burgess recognized that variations in such factors as local topography would distort the ideal symmetry and accepted that residential zones may be further subdivided by race. The theory overlooks the development of complementary clusters and the possibility of incompatible land uses with similar access requirements, both of which give rise to focal points other than the central business district. Moreover, the fact that the higher their income the further away a household is likely to locate from the centre, indicates that access considerations are more than offset by preferences for spacious living. If high-income households were prepared to live at the same densities as low-income groups, they would be able to compete the more accessible sites away from low-income housing. From an economic point of view the specialized pattern of land use produced by this theory points only to the importance of access to the central business district. Admittedly this is the most important single factor in many urban areas, but there are other accessibility aspects to consider and additional factors besides accessibility.

## THE AXIAL THEORY

With movement confined to limited routes, sites a given distance from the urban centre may not be equally accessible to that centre and the regularity of the concentric rings would be disturbed. The superimposition of transport axes on the concentric pattern produces a star-shaped pattern (Babcock, 1932). Here accessibility is considered in time-cost terms in relation to a given transport system. Development proceeds outward from the central business district along major transport axes for a greater distance than in the interstices. Expansion along the axes is limited by competition from areas nearer to the centre which, though less well served by rapid transport facilities, can compete in time-costs to the centre because of lesser distance. In Fig.

4.3b, sites $L$ and $M$ would be in the same use since they are equally accessible in time-cost terms to the central business district. Except for recognition of the spatial inequality of accessibility to the central business district, the axial theory offers little improvement over concentric zoning.

## THE SECTOR THEORY

The sector theory also recognizes the importance of limited transportation in urban areas but suggests that specialization of land use takes place according to direction rather than distance from the position of greatest accessibility (Hoyt, 1939). The differential access advantages associated with certain radial routes attracts particular uses to that radial sector as well as causing marked sectoral variations in land values. In this sense the theory represents a transport-land-use model. Empirical evidence was derived primarily from residential land use but non-residential land uses, such as industry and warehousing, fit better into this scheme.

Once established, contrasts in land use, arising from the differential advantages of radial routes, tend to be perpetuated. With residence, high-income groups can afford the best sites which are likely to be associated with superior access characteristics and future development continues outward in that direction. Certain factors influence the original location of high-income housing such as the desire to avoid proximity to industry. Thus high-income housing forms a sector and not a continuous ring, at a given distance, around the central business district. As Fig. 4.3c shows, the high-income housing is hemmed in on each side by middle-income housing, leaving the low-income housing nearest industry because in accessibility terms or rent paying ability it is the least flexible.

Although the highest income groups are able to afford the sites available in the most accessible sector, they do treat accessibility as an inferior good and can choose to live anywhere within the urban area; hence the importance of amenity. Indeed, the original location of high-income housing may be due either to chance or to non-economic factors (Firey, 1947). Low-income housing, however, continues to be tied to locations giving low-cost access to places of work.

THE MULTIPLE NUCLEI THEORY

This theory observes that urban areas may have more than one focal point, each of which influences the location of certain land uses (Harris and Ullman, 1945). In some urban areas such nuclei existed from the beginning as subsidiary settlements which were swallowed by the growth of a large urban area. In other cases additional nuclei appear with increased specialization. Separate nuclei arise because of the differing access requirements of activities, the grouping of complementary activities, the mutually repellant nature of certain land uses, and the fact that some uses cannot afford the most desirable sites. The number of nuclei depends on the size of urban area, and, besides the central business district, may include heavy and light industrial areas, cultural and entertainment concentrations, suburban business districts, and dormitory settlements. Residential use of land will be arranged with respect to the various nuclei as illustrated in Fig. 4.3d.

The most irregular pattern of urban land use is produced by this theory since development can proceed from more than one centre and peculiarities of areas, sites, and historical factors can be allowed for. It cannot, therefore, produce a simple model of urban structure. What is more likely is that each urban area will have a unique pattern of land use as a result of the application of the principles outlined within different frameworks.

Since factor explanations of urban land-use patterns will hardly ever be plausible, most urban areas exhibit, in all probability, elements of each of these four generalizations. For example, Mann (1965) combines the concentric and sector approaches in attempting to explain land use in medium-sized British urban areas. Among factors neglected by all these theories, especially important is the provision of non-profit uses of land by public authorities. Overall urban shape is relatively compact in all four cases, but urban shape differs and this has repercussions for internal land use because the location and scale of operation of certain activities is linked to urban shape. A more comprehensive theory must await a detailed analysis of the behaviour of the decision-making units which decide the location of shops, factories, offices, and houses within urban areas.

# CHAPTER 5

# Urban Location Decisions: (1) Businesses

## The Nature of Locational Analysis

Location may be viewed from either a processual or a systematic point. Viewed as a general system, the focus of attention is the site, and the concern is with the forces that determine the activity to be carried out there. At its minimum this is an industry-wide approach, as reflected in agricultural location theory (e.g. von Thünen, 1826; Dunn, 1954). Also typical of this approach is urban land-use theory where the arrangement of activities in space, as described in Chapter 4, results from the operation of a mechanism such as the urban real property market. The alternative, or processual, approach examines location in terms of what is best for the individual enterprise or activity unit. Here focus is on the activity, and the behaviour of the individual decision-making unit is analysed in the light of various influencing forces. Such is the emphasis of industrial location theory (e.g. Weber, 1909; Hoover, 1937, 1948) and choice of retail locations (e.g. Applebaum and Cohen, 1961). It is the latter approach which will be applied to intra-urban location decisions in this chapter and the following one.

Location theories provide not only an explanation of actual location patterns but also suggest optimal patterns which reflect a selected criterion such as profit-maximization or transport cost minimization. These theories are, therefore, normative in the sense that they indicate what "should be". There will always be a need for such normative theory. Actual and optimal do not coincide. Society seeks to improve upon existing situations, and a comparison of actual with theoretically optimal patterns may provide guidelines for achieving such improvement. The optimum pattern suggests there is a clear-cut location for each unit of activity, but this is not so in practice. Whilst not suggesting that actual patterns are the result of whim or chance, in practice it is seldom found that there is a single clear-cut location which offers an activity overwhelming advantages. The best location in practice is not wholly ideal, for no location has a monopoly of advantages and a complete absence of disadvantages. Moreover, whilst in real life irrational decisions can carry a heavy penalty, some such decisions will be adopted by the economic system. For example, given a theoretical pattern based on profit-maximization, activities can exist in real life at lower, but still positive, levels of profit because there are varying degrees of profit-taking that allow activities to continue operating.

Businessmen have to decide not only where to locate their plants, but also what line of business to enter, at what level or scale the plant should operate, and in what proportion factors of production should be combined to produce at a chosen scale. For the individual business unit, locational choice should be viewed as part of the total investment decision. Location will influence availability of factor inputs and scale of operation. Factor input requirements can influence locational needs. However, in most cases, instead of a fully integrated investment decision, the problem of location is the last one in the investment process, taken after commitment to a given scale of output and a particular method of production. Furthermore, choice of site is a second-stage operation after the choice of locality. Choice of site, however, is of particular interest for urban land use. Choice of locality is important at the aggregate level of the urban area since this influences the amount of new investment taking place in an urban area and, therefore, its growth prospects.

### Locational Analysis

Location theory, with its emphasis on manufacturing and agriculture, has been especially concerned with those quantitative factors, both inputs and outputs, capable of expression in cost–revenue terms. Tertiary activity, excepting retail, and consumptive activity have, until recently, been less frequently the subject of detailed analysis. The latter are, however, extremely important users of urban land. Thus the findings of location theory are very much more applicable to an explanation of the distribution of manufacturing throughout the urban system as a whole than to the intra-urban location of a variety of activities. For example, the unique array of internal, external, and urbanizational scale economies available at urban locations help explain the growth and specialization of urban areas and the limitation of a large-scale manufacturing development to a few urban areas (Pred, 1966). The techniques contained in this regional level approach may or may not be relevant to intra-urban location since the parts need not resemble the whole. A brief examination of traditional location theory will reveal its strengths and weaknesses in respect of intra-urban location decisions.

Costs and revenues may vary with location. The choice of a location is made only after an assessment of the relative advantages of alternative locations for the activity in question. Therefore every location decision is the result of an amalgam of interacting forces. Within an assumptive framework covering material sources, markets, production methods, and transport systems, location theory has dealt largely with the one-plant, single-product, owner-controlled firm. Transport factors were emphasized because, generally, both products and factor inputs are spatially mobile and substitutable. Orientation to labour, power, or the like was viewed as a deviation from the optimum transport location. Production costs and sales revenues varied from one location to another depending on access at competitive costs to product markets and to factor sources. Resultant locations could be classified as material- or market-oriented depending on whether the pull to factor sources or to the market was the stronger, or intermediate where neither of these pulls were important. Urban areas attract activities because they offer all three types of profit-maximizing location. However, a growing share of output comes from multi-product, multi-plant concerns which are shareholder-controlled, and techniques such as industrial complex analysis (Isard, 1960, ch. 9) must be employed to find the optimal spatial pattern of such firms since it is the profit of the whole group of firms and not the profit from a single member plant which is to be maximized. Within a given urban area, manufacturing concerns are most likely to have only a single producing plant, but in retailing a chain of shops under single management is quite common in a particular urban area. In this case the location of any shop in the chain must be related to the others. In traditional theory, as applied to manufacturing, the strength of the locational pull of markets as against factor sources depends on the ratio of transport costs on product distribution to those on factor assembly. This ratio usually results in orientation to the market, or the factor source, depending on a number of factors. Firstly, the relative physical qualities of the materials and products to be transported must be evaluated. Profit-maximizing locations at material sources are likely where the material loses considerable weight or bulk in processing, where the material is more perishable than the product, or where for other reasons the material is more expensive to transport than the product. Market locations would occur in the reverse circumstances. Secondly, the structure of transport rates also influences the ratio for pricing policies differentiate between commodities, journey lengths, and shipment sizes. If raw materials are carried at a lower rate per ton-mile than finished products, then a given amount of materials can be moved a greater distance for a given transport expenditure than the same amount of products. This would favour a market location since materials can be assembled more cheaply than products can be distributed.

The foregoing analysis assumes the producer is directly responsible for all transport costs incurred in material assembly and product distribution. This is not always so, and variations in responsibility can have significant consequences for intra-urban location. There is a wide range of possibilities reflecting pricing policies of producers and charging practices of transport firms. Most relevant to the intra-urban scene is the case where the consumer incurs the direct costs of product distribution. This happens when the consumer comes to the producer's location and takes the goods away with him. Price to a consumer at the producer's location will be fixed irrespective of the consumer's place of residence. This describes the practice common to a large part of retailing where the producers are shops supplying final consumers in a spatially limited market. Such shops have a critical need of a site which affords ease of access for the prospective customer. As a result this type of activity is generally associated with the highest land values in an urban area. Where the producer is responsible for delivery and makes a charge to cover the full cost of that service, again revenue per sale is a constant and the number of sales a function of location since the greater the delivery charge the smaller the volume of sales. However, where price to the consumer is fixed and the producer assumes costs of delivery, whether wholly or partly, the volume of sales and profit per sale will vary with location, and the producer is more likely to locate in respect of the ease of delivering goods than the mass transit facilities which assemble consumers. For example, the location of department stores is dependent on mass transit facilities, but their warehouses for supplying bulky goods ordered by consumers are located where there is better access to goods-handling facilities and delivery areas. In any given urban area such considerations are unimportant for producers supplying national or regional markets and are unlikely to influence their intra-urban location. Thus, within an urban area, whether the producer or consumer bears the costs of product distribution will have repercussions for intra-urban location in the case of local market activities.

Although appearing to face the disadvantage of two short hauls, which graduated freight rates make relatively more expensive than a single, longer haul from material source to market, intermediate locations between material sources and markets are possible. There are several situations in which intermediate locations are profitable. For example, where there is a break-of-bulk point or a transhipment point. In both cases an additional handling of goods is involved, for the former requires the splitting up of a cargo into smaller shipments and the latter a change of transport media. Usually the two operations are combined. Where transport costs represent a negligible proportion of total costs of a firm, other factors, such as the availability of labour, may influence choice of location. Peculiarities in transport rate structure, such as the fabrication-in-transit privilege which allows the advantage of the single long-haul rate for what is, in effect, two journeys, can also result in intermediate locations. These considerations bring about variations in the distribution of industry throughout the urban system rather than within a single urban area.

Intermediate locations are perhaps most common in practice where the markets and material sources of firms assume a scattered rather than pointform spatial character. This is particularly true of firms catering for the final consumer market, but firms with multiple factor inputs and no dominant factor may find their supply sources widely scattered. Intra-urban locations of activities may be affected. For a firm serving a national market the demand for a good from a given urban area will appear pointform, especially if that firm supplies a wholesaler who is responsible for distribution to retail outlets in that urban area. At the level of the individual urban area, it is the spatial spread of consumers that is important, especially to retailing. Market location in such cases is a relative term, for locational choice involves the determination of that location which is best for carrying out a given set of market contacts. Intermediate sites thus assume importance where an activity faces both wide factor supply and market demand areas, and whilst this reasoning may account for the presence in any urban area of an activity it is also influential in the locational decisions of local market activities. Industries with the greatest chance of having pointform market and/or supply areas are those dealing with components and semi-finished products as inputs or outputs. For example, a firm supplying components to a single, large assembly plant has a pointform market and is likely to be drawn to a location within the urban area in close proximity to the assembly plant.

Overall location patterns reflect not only market factors but also technological ones, especially the use of indivisible factors in large-scale productive units. Given the level of demand, fewer large plants than small plants will be needed to satisfy that demand. This applies equally to activities able to realize such scale advantages within an urban area. Where the national market or an urban market can be served from a single location because of the extreme importance of internal scale economies, the excellence of other sites, in other urban areas in the first case and within an urban area in the second, would avail nothing once a producer had pre-empted the market from an alternative location. Competitive firms tend to repel each other locationally so that a dispersed pattern emerges as each tries to obtain a spatially protected market. However, external economy advantages bring competitive firms together in space, as do economies of urban concentration, since a high proportion of these economies are spatially immobile and not available to firms irrespective of their location. Industrial complexes comprising firms exhibiting various degrees and types of complementary linkage develop. The vertical and, especially, horizontal disintegration that accompanies the rise of an industrial complex need not always produce spatial clustering, but where this does happen the complex must be associated with an urban area where a specialized industrial nucleus will accommodate the group of firms.

Location theory has examined various competitive conditions, e.g. oligopolistic competition (e.g. Hotelling, 1929) and monopolistic competition (e.g. Chamberlain, 1933), but these have not been fully integrated with general equilibrium studies. These approaches may be relevant to intra-urban location since overlapping market areas of imperfect competition are common in urban areas. For example, conditions of monopolistic competition may well parallel the situation in urban retail grocery and oligopolistic situations describe competition between department stores in an urban area.

Perhaps the most serious shortcoming of traditional industrial location theory in respect of intra-urban manufacturing location is the neglect of site rents (Logan, 1966). Although differences in land costs between urban areas may not be as significant as other inter-urban factor cost differentials, variation in land costs between parts of an urban area may be highly significant in determining intra-urban manufacturing location because of the relative ability of manufacturing to compete for urban land. This is especially the case when scale of plant is related to the total amount of land needed. Scale of operation thus becomes a significant factor determining actual location within an urban area. It must also be considered whether relative intra-urban location influences the proportions in which factors of production are combined. For example, if peripheral urban locations have a restricted laboursned, this may lead a firm to use more capital equipment or part-time labour.

Summarizing, the role of general equilibrium theory in its locational context throws light on the type and amount of productive activity found in a given urban area. The explanation is made more complete when random or chance factors in innovative behaviour and irrational decisions are incorporated. Although the same principles apply to the choice of intra-urban business locations, the weight given to influencing factors in the case of these site decisions may differ from the weight these factors carry when influencing an activity's choice of region or general locality. As pointed out, the importance of land or site characteristics looms larger within the urban area than the region. Distinctions between the territorial coverage of markets brings the association of highest-valued urban sites and those activities whose market corresponds to the urban area itself. Such differences in emphasis will be illustrated by reference to the locational decisions of manufacturers and retailers in particular.

## Locational Change

Determination of the theoretically optimal location of a plant, as described above, is carried out under static conditions, i.e. unchanging factor sources, market areas, and so on. It can be argued that, given the change in underlying conditions, the existing technique allows the determination of the new optimal location. Indeed, much can be inferred from such comparative statics at the general level of analysis, but it must be remembered that underlying conditions are always changing and at the level of the individual urban area, where equilibrium is never attained and adjustments are continually being made, such generalization may detract from the applicability of the conclusions. Locational trends over time at the level of the individual urban area deserve some comment. However, the locational economics of a given firm in a continuous time dimension involves the study of all alternative locations and the internal dynamic economics of the firm (Dziewonski, 1966).

Certain forces promote stability in locational patterns. One obvious case is where an activity is located in its optimal position, but disturbed or partial stability is also possible. For example, where a location is sub-optimal, certain inertial and frictional factors impede the relocation of activities. Inertial forces, such as sunk costs in immobile factors, bind an activity to a given site. Geographical inertia may, therefore, be an important factor explaining the presence of an industry in a particular urban area or part of an urban area, although the locations in both cases are obviously not the best ones today. Initial advantage is tremendously important in this context, for businessmen are most willing to expand at existing locations and others will be attracted to what is apparently a successful location. Vertical and horizontal disintegration may bring greater dispersion, but they may also emphasize locations with already built-in advantages.

The concept of optimal location is most relevant to a state of locational mobility when new locations are under assessment by new and existing firms. In practice, changes in locational patterns probably come about more as a result of changes in the population of firms comprising an industry than as a result of the physical relocation of firms comprising that industry. The death of firms in outmoded locations and the birth of new firms in superior locations bring changes in regional and intra-urban location of economic activity. Such is often the explanation of the relative decentralization or supposed movement of activities from central to peripheral parts of urban areas in response to changing local forces. Existing firms contribute to changing patterns in so far as they are successful and seek to expand capacity either at their present location or by establishing branch plants. Where relocation of a firm does occur, local movement, e.g. within an urban area, is probably more frequent than long-distance movement. The impact of changing technology and transport in the twentieth century has been especially noticeable at the urban level. The dynamic analysis of locational change helps to explain not only changes in locational patterns at the intra-urban level, but also changes within the urban system as a whole.

## Manufacturing

The proportion of land used for manufacturing shows wide variation between urban areas due to differences in economic base. Areas specializing in heavy industry have the highest proportions of land in industrial use, although all urban areas have some industry, if only to satisfy local demand. The importance to manufacturing of a location within an urban area has increased (Czamanski, 1965). Not only are access to a large consumer market, to labour supplies and transport facilities, to sources of materials, parts, and components, and to increased opportunities for external economies important attractions of urban areas but, increasingly, location within an urban area, compared to location outside, can save a firm capital outlays on water supply, sewage, and similar facilities since these are adequately provided by urban public authorities. What attracts industry to a given urban area? Manufacturing often serves markets outside the urban area and attraction then depends on the comparative advantage of the urban area as a location for industries serving a wider market than the urban one, i.e. the advantages it offers to local export firms engaged in interregional competition. In the case of this type of industry especially, urban areas are likely to have a non-random distribution of industrial plants by age since changes in locational factors can alter comparative advantage and, therefore, locational choice. The older industrial urban areas will have the greater share of the oldest factories. The amount and type of industry whose market is restricted to the urban area involves a threshold concept related to urban size. With increased size the threshold of profitable local production for the local urban market is passed by one industry after another. The first industries to appear are activities with high transport costs and modest scale economies; the last to appear, activities with low transport costs and large-scale economies.

CHOICE OF URBAN SITE BY MANUFACTURERS

As pointed out above, the reasons why a manufacturer chooses a region or urban area in which to locate his factory may well be different from those influencing his choice of a particular site within that region or urban area. Indeed, McMillan (1965) argues that factors such as markets and availability of materials are prerequisites to operation, not determinants of a particular location, and that the manufacturer has no choice but to locate his factory in a region or urban area providing these basic requisites. Given the basic requisites in an urban area, the manufacturer does have a choice as to where in that area he locates his factory. In the case of equality of certain other factors between alternative sites, the golf course may then become a determining factor. It is important to realize that the choice of site by a manufacturer can be influenced by local factors such as amount and cost of land, residence of managing director, availability of public transport for workers, access to ancillary activities, attitudes and policies of local government (Logan, 1966), availability of public utility services, and local tax differentials. The importance attaching to these factors differs between firms depending on size of firm, its capital reserves, and the quality of its management.

Overall urban industry exhibits orientation to transport routes and transport media. For example, the concentration of manufacturing around major rail intersections and trunk-line goods handling facilities is prompted by costly terminal and transfer charges since locational adjacency of activities can eliminate multiple transhipments of product mixes. The pattern of intra-urban manufacturing distribution tends to be dispersed away from the core in the case of specialist industrial urban areas (Loewenstein, 1963), with a marked lineal appearance where associated with rail and water transport and even with radial and ring roads. Labour requirements, linkages with other firms, and the geographical market served determine the degree to which any firm locates off centre. The size of urban area is important in this context since only in large urban centres will significant differences in costs exist between alternative locations within an urban area.

*Market Considerations*

Where the market for a product is geographically dispersed rather than pointform manufacturing may well be dependent on markets outside the urban area in which it is located. Within the region providing access to such a market several urban areas may offer equal opportunities for tapping sales, and total revenue would be the same for location in any of these urban areas. Similar reasoning applies to the location of an export firm in a given urban area, for choice of site is unlikely to alter revenue/sales possibilities. Therefore locational choice becomes a matter of cost-minimization for the output involved. Thus where an industry or firm makes a substantial proportion of its sales outside the urban area it is unlikely that any one site has an advantage over any other when it comes to volume of sales but differences in costs, of land, of access to labour and transport, will be important. Profits will be maximized after a comparative cost study has revealed the cost-minimization location. Such profit-maximizing locations for firms serving national or regional markets are likely to be at the periphery of the urban area so as to avoid the congestion of the central part of the urban area (Stefaniak, 1963), and to minimize distribution costs. A special category of market orientation occurs at intermediate stages of production where the swarming of closely linked small firms benefiting from external economies creates opportunities for pointform markets.

Industries gravitating naturally to urban areas are those producing final consumer goods and whose market is mainly confined to the urban area itself. The larger the urban area the more numerous these industries. Until an urban area reaches a certain size, it must import certain of its needs from more complex urban areas, but with increasing size the threshold is attained for the appearance of additional industry catering to the local market. New industries are introduced, and activities previously performed by businesses or households themselves are demanded in sufficient quantity to support specialized production units. The appearance of industry need not coincide with the threshold attainment, but tends to occur in an entry zone overlapping both sides of the optimal entry level. For threshold industries supplying the local urban market, such as bread and newspapers, distribution costs rise steeply with distance from the urban centre. Transport costs must be minimized because of the relatively low value of the product, and deliveries must be closely timed to maximize sales. Such industries tend to locate nearer the urban centre than those with wider markets, and are characterized by high transport costs and small-scale economies. Where the efficient unit is small enough and transport costs high enough, these industries will be found in even the smallest urban areas.

## Heavy and Light Industry

The influence of transportation factors on intra-urban manufacturing locations is reflected, particularly, in the choice of sites by heavy and light industry. Heavy industry usually requires access to some raw materials from outside the urban area; thus access to heavy freight transport facilities is essential for raw material assembly as well as for product distribution. Heavy raw materials, such as iron ore or grain, are often weight-losing in the production process, and the factory will be located alongside the route affording the cheapest transport, probably at a point where transhipment is inevitable. Canals, other navigable water, and railways with sidings provide the cheapest means of movement for heavy materials, and products and profit-maximizing sites will be adjacent to these facilities unless offset by additional costs such as the need to comply with zoning or clean-air regulations. Sites served by heavy freight transport in any urban area are limited in number, thus restricting the choice of alternatives for heavy industry. Two contrasting intra-urban locations are occupied by heavy industries. Firstly, relic locations, in what is now the transition zone, associated with rail movement. Of course, at the time of development this was the outer edge of the urban area, and the heavy industry has since been enveloped by subsequent urban growth. These are old factories, but heavy industry continues to use them because of the importance of sunk costs in existing locations. Secondly, peripheral location follows recognition of the hazards associated with much heavy industry. Because of noise or fume levels, fire hazard, or effluent disposal, heavy industry may be regarded as incompatible with many other urban land uses, and the resultant nuisance legislation makes central sites prohibitive in cost terms. Peripheral location is further favoured because these industries require large tracts of land, and their operations cannot be adapted to the block pattern of existing central urban road patterns should they seek a near-central location. Such peripheral locations alongside suitable transport facilities, giving a general lineal appearance, are frequently confirmed by local zoning regulations.

Given a well-developed intra-urban transport system, light industry, producing a less bulky and less weighty product, is largely "footloose" regarding its location within an urban area. Despite the much wider choice of location available to light industry, again a core-periphery contrast can be distinguished. Central locations on the edge of the central business district are occupied by light manufactures with specific skilled labour requirements such as precision instruments, or serving the central business district, as with printing and clothing. These locations are shared with warehousing and wholesaling with stocks. Suburban locations along radial or outer ring roads are favoured by other light industries, e.g. food processing and electrical goods because they depend on motor transport for material assembly from, and product distribution beyond, the urban area. They also operate on a larger scale than the near central light industries. Grouping is again evident because these industries seek similar transport advantages at the level of the individual urban area.

*Size of Plant*

The core-peripheral distinction is also supported by plant size considerations. Small plants need less land having lower ratios of land per plant and land per worker and, as relatively intensive users of land, are, therefore, able to compete effectively for near central sites. The small firms of the urban centre are virtually all single-plant firms, concentrated in industries with ease of entry for new competitors because heavy capital equipment is not necessary. Existence is on a hand-to-mouth basis as reliance on outside suppliers is high. Speed and flexibility of operation are essential to survival in a product market where demand is unstable and limited. These industries—high-style clothing, military electronics, job printing, publishing, toys and games, sporting goods, etc.—are especially characteristic of large urban areas (Vernon, 1962). The firms concerned are frequently marginal ones and their location is positively associated with the location of old, poorly maintained structures (Wingo, 1966). Thus their ability to compete for sites on the edge of the position of greatest accessibility also reflects an ability to adapt their operations to existing buildings. Uncertain as to their future and short of capital funds, the availability of cheap rented premises in the transition zone is an obvious attraction. Small firms make greater errors in sales forecasts, often suffer higher labour absenteeism and turnover (Hoover and Vernon, 1959), and a near central location allows them access to many industrial and commercial services which help mitigate these difficulties. For example, the availability of facilities for small freight shipments and the frequent and special delivery services allows the individual firm to do without stockpiles of materials and products; employment services enable these firms to recruit replacement or short-term labour with comparative ease. Access to a large trained labour pool is especially important, for these small plants lack funds to train their own personnel. The need for face-to-face contact brings about a pronounced clustering of complementary small firms, e.g. in metal plating, printing machinery and parts, and printing works or garment workshops, designing, styling, and the making of costume jewellery and other accessories.

With growth in size through vertical integration, a firm becomes less reliant on external economies of scale, for it incorporates within itself

certain processes previously supplied by other firms. Being less dependent on other firms, it is able to locate further away from the position of greatest accessibility and complementarity. Moreover, with an
increase in scale of business a greater territorial division of functions
formerly contained in one plant is possible as long as the additional
benefit to the firm offsets any higher management costs. Large plants
are able to locate successfully in suburbs where there is no other manufacturing, e.g. United Kingdom and United States subsidiary firms
around Sydney, Australia (Logan, 1966). However, large firms can
have very demanding site requirements, especially in terms of the
amount of land required, since there is a tendency to purchase sufficient
land as insurance against the uncertainty of future space requirements.
This capital investment, representing high fixed costs, is likely to give
these large peripheral plants the same permanence of location as seen
with heavy industry in the transition zone. Factory buildings can take
on an advertising or prestige value where there is a restricted number
of firms in an industry all located in the same urban areas. Such oligo-
polists substitute quality for price competition, and the choice of a
prominent suburban location may boost sales. The process of obtaining
newly built factories, sites for which are generally available only at the
outer edge of the urban area, really concerns only large firms, for small
firms can rarely finance the building of their own structures. Any shift
of small firms is an aftermath of movement of the larger in so far as the
former rent accommodation vacated by the latter.

## Labour

The intra-urban manufacturing location pattern is also confirmed by
the labour orientation of many firms. For certain goods, especially
where high value added during processing, labour may be the most
important factor input, and the firms concerned are attracted to those
urban locations providing the necessary access to supplies of suitable
labour. Many new or expanding industries have minimum labour
thresholds, and the size of the local labour pool becomes increasingly
significant as the size of plant increases. Thus certain urban areas may
not be able to support a given type of plant or, in other urban areas, that
plant cannot be found in the suburbs. Within the urban sphere certain

industries are labour-insensitive because they depend on access to the local market, such as brewing, ice cream, and construction, whilst others, like research activities and industries producing goods to consumer specification, are labour-sensitive because oriented to skill (Segal, 1960). On the one hand, firms depending on relatively low-paid unskilled labour cannot move away from older, near central locations so long as the supply of cheap housing is predominantly located there, unless they provide workers' transport. On the other hand, the preference of certain highly paid skilled and professional workers for the suburbs has influenced the location of industries requiring such labour, e.g. electronics and missiles.

## *Urban Industrial Complexes*

The advantages manufacturing units derive from clustering give rise to the development of urban industrial complexes. The grouping of like firms gives mutual advantages such as a large local supply of specific and skilled labour created by their own combined demands. The location of a large firm may encourage the growth of such a complex by providing opportunities for small specialist firms to come into being. Linkages emerge, although this need not mean proximate locations unless there are overwhelming advantages as might attach to the existence of a pointform market for a small components specialist or where the degree of interdependence between industrial managers requires face-to-face contact to discuss common technical and marketing problems. Historically, such clusterings became important in the later nineteenth century when external economies were less mobile and before congestion and rising land costs began to drive large plants to outer locations. Although today immediate adjacency is not necessary for the enjoyment of external economy benefits, there are many general advantages which result from the grouping of all types of industry in an urban area, and this is reflected in the creation of industrial estates, as at Slough, catering for large and small firms.

## CHANGING PATTERNS OF INTRA-URBAN MANUFACTURING LOCATION

Whatever tendencies exist for movement to optimum locations, this may be severely restricted in the case of manufacturing by the existence of sunk costs in the present location. Costs of disinvestment are high and will include the cost of new land and buildings, the cost of transfer of equipment, the loss of interest in money tied up in the old site before it is sold, and the value of any immovable equipment that has to be written off. If relocation is to take place, profits at an alternative site must be greater than those at the present site by an amount greater than the costs of disinvestment. Initial advantage, coupled with the external economy advantages gathered round a firm, mean that existing locations are characterized by tremendous inertia. Indeed, this compounding of advantages at existing locations exerts a considerable influence on subsequent plant locations. Complete relocation is, therefore, less common than other forms of adjustment and usually occurs only where a firm is forced to move, as in a redevelopment scheme. Wherever possible managements prefer to augment existing capacity than relocate, especially where the latter decision involves a large capital expenditure.

However, central area plants are outdated because of technologically obsolescent layouts on inadequate sites. The amalgamation of surrounding sites with the existing one to give room for expansion is virtually impossible. Expansion, therefore, is frequently achieved by establishing branch plants, and although this allows advantages to be taken of new and separate locations, access to the parent plant becomes a factor in locating the branch. If the individual urban area is large enough to support parent and branch plants, then the branch plant will be constructed at the urban periphery of the same radial sector which includes the parent plant (Martin, 1964, 1966; Keeble, 1965), since this involves the minimization of costs incurred in maintaining necessary linkages with the parent plant (Hamilton, 1967, p. 412). Such branches usually manufacture components for assembly parent plants, but variations in transport, administrative, and overhead costs between parent and branch plant influence the type of branch plant developed at varying distances from the parent plant (Luttrell, 1962) and other branches, less fully integrated with the main plant, may be found greater distances away and, hence, in other urban areas. Preference for short-distance displacement is shown by firms which have to move out of urban centres (Gottman, 1961). In fact the centre may serve as a nursery with the firm moving to the suburbs after it has grown to a certain size (Neutze, 1965). Where the development of a multi-plant concern leads to the establishment of plants in various urban areas, then contact between plants demands a location, in each case accessible to multi-transport interchanges which are likely to be found in only the larger urban areas.

Most of the near central sites suitable for manufacturing have been appropriated by industry of an earlier era, thus expanding, and particularly, new industry in an urban area has to resort to more and more distant sites. Such intra-urban decentralization reached a new maturity as improvements in transportation broke the locational monopoly of central sites and was accelerated by technological developments in production. Journey-to-work improvements removed the necessity for the close spatial proximity of housing and production. Outer urban locations became increasingly possible and economic as transport and communications development made land more homogeneous from a manufacturing point of view and reduced the need for locating all functions of a given firm at the same place. Management control could be centralized and production dispersed to the periphery or even to satellite centres. Containerization, for example, acts as a decentralizing force for production since, combining the line-haul economies of rail with the flexibility and economies of truck organization and terminal shipments (Meyer *et al.*, 1966), it extends the range of industry that can locate away from railway sidings.

The development of space-extensive technology has reduced the demand for central locations, for the urban block represents an obsolescent site for modern plant. Improved production methods affect mainly the internal space requirements of a firm, but also generate different movement demands and certainly alter the balance of locational requirements in terms of trade-offs between centrifugal and centripetal forces. It is technologically impossible to employ most continuous material flow systems with their automatic control of processing and handling in old buildings. A tailor-made single-storey structure is preferred. Indeed, the production process is designed and a building wrapped around it, or, as in the case of chemical plants, it may remain unenclosed. The increasing ratios of land per plant and per worker associated with new production techniques favour large sites as do the high disinvestment costs which prompt firms moving to the suburbs to buy large areas of land to safeguard future expansion prospects.

For urban manufacturing the choice of sites is being increasingly widened by transport improvements with regard to material assembly, product distribution, and journey-to-work. This allows productive activities to take advantage of the economies associated with modern techniques in new buildings on large sites away from congested urban centres. Most firms, therefore, have a reasonably free choice of site within an urban area and all, except external economy industries and certain local market industries, have been favouring open spaces. Industries which are growing most rapidly and industries with large plants have been leading the move to the urban periphery.

## GOVERNMENT INFLUENCE ON INDUSTRIAL LOCATION DECISIONS

Government measures, more fully discussed in Chapter 12, are foremost amongst factors external to the production process which influence intra-urban industrial location decisions. These measures now largely determine whether or not a new industrial development or expansion programme will take place in a given urban area. They are, moreover, instrumental in deciding where within the urban area the permitted development will be located.

For example, national and regional controls of industrial location will influence the relative advantage of competing urban areas for the industrial activity in question. The influence may be positive, by augmenting any original advantages by cash grants, etc., or negative, by causing an otherwise attractive location to be passed over, as when an industrial development certificate is refused for development in a given urban area. Urban governments, by means of promotional activity, can also enhance the attractiveness of their areas for industry. Such activity may range from the straightforward supply of information about facilities and opportunities in the area to the provision of buildings, loans, etc. Where a comprehensive system of land use controls exists industrial firms will have to obtain planning permission for any proposed development from the urban planning authority (in addition to any national/regional permissions required). In this case urban governments have effective control over the location of the new industrial development, and by zoning land for industrial use they can actively promote the formation of industrial estates and complexes in positions which are optimal from the urban community's view as well as being integrated with the urban and regional transport net.

## Retailing

Retail productivity is highly dependent on location. Within short distances the advantages of sites for retail use can change dramatically, not because of differences in operating costs but due to the influence of location in determining the volume of sales and often, also, the selling price of goods. Given the need to attract customers to the retail site, the number of sites in an urban area which can be profitably used for retailing, especially of high-order goods, is strictly limited. Consumer orientation of retail facilities is, therefore, a first principle of any theory to explain retail location, whether at the aggregate or the individual level. The critical dependence of retail location on consumer access leads retailing to offer the highest prices for sites with the greatest relative access advantages. In this sense it can be suggested that retail use forms a skeleton of urban organization about which other uses are arranged according to their ability to pay. In the long run, however, there must be a mutual interaction of locational influences between retailing and all other urban uses. For instance, the mutual attraction of shops and residences is reflected in retailing following population, but when shops go into an area they can command the best sites. Good retail facilities, amongst other factors, may encourage residential development in certain parts of an urban area. Before discussing the individual shop location decision, a brief review of the industry level approach of central place theory is illuminating.

## CENTRAL PLACE THEORY AND INTRA-URBAN RETAIL LOCATION

Central place theory has been extended to cover not only the distribution of retail and service activities between urban areas, but also their distribution within urban areas (Garrison *et al.*, 1959; Mayer, 1965; Berry, 1967). The two key concepts of threshold and range still have meaning at the intra-urban level although boundary determination is nowhere near as clear-cut. The range of a good can have both an upper limit, beyond which a shop or business centre is unable to attract purchasers for a good, and a lower limit, which incorporates the threshold purchasing power needed for the good to be offered in the first place. The two limits would coincide in a perfectly competitive equilibrium situation. Range thus defines the market area of the shop or business centre for a good. The threshold represents some minimum size of market below which a shop or centre will have no economic justification in supplying a good and corresponds to that volume of sales which permits a firm to earn normal profits. The threshold sales level is, therefore, a minimum scale or entry condition.

Shops and consumer services are located to supply their own thresholds most efficiently. Under competitive conditions, in the long run, shops would earn only normal profits and these only if the threshold sales business is transacted at minimum costs which require a location minimizing delivery costs or consumer movement where the consumer comes to purchase the good. This equilibrium, in practice, would be representative of monopolistic competition coming at the point of tangency between the demand curve facing the firm and its long-run average cost curve. The level and distribution of demand is an important determinant of the number and location of shops in an urban area. Shops, assumed to be retailing one and the same good, tend to be competitive and, therefore, seek spatially separated locations. However, in urban areas clear-cut market areas may not exist and, in densely populated parts of an urban area, where demand is several times greater than the threshold level, several traders may be supported in the same centre. For any given commodity alternative methods of retailing may give some variation in threshold size and introduce a measure of irregularity into the spatial pattern. Innovative differences and variations in judgement bring additional spatial elements into the pattern, for varying degrees of profit-taking allow firms to continue at other than optimum sites. At any given time the intra-urban distribution of shops retailing a particular good is critically conditioned by the distribution of purchasing power. Shops are more closely spaced where purchasing power in an area is high and, as the amount of purchasing power per unit area decreases, the range needed to encompass a given threshold increases and shops of a given type will be more widely spaced.

If sales in the whole urban area are slightly greater than an exact multiple of the threshold but not great enough to justify another firm, then excess profits may be earned and ranges reach more competitive upper limits. Competition is for demands in excess of the threshold and located between threshold market areas, i.e. competition for surplus demands over which the shop does not have a spatial monopoly in terms of access. The theory as developed is largely a single product one, but shops sell a variety of goods, and the long-run equilibrium of the multi-product shop demands that all products for which marginal revenue exceeds marginal cost are added to the sales' line and their sales expanded to the point where marginal revenue equals marginal cost (Holton, 1957). This recognizes that commodities have differing elasticities of demand. Where shops provide sets of goods it is likely that only the hierarchical marginal firm earns normal profits. What has been said holds true for distribution of retailing within and between urban areas, but within urban areas clear-cut market areas disappear and the overlapping of market areas is common. This is because at high population densities customers have many shops or centres of differing attraction available within the maximum distance they are prepared to travel, and it is likely that they visit none exclusively but each at some time with some probability. Thus at any given level in the intra-urban hierarchy an index of customer access potential, recognizing the probability of consumers interacting with any particular shop or centre, is a useful guide to optimum retail location.

## CONSUMER BEHAVIOUR AS A LOCATIONAL FACTOR

The principles summarized by central place theory emphasize the relative distribution of retailing throughout an urban area but also recognize the access factor as a determinant of the location of an individual enterprise. Central place theory emphasizes customer attraction which is natural, since the consumer wishes to minimize the disutilities involved in shopping and obtaining services. A shopkeeper may be able to cash in on the effort needed to go to his next nearest competitor. Consumer trips are varied as persons are prepared to travel different distances for different purposes. Much depends on the type of commodity required, the immediacy of the need, the frequency of purchase by any one consumer, the degree of selection desired, and the value of the commodity relative to the consumer's weekly income. Amounts of goods consumed by the customer are a function of price to the consumer at his residence. Costs of shopping trips may be related to the value of purchases to get a measure of the advantage of proximity to shops (Hoover, 1968). If an extra half hour's travelling time is valued by the consumer at 25p, it would be worth that consumer incurring the extra travel time in order to save at least 25p on his purchases. This represents 25 per cent on £1 of groceries, but only $1\frac{1}{4}$ per cent on a £20 suit, and it is logical to suggest that the consumer would be willing to incur twenty times as much travelling time in shopping for a suit as for groceries. This illustrates an important distinction between low- and high-order goods in terms of consumer behaviour. Low-order or convenience goods are purchased by consumers at fairly regular, short intervals, they are often needed every day, represent a small fraction of a person's weekly income, and selection is relatively unimportant. Groceries, fruit and vegetables, and household cleaning items fall into this category, and customers tend to purchase such items from the nearest shop to their residence. The shopkeeper retailing low-order goods must therefore locate close to customers' homes, and his profit-maximizing site would be that position in a residential area which affords the greatest access to the local population. This is largely a reflection of local road patterns, e.g. the intersection of two of the more important suburban roads or access roads to suburban railway stations. In the oldest residential areas the corner general shop is an expression of exploitation of local access advantages.

In contrast, high-order or shopping goods are only purchased by any one consumer at irregular and infrequent intervals; they represent in many cases a multiple of persons' weekly incomes, and the purchase is delayable in order to compare as wide a range of models as possible. In the purchase of furniture, electrical equipment, and similar items, consumers take more time over their purchase and travel further in order to compare between shops as well as within a shop. Shops retailing high-order goods need access to larger populations since the purchases of any one customer are much less numerous than in the case of convenience goods, thus giving a higher threshold. Access is needed to the urban population as a whole, and such retail units therefore locate at focal or convergence points in the mass transit network. The minimum number of items necessary to induce a consumer to shop at a given shop or centre will increase with distance from the consumer's residence.

Variations in consumer tastes can create variations in retail structure. Where persons of different incomes have different tastes and their residences are spatially separated, then certain goods will be provided in low-income areas and others substituted in high-income areas. For example, fish-and-chip shops in low-income areas may be replaced by delicatessens and gourmet food shops in high-income areas. Access to purchasing power, rather than number of consumers *per se*, can be influential in the location of shops selling high-order goods. Thus the fashionable shopping areas of London, such as the Oxford Street–Regent Street or West End area and the outliers at Knightsbridge and Kensington, cater for the middle- and upper-income groups who were most numerous to the south and west, whilst the East End, associated with lower income groups, did not develop fashionable shopping areas.

The principles of location outlined will hold true unless there is good reason for a consumer to behave differently. For example, where a restricted number of shops offer credit facilities on low-order goods a particular customer may ignore his nearest shop because it does not offer such facilities, but there will be a close limit to his search for an alternative. In urban areas, where overlapping retail market areas are common, factors such as this and the availability or otherwise of a delivery service, the cleanliness of the shop, or the congeniality of the shop staff may contribute to the explanation of consumer behaviour in terms of shops patronized. The actions of the mass are predictable, and the gravity principle will account for the behaviour of large groups of people. It rests on the assumption that group behaviour is predictable on the basis of mathematical probability because the idiosyncrasies of any one individual tend to be cancelled out (Huff, 1962). This is especially relevant to the intra-urban case, although the gravity principle itself tells nothing of why the regularities occur.

## SUPPLY FACTORS

Within any urban area the spatial distribution of retail and service outlets is largely a reflection of aggregate demand conditions, i.e. population density, purchasing power, and spending habits. The number of out-of-town customers contributes to the functional array of high-order uses found in centres such as the central business district. However, the number and size of retail units and the degree of local spatial separation must also reflect certain economic characteristics of the supply side. The fixed investment in building and equipment required for retail trade location is relatively small in relation to the advantages which accrue from exploiting a superior site. The retail unit is a relatively flexible or divisible unit, although various branches of retailing have a unique internal structure based on economies of scale to the shop or sometimes to the multiple organization. Thresholds increase with increasing indivisibility of shop units and, especially, with increasing specialization of supply units. The more specialized and indivisible the individual retail units, the greater will be their local spatial separation.

Sources of saleable goods are a negligible influence on the location of shops since reliance on motor transport provides a flexible means of assembling goods for sale. Similarly, availability of labour is no problem since supplies are obtainable from the residential areas served. Where there is freedom of entry for new firms in the long run, this may determine whether existing units can maintain their present location in competition with new firms.

## SHOPPING CENTRES

Analysis has concentrated on the single shop, but what is true for one shop may be true for others. Therefore low-order convenience outlets may compete with each other to obtain positions with relative local access advantages and high-order uses compete with each other for positions in higher order centres. Convenience goods shops will cluster in positions affording the greatest local accessibility. In the smallest clusters, the number of functions may be greater than the number of shops, since shops may perform more than one function. It is likely that all the retail outlets in a cluster are complementary because persons visit more than one shop. Indeed, competition is often specifically prohibited where all the units in a cluster are leased from a single developer. Two or more greengrocers may compete for the one shop in the cluster that could be used for selling fruit and vegetables, but once this shop has gone to the highest bidder, the unsuccessful bidders will have to look to alternative clusters. Thus low-order neighbourhood shopping centres are likely to contain shops such as grocer, butcher, greengrocer, newsagent/confectionist, baker, fishmonger, hardware store, hairdresser, laundrette, etc., with the actual range in any centre depending on density of population. Land has only to be competed away from residential use and within the cluster shops compete for the best positions such as corner sites. In the largest neighbourhood level centres the number of shops may exceed the number of functions, indicating competition in certain lines, e.g. the grocery trade may be represented by self-service and traditional type shops.

There are similar, indeed additional, economies to be gained from the clustering of high-order retail outlets. Persons on multi-purpose shopping trips may need to visit more than one shop to obtain the items needed or, where only one item is sought, they may visit more than one shop in order to compare models. Persons use various means of transport to get to such a centre, but, once there, undertake their shopping by walking from shop to shop. Clustering of similar shops thus promotes sales by attracting customers and facilitating comparison between shops. Such high-order retailing is a primary function of a business centre. Even where shops are selling like goods, such as shoes, they are often complementary, for different shops concentrate on different grades of commodity or serve different classes of customer. Competition between shops will determine the allocation of sites within the position offering the necessary access conditions to the urban population. For example, department stores serve such large numbers of persons that they can outbid even the most exclusive shops for the best sites. Ability to obtain a particular site in a regional-level shopping centre, therefore, depends on earning ability, and this reflects the threshold of the activity concerned. The higher the order of the good, the greater the threshold, the more critical is an accessible site, thus the highest order uses in a centre are usually those which need and are able to pay for the best sites within the centre. Ability to pay, therefore, appears to reflect the order in the central place hierarchy and the internal zoning within centres mirrors the level at which functions appear in the hierarchy (Garner, 1966). Within a shopping centre, functions of the highest threshold are at the core, such as department stores, jewellers and clothing shops, together with those uses, like tobacconists, whose sales are critically tied to pedestrian volume. At the periphery are personal service establishments of neighbourhood level, e.g. laundrettes and grocers, whilst the intermediate zone mixes neighbourhood and certain higher order uses, as with bakers and household appliance and furniture stores.

Department stores only appear in a shopping centre when the accessible population has reached a certain minimum size and, the larger the population within reach of the store, the more specialist departments it contains. For example, the greater the demand the more likely it is that electrical appliances are split between several departments, dealing with television, radio and gramophones, washing machines and refrigerators, or that furniture is divided between departments for beds, kitchen furniture, garden furniture, etc. This, and likewise the number of specialist shops in a centre, is simply a function of the size of the market.

Given a very dense population, a number of high-order shopping centres may evolve in large urban areas, and these centres will be competitive because they are not afforded the natural protection of distances. Such competition may frequently take the form of differentiation. The other urban retail pattern, that of the business thoroughfare, serves a different demand from these nucleated shopping centres, and clustering is not necessary to the minimization of shopping costs since the customer often shops from an immediately parked car. Business thoroughfares are, therefore, related to the road network and, especially, traffic flows within the urban area.

CHANGING INTRA-URBAN RETAIL PATTERNS

Low, fixed investment and freedom of entry of firms means that the retail trade, considered as a whole, can and must adjust rapidly to changes in the location of demand. At any point in time, with few qualifications, the location of retail activities can be considered in equilibrium in response to market forces, in which case subsequent changes represent adjustments to changes in demand and in supply technology rather than adjustments to a pre-existing disequilibrium (Harris, 1968, p. 383). A rise in suburban residence brings retail and personal service activities in its wake because such activities must follow their markets. Diffusion of these consumer-oriented activities proceeds at varying speeds according to the type of trade. Low-order or convenience activities are most responsive, with the grocery super-market trade moving most rapidly, closely followed by personal and repair services. These products or services are comparatively standard-ized, and as the consumer buys from the nearest outlet to minimize his shopping costs they must be marketed as close as possible to the con-sumer's residence.

The central business district's share of urban retail sales was certain to decrease with urban growth, but the trend has been accelerated in large urban areas where high-order retail activities have also en-deavoured to pursue the consumer by establishing suburban branches. Enhanced purchasing power at the urban periphery, combined with the mobility and flexibility afforded by the motor-car, makes the development of satellite regional shopping centres feasible. Indeed, in the United States improved merchandizing techniques alongside cus-tomer's use of the car has changed the unit of development from the single store to the entire planned shopping centre (Berry, 1967, p. 53).

Whilst population expansion and redistribution account for the overall spatial pattern of retail change in urban areas, other factors, such as scale shifts, road improvements, or increasing real incomes, affect the total volume of change. For example, with increasing real incomes, the number of high-order retail outlets increases, often repre-sented by the growth of small specialists in luxuries, such as florists, pet, or photographic equipment shops. There may even be an absolute decrease in the number of low-order retail outlets since their goods face an income inelastic demand, and other factors favouring a larger size of shop bring about centralization. Within the grocery trade the decline of resale price maintenance favours the more productive, self-service, large shop, and small shops—no longer protected from competition—go out of business. In general, new facilities tend to enter areas which offer the highest income earning opportunities. These will be areas where demand is increasing more rapidly than facilities and price is high.

Economic solutions to retail location problems and, especially, market area delimitation, are at the best only approximations, for persons are generally unaware of fine economic distinctions, and boundaries take on a certain non-economic character. This extends the range of locations that can support retail uses. Urban shopping centres no longer dominate an immediate market area; instead, several centres serve the same community of interest areas and consumers visit them all at some time.

## THE SCOPE FOR PLANNING INFLUENCE ON RETAIL LOCATION

The changing spatial pattern of retailing at the urban level, particularly the trend towards large out-of-town shops and shopping centres, is amenable to planning direction. In this respect planners must work within certain constraints. For example, they must recognize both the changes in shopping habits and the changes in the character and structure of retailing that are currently taking place. It is necessary for planners to understand the forces generating the pressure of demand for widespread out-of-town retail developments. Population, at the urban level, has been decentralizing, and this has placed many existing, in-town shopping centres at a relative disadvantage. This disadvantage is heightened for many existing centres in spite of increased mobility of population based on the use of the motor-car, by congestion, and parking restrictions, which make things increasingly difficult and inconvenient for the motorist-shopper. With car travel the central business district has lost its accessibility *raison d'être* (Schiller, 1971). Increased home storage possibilities, such as refrigerators and deep-freezers, mean persons need to shop less frequently. "One-stop shopping" at out-of-town locations, which allows persons to combine the purchase of bulky food orders with mass-produced durables, especially soft-goods, and any more frequently needed items, would, therefore, appear to be an obvious attraction.

Retail units are growing larger and the changes in their internal and external space requirements favour out-of-town locations where adequate land is available. The increased efficiency of the large unit is reflected in a higher turnover per square foot of floorspace and has been brought about by improvements in stock control systems, innovations in shop-floor layout and display, refinements in processing and packaging, and economies in internal handling achieved by transferring work to the customer via self-service and to the wholesaler/supplier via prepackaging. The benefits of these economies of scale can be passed on to the customer in terms of lower prices, and this has been assisted, in the United Kingdom, by the gradual abandonment of resale price maintenance. Other economic pressures, such as rising wages and the introduction of selective employment tax, have further encouraged the substitution of capital for labour. As a consequence new forms of retail unit may evolve—the cash-and-carry retail warehouse, the discount store, the hypermarket or superstore—where an adequate choice over a very wide range of goods is provided by one large establishment. Catering virtually exclusively for motorist-shoppers such a unit requires extensive, adjacent parking facilities; hence, the attraction of out-of-town locations.

The influence of these changes on retail location depends on the type of shop. Schiller (1971), using a three-group classification of goods into convenience, fashion-content, and high-threshold specialist categories, suggests that clustering in a traditional central business district is now important only for fashion-content goods where the desire for comparison facilities remains strong. It is, however, to the advantage of convenience and high-threshold specialist retail outlets to leave urban centres. In the case of convenience goods this is consistent with traditional theory in the sense that, by following population, the effort of shopping is minimized. High-threshold specialist outlets, such as antique shops, antiquarian booksellers, and boutiques, which are the focus of a single-purpose trip and depend on advertising and word-of-mouth recommendation, do not fit into the theory so easily. Their choice of out-of-town locations in a metropolitan region may, in fact, correspond to small, high-class urban areas/villages, providing adequate parking is available.

Being dependent on motorist-shoppers, out-of-town retail locations require maximum access to the road network of a large suburban/exurban catchment area. A driving time of half-hour each way probably provides an outer boundary to the market area. Such centres will be adjacent to, not athwart, a major road, and, in metropolitan regions, a preference for radial and ring-road routes is noticed (Cohen and Lewis, 1967). Problems of immediate access/egress to the major road need to be solved in order to provide the ready access needed by customers' cars as well as by the heavy commercial delivery vehicles. Since out-of-town retail units are larger than inner urban ones they will be fewer in number and more widely spaced, although a tendency towards clustering of centres is noticed where product differentiation rather than location differentiation is practised. Out-of-town locations are also prefered because of the need for very large sites to accommodate the development of extensive single-storey buildings and enormous associated car parks.

Faced with these trends, planners can influence not only the locational pattern of out-of-town shopping centres but also the extent of such developments. Moreover, the latter may be extremely important when planners come to deal with the problems of the central business district. Indeed, many urban planning authorities have attempted to mitigate the disadvantages of their central business districts by introducing comprehensive traffic management schemes which include, for example, parking provisions designed to favour short-term parkers. However, an element of inconvenience remains, and unless planners can create conditions similar to those possible at out-of-town locations (and this may be feasible in the case of comprehensive redevelopment schemes), the outward movement of retailing may be accelerated.

Indeed, out-of-town shopping centres could offer planners an opportunity to improve an urban area's commercial and social infrastructure. This could be especially attractive in the United Kingdom where much inter- and post-war suburban residential development outstripped the provision of other facilities. These areas now lack adequate shopping centres. Development of out-of-town shopping centres should, therefore, be encouraged on sites offering the necessary access conditions, providing such developments include the full range of commercial and social provision expected in a district business centre and there are no objections on amenity grounds. The preferred location is therefore adjoining the edge of the existing built-up area (Department for the Environment, 1971). In this way the centre can be more effectively integrated into the existing public transport system and so cater for the 25 per cent of population who will still lack cars in 1980. Furthermore, the restrictions on opening hours in the United Kingdom also place a locational constraint on such centres and favours location adjacent to existing population concentrations. Moreover, isolated development in a green belt/green fields location is unlikely to provide as full a range of facilities and would probably be objected to on amenity grounds. Such out-of-town developments of retailing could pre-empt good industrial sites, and it should be noted that cash-and-carry retail warehouses have appeared on some industrial estates.

It must be emphasized that it is not the function of the planner to prevent competition in retailing, nor to favour one shopping centre, be it already in existence such as the central business district, over another. However, over-provision of shops on a large scale represents an inefficient use of resources, and American experience has shown that out-of-town locations may be unprofitable if too many are developed. In the United Kingdom, therefore, under comprehensive planning controls the number and relative success of out-of-town centres will depend, in large measure, on the actions of planning authorities. Too many out-of-town centres will not only jeopard the success of any one such centre but could also result in such a loss of trade for existing centres, especially the central business district, that central area redevelopment is prejudiced. Such is the planners' dilemma.

### Other Activities

If every productive activity was examined in the same detail as manufacturing and retailing, it would be found that similar principles determine the profit-maximizing locations of units of those activities. To a greater or lesser extent, depending on the activity in question, similar tendencies toward clustering at the intra-urban level would be revealed. For example, offices are relatively more concentrated in the central business districts than other activities, a dominance in locational terms which continues up to metropolitan size.

The rationality of locational choice also varies between activities. Indeed, in the case of offices it has been suggested (Vernon, 1962), that the chance of a rational location pattern is less likely than with manufacturing, because the product, being less easily defined, makes the comparative costing of alternative locations difficult. Offices outside the central business district are limited. Firstly, most manufacturing firms need some office space for on-the-spot administration of personnel, wages, stocks, and distribution, and, where this cannot be separated from production, location of the factory determines the location of the office element. Secondly, street or field offices of insurance, banks, public utilities, and the like have to locate where their customers are found in the same way as retail units.

What of the rationality of the other offices located in the central business district? Offices use labour and space intensively. The need for a labour supply with a median educational attainment above that of the population as a whole demands a central location in order to assemble the necessary labour force. Within the central business district, major offices will cluster because many of the dealings during the working day are inter-office, which means that these offices are communication oriented. Face-to-face contact in such cases may be traditional, but good, reliable information is needed in a hurry in order to minimize risks, especially for financial offices (Robbins and Terleckyj, 1960), and the speedy movement of the large amount of paper between offices is facilitated by proximate locations. The demand for services within any one office may be unpredictable, and as each firm cannot keep a full complement of analysts and advisers, clustering makes it possible to enjoy external economies of sub-contracting to specialists. A central business district location may provide an office with a prestige address which is a boost to the volume of business transacted.

Locational change at the intra-urban level is continually taking place. Even the intense concentration of offices in the central business district is being eroded by changing locational pressures. Urban growth increases the competition for central, accessible sites and raises the price to be paid for central location. This makes it expensive to keep r outine office activities in the centre. Changes in the organizational structure of office firms consequent upon the automatic handling of data and records allows high- and low-order office functions to be spatially separated. Purely routine office activities may then be located at non-central positions in the urban area where those activities can be undertaken at minimum costs. Remaining in the centre is the top of the office hierarchy, a cluster providing a point of confrontation for those who need to produce answers to non-standardized problems and a machine for producing, processing, and trading specialized information between a group of highly skilled professionals engaged in decision taking and strategy formulation (Dunning, 1969).

Warehousing and wholesaling also show particular intra-urban location patterns (Loewenstein, 1963), and definite responses to changing location conditions (Gottmann, 1961, p. 521; Meyer *et al.*, 1966, ch. 2). Likewise other urban land uses. Indeed, the locational principles referred to in this chapter may be equally applicable to certain non-profit uses of land, e.g. churches (Goodall, 1969). Location of local authority offices and regional or local offices of central government bodies are also influenced by accessibility and complementarity considerations, although they could equally be treated as independent of such considerations if government so desired. However, the latter situation would either increase the costs of operating those offices or increase the costs of persons needing to visit them, neither of which is desirable from the point of view of efficiency in the use of urban resources. Locational decisions by businesses at the intra-urban level confirm the view of the urban area as a mechanism contributing to efficiency in the use of resources. It is also recognized that there are limits to the level of efficiency actually achieved because of the nature of the framework within which these location decisions have to be made.

# CHAPTER 6

# Urban Location Decisions: (2) Households

## Location Theory and the Choice of Residential Location

Location theory has, for the most part, until recently, centred on productive activity. An implicit assumption was that population would respond to economic opportunities; thus the relative economic growth of one region or urban area would be accompanied by immigration of population consequent upon the higher wages now available in that area. Most persons, therefore, choose a residential location because of the income earning opportunities it provides access to, as well as considering the consumption opportunities afforded by the location. The household may be taken as the basic decision unit involved in the choice of residence, and its functions are (a) to assemble consumption inputs at its residential location, and (b) to distribute the labour which the household contributes to productive activity. In nearly all cases the costs of marketing a household's labour over any considerable distance are greater than the costs of assembling its consumption inputs at its residential site. In general, therefore, the distribution of population by place of residence will correspond to the regional distribution of economic opportunity so that factors explaining the general location of productive activity also account for the general distribution of consumptive and residential activity.

For some persons, however, choice of residential location only interests them in so far as it affects their consumption possibilities. These exceptions are basically households which do not contribute labour to productive activity, such as retired persons or those of private means, and their residential location is decided in terms of maximum access to the consumption inputs they require. For the rest, the extent to which they can obtain the consumption inputs they require depends on the income they can derive from contributing to current productive activity. These households need to be accessible to job opportunities and this restricts the spatial influence of consumptive factors on their choice of residence to the commuting range of job opportunities. The force of consumptive factors may be particularly strong for these households over shorter distances, such as within an urban area. Where households move in search of alternative accommodation it is found that three-quarters of those who moved found a house within one hour's journey of their previous home (Donnison *et al.*, 1961).

In the use of any site for residential purposes, a household incurs transport costs on both its labour distribution and its consumption input assembly. As transport costs involving personal movement exhibit a certain regularity in their spatial change from any given point, it is to be expected that residential location patterns will show spatial regularities associated with the transport factor. This is because travel represents a disutility or loss of satisfaction for households and suggests that households seek to minimize the disutilities of travelling and that their choice of residence is responsive to differences in transport costs incurred in carrying out their activities. Where minimization of travel disutility leads to maximum satisfaction for households, there will be a demand for the residential use of sites with relative accessibility advantages. The choice of residential location is complicated by other factors that are difficult to quantify: amenity, space and privacy, health and fresh air, safety, quiet, and social segregation or integration. The prospective residential user of a site has to place a money evaluation on these attributes. The location decision is, in many cases, a compromise since, for example, greater amenity is often attainable only at the expense of lower accessibility, i.e. added travel disutility. Indeed, accessibility appears to behave as an inferior good (Alonso, 1964). The quantifiable variables involved, therefore, for any household are location and amount of space, and the choice of residential site involves balancing the transport costs involved in the use of a location, the land costs, the costs of other goods, and the amenity value of the site.

A distinction should be made between the choice of residential locations by households and the choice of locations to be used for residential purposes. The majority of housing choices are made from the existing stock. New housing in Great Britain represents an addition to stock of about 2 per cent per annum. However, one-tenth of households move house each year. In addition new household units are being continually formed as population expands, so there are insufficient new houses for all those seeking accommodation at any one time. Thus most of the decisions regarding the choice of land used for residential purposes were made at some time in the past and the explanation of the choice of that residential location by the present inhabitants may be very different from the explanation of the original situation. In seeking answers to the questions of who lives where and why at the present time, it must be accepted that consumer freedom of choice is largely restricted to the distribution of existing residential locations.

It was, of course, argued in Chapter 1 that the price mechanism brings forth those goods demanded by consumers in the quantities required, which would suggest that houses of the type and in the locations demanded by consumers would be provided. This would only be true under conditions of perfect competition. In practice, under conditions of monopolistic competition, the consumer may influence and, in turn, is influenced by, the housing developer. It would appear that the developer of land and the builders of the houses are most directly involved in the location and physical design of housing, for the majority of new housing is speculative housing. So even with new housing the consumer is constrained in the choice of location to what is provided, although the actions of present consumers may influence the location and type of future residential packets. It is the developer who, therefore, makes the initial, speculative commitment to location. Factors influencing the developer's profit-motivated location decision are by no means limited to the characteristics of consumer demand, but include other influential factors such as site and developer characteristics (Weiss *et al.*, 1966; Kaiser, 1968). Actual residence patterns, therefore, depend only partially on how the housing stock responds to demand for new construction is only a small and unrepresentative part of the demand for housing. Choice is, therefore, limited by the durability of existing housing. As the stock of houses changes sluggishly in size and character, analyses concentrate on explaining the distribution of households in respect to the existing housing stock and make only minor reference to the actions of developers. It is, however, important to realize that, in the free market, it is the profit motive which in the past has brought, and today brings, land into residential use. Residential use remains the highest and best use of this land so long as the subjective values of prospective residential users, which reflect the satisfaction to be derived, are greater than the values offered by alternative uses.

## The Household's Residential Objectives

In buying housing, a household is in fact buying a number of things, e.g. living space, location, physical and service amenities, and prestige values. Of these factors, some cannot be measured objectively and must be evaluated subjectively by a household before making its final choice. However, that part of the price paid for location and space is difficult to isolate since the indirect and intangible returns a household expects to receive frequently influence the price it offers. Every household seeks to maximize its satisfaction and will achieve this by spending its income in such a way that it consumes commodities in such proportions that the marginal utility or satisfaction per pound spent is the same for all. This will apply to the consumption of housing and the household's equilibrium or satisfaction-maximizing position can be expressed as follows:

$$\frac{MU_{housing}}{P_{housing}} = \frac{MU_a}{P_a} = \frac{MU_b}{P_b} \dots = \frac{MU_n}{P_n}, \qquad (6.1)$$

where $MU$ represents the marginal utility derived from an additional unit of a commodity, $P$ the price of that unit, and $a, b, \dots, n$ are other goods. As people are different and have different values, households' preferences for housing relative to other commodities will vary. The equation allows for this, given the preferences of households. For some households additional spending on accommodation will yield smaller increments of utility than additional spending on other commodities, and these households will purchase smaller amounts of accommodation than households of similar income for whom the marginal utility derived from additional spending on accommodation diminishes less rapidly relative to their additional spending on other commodities. Every household, therefore, chooses its residential location and amount of living space so as to maximize its satisfaction overall. For some this will mean maximizing the amount of living space that can be purchased for a certain housing expenditure, for others maximization of access, whilst others may substitute maximum amenity for other attributes. Income will determine the extent to which any household can indulge its preferences.

In evaluating a given property as a possible residence, a household normally takes into consideration three major groups of factors—the characteristics of the dwelling, the characteristics of the neighbourhood, and the spatial relationships of the site with the rest of the world. What weight attaches to these three groups of factors? It has been argued (Kaiser, 1968) that the consumer's choice of housing is based largely on the house itself rather than its location attributes. Certainly the characteristics of the house, whether old or new, large or small, detached or multi-unit, and the quality of internal fitments, etc., relative to the costs of occupying the house, are important determinants of choice. As building costs rule out a new house for substantial parts of the population, the idealized consumers' choice of residence is limited in practice by the availability of suitable structures and locational alternatives. Even where the characteristics of the house are the most important factors determining choice, the character of the surrounding neighbourhood and the general spatial relationships of the location must be considered. Desirable neighbourhoods, irrespective of density, are homogeneous in terms of the economic and social characteristics of their inhabitants. Accessibility of the residential site to commercial, industrial, and other land uses in general must be considered and, in particular, the job access of the head of household. There must come a point for any household where the attractive characteristics of a house are more than offset by its locational disadvantages as reflected in the higher transport costs incurred. Income, job, and family status appear, in practice, to be significant factors in the choice of residential location.

## Factors Influencing Choice of Residential Location

### INCOME

Accommodation would appear to be a necessity for every household, and it might be argued that the demand for housing is inelastic in respect to price and income. However, with a given income, the household can vary the proportion of income it spends on housing within certain limits, whilst it can also vary the type and amount of housing it purchases. The demand for housing, especially in terms of space, appears to be elastic over most of its price range. Where demand exceeds supply, any increase in housing prices brings a decrease in per household consumption of housing, and is likely to lead to increased residential densities as a result of the doubling-up of households in existing properties. As income rises, housing behaves as a superior good, for the household spends proportionately more of its increased income on purchasing larger and/or better quality housing. Thus there is an increasing propensity to consume housing, for the greater is household income the greater—absolutely and relatively—its expenditure on housing. The demand for housing is income elastic; indeed, the long-run schedule is probably highly elastic (Muth, 1968, p. 286).

Income, preferences, and choice of residence are positively related since the greater is household income the wider is its range of choice of housing type and location and the greater the likelihood that its preferences are more fully met. The higher a household's income the stronger is its preference for more residential space and for newer housing. Net residential density declines consistently with increasing income as high-income households buy more space per household. Persons with high income and high-quality preferences may not be satisfied with the best of the housing stock for long and, therefore, there is a strong tendency for high-income households to inhabit new houses.

Ability to pay for the better, newer, most desirable residential facilities and locations is a major determinant of the distribution of population within an urban area. Moreover, where residence is to compete for the most accessible sites it has to use land intensively, i.e. at a high density, if land is to be competed away from alternative uses. A high price must be paid for accessible sites because of competition from productive uses whose profit levels depend on accessibility. Therefore, given the level of income, households can buy less residential accommodation in the position of greatest accessibility than elsewhere. More accommodation or space can be bought as distance from that position increases, because land prices decrease as the supply of land increases as the square of the radius from that position and as transport costs to that position become more expensive. The choice facing the household is that it can buy more accommodation with increased distance from the centre but at the expense of increased journey costs. A household seeking half an acre of land needs only a £1 per acre decrease in land prices to offset an extra 50p in commuting costs, but a household with one-twelfth of an acre needs a decrease of £6 in land prices as compensation for the same increase in commuting costs. Much will depend on the relative rates at which land prices decrease and commuting costs increase with increasing distance from the position of greatest accessibility. Where households of unlike income live at distances where they incur the same amount of commuting costs, the household with the highest income will occupy the best accommodation and the largest amount of space.

Given that the preference for space and privacy is stronger, the higher is household income, then high-income groups will use their superior purchasing power to buy low-density housing (Hoover and Vernon, 1959, ch. 7). If, in addition to large quantities of space, high-income groups prefer new houses, densities will be lowest in areas of new housing and the proportion of households living in multi-family structures will decline as household income rises. However, high-income groups may tend to live in single-family detached dwellings more frequently because of the greater savings they realize from the tax advantages in countries such as the United Kingdom and the United States (Muth, 1965). Since urban growth, in age terms, shows a concentric pattern, older, high-density houses are near the centre, and high-income groups can only find the low-density and new housing they require at the periphery of the urban area. Thus high-income groups seek locations in the outer urban area because (1) of their stronger preference for space and privacy, (2) greater savings in land costs are possible as land prices are lower away from the position of greatest accessibility and single-family detached houses can be provided more cheaply, and (3) they are affected relatively less by higher commuting costs as these are spread over larger sites. Consequently high income households are price-oriented and low income location-oriented and with less access being bought as income increases the apparent paradox of the poor living on expensive central land and the rich on cheaper peripheral land may be explained (Alonso, 1965, p. 109). It is important to realize that there is nothing intrinsic in an area of land which creates a high-class residential area. Obviously, high-income groups can pay for sites with attractive physical qualities like lake- or hill-sides, but such features do not exist in all urban areas, whereas high-class residential areas do emerge in all urban areas. This explanation of the location of high-income residential location relies heavily on the assumption of the strength of the preference for space and privacy. Whilst this may be largely true for the majority of high-income groups in the United States, the United Kingdom and similar countries in many southern European, Latin American, and African countries, the preference of high-income groups may be for central living in which case a very different intra-urban distribution will occur. For example, workers generally in Latin countries like to go home from work for their midday meal (Clark, 1968, ch. 9).

Low-income groups have a restricted range of housing choice, having to take the least acceptable housing available, i.e. the oldest, most cramped, most obsolete and deteriorated segment of the housing stock (Wingo, 1966). The older the housing the more cheaply it can be converted to occupation by lower income groups, thus the oldest central housing areas become a repository for those living around subsistence level. Low-income housing is concentrated towards the centre of the urban area and is also oriented toward urban manufacturing irrespective of the latter's distance from the urban centre. Striking contrasts in housing are possible in the urban centre as the luxury apartments of certain high-income groups give way immediately to low-income housing as middle-income groups cannot afford the type of apartment they would prefer and seek alternative accommodation in suburban areas.

The mean quality of the housing stock improves with distance from the central business district. The value of the house also increases with distance from the centre, whereas land value drops; hence house prices or rents per dwelling are inversely related to land values and accessibility. The patterns discussed are characteristic of free market conditions. The enactment of rent control and the provision of subsidized public housing may increase the choice of location for the lowest income groups, although the location of subsidized housing may be as rigorously determined as other housing for low-income groups.

## JOB ACCESS

At the level of the individual urban area the distribution of jobs may influence the distribution of residential population more than any other single factor. Given the place of work of the head of household a household has to weigh access to work against various possible combinations of commuting costs, accommodation prices, and its other needs for urban contacts and amenities. The same applies where a person in a given job wishes to change his place of residence. Certain residential locations would have an economic advantage in terms of

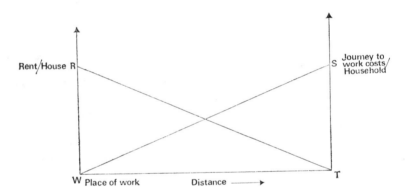

Fig. 6.1. House rents and journey to work costs in relation to distance from place of work.

access to work for locations near to the workplace enjoy lower commuting costs. However, where access to workplace is the only factor to consider, the price or rent of accommodation will decrease with increasing distance from the workplace. Assuming a single place of work (*W* in Fig. 6.1), homogeneous housing and plots, and that each household makes one journey to and from work each day, then, taking a transect in any direction from *W*, *WS* will represent a household's weekly journey to work expenses for increasing distances from *W*.

Assuming the place of work is not repulsive to residence, competition between households for houses nearest to $W$ will bid up their rents by an amount equivalent to the savings in commuting costs possible from the use of those locations. Thus the rate of decrease of $RT$, the rent per house per week, is inversely related to the rate of increase of $WS$. Given the wage per week, residential development will not be worth while beyond $T$. The locational advantage of the residential site is absorbed as rent. Housing is not homogeneous, and the savings any particular household could make through a longer journey to work would depend on the amount of residential space it consumes.

Where an urban dweller is considering changing jobs, the work access advantage of various residential locations may be a key factor. How should various job opportunity locations be discounted for distance? Do 300 jobs 4 miles away have the same attraction as 150 jobs 2 miles away? A gravity–potential approach to interaction over distance would suggest that the employment potential of a site varies directly with the employment opportunities surrounding it and inversely with the distance between it and these employment opportunities (Brigham, 1965). Transport studies show how people react to the present set of choices.

Competition for land use means that if residence is to occupy sites in and around the position of greatest accessibility, the price of accommodation must be high. Therefore, where persons wish to live close to their place of work those employed in the central business district must pay higher prices for their accommodation than persons employed in other parts of the urban area. Alternatively, persons working in the central business district make longer journeys to work, incurring higher commuting costs, than those working elsewhere in the urban area. Viewed overall, journey-to-work lengths decrease with increasing distance of workplace from the central business district. If the urban area is thought of as being divided into concentric rings, the proportion of each ring's workers residing in the same ring as their workplace increases as the workplace ring distance from the central business district increases. The more dispersed are employment opportunities throughout the urban area the less the premium households are prepared to pay for central locations and the less steep are price and density gradients.

Separation of workplace and residence is greatest for persons working in the central business district because the urban transport system in focusing on the central business district permits a much wider dispersal of residences in the case of such workers. Length of journey to work also increases as a function of income, so that the highest income workers have the greatest separation of workplace and residence. Although journey time is relatively constant, distance travelled and means of transport vary with a worker's socio-economic status, so that high-income workers, by using more rapid and flexible means of transport, can travel considerably further to work for the same time expenditure. In money terms the journey to work may cost twice as much for high-income workers.

Where low-income households have to pay the full price for accommodation and commuting, they need low-cost access to their unskilled work in services, factories, and goods handling. They live near to their work, thus achieving a short journey to work, and generally their residence is to be found in the same ring as their workplace irrespective of distance from the urban centre. They are linked to jobs in the older part of the urban area by the public transport system and well-worn labour market information networks. Very high-density living is necessary to compete sites away from alternative uses. This accommodation may have been purpose-built as with tenements or may represent once better-class housing converted for occupation by lower income groups. Households resident in multi-family structures, therefore, have shorter journeys to work than those resident in one-family houses. Thus low-income residential areas correspond to areas adjacent to industry, allowing persons to walk to work or to high density, near central areas reliant on public transport. The relative number of manufacturing workers living in a residential area varies with both the area's position in the sequence of urban expansion and its access to manufacturing jobs (Duncan, 1964). Other workers who must live close to their workplace are those with irregular working hours, as in certain retail, transport, and service jobs.

With the exception of the top white-collar groups, the professional and managerial, each group of workers tends to live in the ring where their jobs are concentrated or in the next outward ring. The other two groups have incomes which give them freedom of choice of residence, and their preference is either for high-cost residence, short work-journey, spur-of-the-moment access to the bright lights, or for spacious country living with expensive commuting bills. The former is likely where two-member households contain two wage earners who both work in the central business district, for this strengthens the pull of inner residence, the more so as such households make above average number of trips to the central business district for social and recreational purposes.

## FAMILY STATUS

The presence of children in a household has important repercussions for a household's space preferences, for the higher the proportion of children the stronger the incentive to seek low-density, peripheral, single-family housing in an agreeable neighbourhood with good schools. Families with children prefer neighbours with children of similar age, therefore, promoting the development of homogeneous and distinctly typed communities. Indeed, this neighbourhood effect is furthered by zoning and construction economics. Family considerations affect, in particular, the residential choice of central business district workers, and a decreasing proportion of such workers reside in the inner rings as their family size increases. However, there may be a tendency for space consumption to fall off as family size increases beyond a certain point as the household's demand for other goods and services causes it to forgo higher space consumption. Childless households prefer access to urban amenities and, having a lower space preference, reside in central locations. Retired persons in the higher income brackets probably have the greatest freedom of choice of residential location within an urban area.

## OTHER FACTORS

Emphasis has been laid on certain factors influencing household's preferences for residential accommodation. For example, a weak preference for quality and space leads households to locate in older areas where the quantity of accommodation per dwelling unit is smaller, whereas a higher preference for space, *ceteris paribus*, leads to larger houses and a longer journey to work. Income and job access are not the only factors which confine certain households to particular, usually poorer, residential neighbourhoods; colour and ethnic origin have a similar effect. Indeed, it can be suggested that class and racial segregation is a good for which many consumers are willing to pay. Ethnic groups are likely to inhabit distinct enclaves near the urban centre. It has been suggested (Anderson, 1962) that the subdivision of an urban area's residential space into neighbourhoods and enclaves may be understood in terms of the growth and social relationships obtaining between various sub-groups which make up the urban population. Certainly the intense competition for status as less-privileged groups strive for advancement is reflected most acutely in housing (Handlin, 1959, ch. 4). Indeed, all income groups may give up the advantages of nearness to place of work for accommodation in a neighbourhood of greater prestige.

Within an urban area variations in public services may be noticed, for newer, often richer, areas have the most up-to-date facilities. Where the urban area is large enough to be subdivided between several local government units, any variation in services provided may influence the choice of residential location, especially by higher income groups. As *per capita* incomes rise and local government performs more services, persons may spend more of their money in buying local government as reflected in product differentiation among public services (Thompson, 1965a, pp. 259–63), or the household, as consumer-voter, will pick that area which best satisfies its preference pattern for public goods (Tiebout, 1956a).

Every household must choose its residential location within an existing framework, and the costs facing a household may not be the true ones involved in the use of a particular site for residential purposes. For example, public utility systems, such as telephone or water, tend to use flat-rate charges irrespective of distance from the utility system centre which weakens a household's preference for staying close to the centre and means that near-in houses subsidize those further out. Also consumer preference for the car, and the extended range of residential choice it affords, is biased by virtue of the fact that most car commuters do not pay anything approaching the marginal costs of congestion inflicted on each other.

Summarizing, the overall pattern is likely to show nearest the position of greatest accessibility the preponderant mass of bottom income, unskilled, manual, and service workers together with recent immigrants. These occupy the oldest and most obsolete of the housing supply at high densities, and they work in the central business district or nearby heavy industry. Also here, in protected enclaves, are wealthy, mainly childless, couples in professional and executive jobs in the central business district. In the next outer ring are middle income residents plus occasional pockets of the other two. These are basically white-collar commuters to the urban centre and semi-skilled workers in industry. On progressing further out, income level rises as skilled industrial and higher white-collar workers are found, and an increasing proportion of households contain children whilst single-family houses are dominant.

## Explanatory Models of Urban Residential Land Use

In many models attempting to explain intra-urban residential location, job access is made the primary motive of household choice of residence. Most are based on rigorous assumptions, especially common being that of a single, central employment focus. Wingo (1961) and Alonso (1965) strongly suggest that residential price and density gradients are a function of household preferences rather than of some form of travel behaviour *per se*. The extent to which these preferences can be indulged by different households depends on their command over resources. However, this conclusion rests heavily on speculations regarding a positive preference for increased space rather than for the convenience of short journeys. In fact very little is known in a quantitative way about the demand function for accommodation in a multi-dimensional framework of space, access, satisfaction, income, and family structure. The theoretical approach can be illustrated by the Alonso model.

Alsonso (1965, p. 17) creates an urban model in which economic factors are paramount in the explanation of residential choice of location. This is done by assuming an urban area located in the centre of a uniform plain so that all land is of equal quality and ready for use without further improvement, a perfect urban land market, and that all jobs and goods are available only in the single urban centre. Each household must decide how near to the centre it wishes to live and how much space it requires. The choices facing a household can be analysed in indifference terms. This involves a comparison of a household's preferences—in terms of those combinations of goods which yield the same satisfaction, with the opportunities available to that household—in terms of those combinations of goods which can be purchased with a given income, in order to establish that pattern of consumptive activity which maximizes satisfaction within the income constraint.

By grouping all purchases other than land costs and commuting costs, all the possible ways in which a household can spend its income are contained in the function (Alonso, 1965, p. 21):

$$\text{Income} = \left.\begin{array}{l}(\text{quantity of land} \times \text{price}) + \text{commuting costs}\\ + (\text{quantity of composite good} \times \text{price}).\end{array}\right\} (6.2)$$

Since income and price of the composite good are taken as given and land price and commuting costs are functions of distance from the centre, the determining variables are the amount of the composite good, the quantity of land, and distance. These three variables can be analysed in indifference terms to form, for a given household, a series of indifference surfaces, each of which represents those quantities of land and the composite good at every distance from the urban centre which yield a certain level of satisfaction. One such surface is shown in Fig. 6.2. The household is indifferent between any of the residential locations represented by a point on the indifference surface. Different households have different-shaped surfaces although in all cases each surface moves upward and away from the land, and composite good axes as distance from the urban centre increases as increased amounts of land and composite good are needed to compensate for the greater inconvenience of increased travelling.

The opportunities open to any household depend on its income and the array of prices for the composite good, land, and commuting. Distance can act in opposing directions on the quantity of land a household can purchase. Since land is cheaper away from the urban centre, more may be bought as distance increases. However, commuting costs increase with increasing distance from the centre, and this would reduce the amount of land a household can purchase. With increasing distance more land can be purchased as long as the marginal savings realizable from falling land prices exceed the marginal increase in commuting costs. Beyond a certain distance, the amount of land a household can purchase must decrease because the rate of increase of commuting costs is greater than the rate of decrease of land prices. The residential locations that may be purchased by a household from its given income can be represented by a locus of opportunities surface which shows, for every distance, all the possible quantity combinations of land and composite good purchasable after the commuting costs for that distance

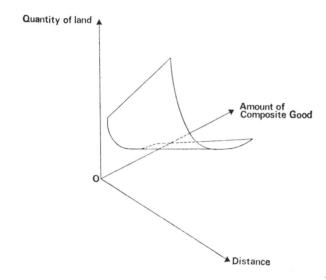

Fig. 6.2. Indifference surface between land and composite good at each distance from urban centre for a given household (see also Alonso, 1965, p. 29).

have been met. Figure 6.3 illustrates such a surface. Thus for any household its equilibrium location would be determined by the point of tangency between its locus of opportunities surface and the highest possible of its indifference surfaces. This point yields the satisfaction-maximizing combination of distance, land, and composite good within the income constraint.

Alonso then proceeds to the formulation of market equilibrium and the integration of residential with other urban land uses. Individual demand curves can usually be derived from indifference situations by varying the price of the commodity, but that is not possible here because of the land–distance relationship. At any particular distance the price of land can be varied to establish the household demand curve for land at that location only. This can be repeated for that household for

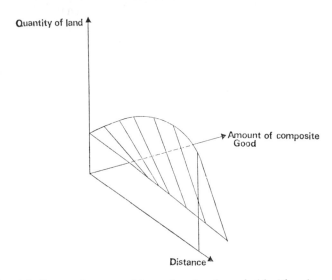

Fig. 6.3 Locus of opportunities surface for a household with a given income (see also Alonso, 1965, p. 25).

every possible location, and it will have a different demand curve for each possible location because the amount of money available after meeting commuting costs differs between locations, and the marginal rate of substitution of land for composite good also varies with location. Likewise for all other households. Which household's demand curve should be used at each location to build up the aggregate demand curve? However, the market solution will decide the location of each household. Unless the location of every household is known, there is no way of knowing which of each household's demand curves to use to build the overall market demand curve.

To overcome this difficulty, Alonso shows how residential bid-price curves, considering land prices and distance in indifference terms, can be established for each household by analogy with farm rents. Under perfect competition each farmer earns normal profit irrespective of location as competition between farmers for land with a relative locational advantage ensures that all surplus profits accrue to landlords as rent. Given the price of the commodity at the urban centre, farmers' adjustments at various distances give an "industry rent function" which can be viewed as the rent any farmer would be willing to pay landlords at each location. Where farmers produce different crops, such a function can be constructed for each crop and represents a "bid rent" since it may or may not be sufficient to obtain land for that crop. For any farmer a family of bid-rent curves is derived, each corresponding to a given market price for the product and a given level of profit for the farmer. Land at each location would be let to the highest bidder after comparison of all bids. In practice the appropriate market price for the crop must be determined simultaneously by establishing that price at which sufficient land is obtained to produce the amount required according to the crop's demand schedule, and this indicates which of the family of bid-rent curves to use.

Therefore, for an individual household a bid-price curve represents a set of prices that household could pay for land at various distances from the urban centre whilst deriving a constant level of satisfaction. The household would be indifferent among locations if the price of land were to vary in the manner described by the bid-price curve. Different households have different shaped bid-price curves because of differences in preference for space *vis-à-vis* accessibility. Alonso obtains a bid-price curve representing a given level of satisfaction for a household by constructing a "derived" locus of opportunities surface (1965, pp. 60–63) which is tangent to the indifference surface representing that satisfaction level at every distance from the urban centre as in Fig. 6.4. This is done by taking a given distance from the urban centre, at which the price of land is known, and finding the equilibrium or satisfaction-maximizing combination of land and composite good for a household at that location. Then, using the indifference surface of which that equilibrium point is a part, finding, for every other distance, the points on that surface which would represent satisfaction-maximizing combinations of land and composite good for those distances. At each distance the maximum amount of the composite good that may be purchased from the income remaining after the respective commuting

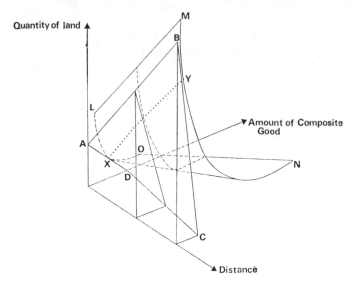

FIG 6.4. Household's indifference surface and "derived" locus of opportunities surface (see also Alonso, 1965, p. 63).

costs have been met is determined. All possible straight lines through that value on the composite good axis are drawn to establish the line which is tangent to the indifference surface at each distance. These points of tangency represent possible equilibriums and together form line $XY$ in Fig. 6.4. Via the substitution of the quantities of land and composite good represented by line $XY$ in the original household income equation (6.2), a bid-price curve for land can be established. This curve will be downward-sloping because transport costs reduce the bid price as distance increases, i.e. the price of land must drop if the household is to maintain the same level of satisfaction at an increased distance from the centre from a reduced effective income. For each household this procedure is repeated for other "starting distances" and hence levels of satisfaction and a series of bid-price curves is obtained. The lower the bid-price curve the greater is the satisfaction to the household.

The equilibrium location for a given household is found by superimposing the actual structure of land prices on the household's set of bid-price curves. Thus in Fig. 6.5 the household's satisfaction-maximizing

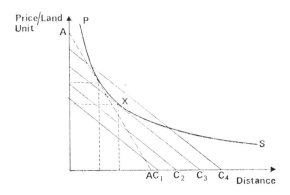

FIG. 6.5. Household's satisfaction-maximizing or equilibrium location.

location would be at $X$, where the price structure $PS$ touches the lowest possible bid-price curve $C_3$. Market equilibrium holds when no household can increase its satisfaction by changing its location or buying less land, and no landlord can increase his revenue by changing the price of his land. The steeper a household's bid-price curve, $AA$ in Fig. 6.5, the nearer the centre it will locate, for it shows the strength of the household's preference for short journeys. The higher is household income the less steep the bid-price curve because of the decrease in relative importance of commuting costs, which follows from the larger land holdings. Alonso's model is a static one designed to explain locational decisions at a given time and produces, under the assumptive conditions, a land-use pattern consisting basically of concentric rings.

Wingo (1961) also views land costs and transport costs as complementary. Together they equal a constant sum determined by the transport costs involved in the use of the most distant residential location. Of personal movements generated by households, work journeys

**168**    *The Economics of Urban Areas*

are considered most significant in terms of order and volume within an urban area, and such journeys have the lowest price elasticity of demand. Other classes of journey are, therefore, assumed to play an indeterminate role in household location (Wingo, 1961, p. 36). With wage or household income taken as exogenous to the system, choice of residential location is again viewed as a budgeting problem—the allocation of income between transport costs and land costs.

Considering distance from a single focal work-point, the net incomes of workers are unequal since their journey to work costs vary, with workers living nearest to the workplace receiving a surplus over and above the marginal value of leisure. Therefore prices of locations with such advantages are bid up to the point where all but one worker is excluded. All or part of the locational advantage is absorbed as rent, and a unique set of location rents can be generated for every worker at every point in space-reflecting preferences for space or short journeys. These play a role in equalizing the net incomes among all workers and at the same time provide a basis for urban site values since the location rent at any site equals the net annual savings in transport costs compared to the highest transport cost location in use. Transport costs, therefore, determine the spatial structure of location rents, i.e. the relationship which must exist among any equilibrium set of location rents, but the market will select the overall level of rents. Any household seeking accommodation will thus find that as it moves towards its workplace rent increases whilst transport costs decrease. Each household will continue to move towards its workplace until it finds the location in which its marginal saving in transport costs is equal to the marginal value of the residential space given up. Through this process of substituting transport costs for space costs locational equilibrium is achieved.

Kain (1962) and Muth (1961) also regard the substitution of transport expenditures for space costs as central to the locational decision of households, with the extent of substitution in any case depending upon the household's preference for high- or low-density living as the way to maximize its satisfaction from a given income. Homogeneity of land for residential purposes and a single urban focus are again essential assumptions. Kain emphasizes work-journey expenses, arguing that a household's other transport costs can either be assumed as invariant with location, as in the case of expenditures on services available within the residential area, or are trivial in amount, as with costs which vary with distance from other urban facilities. Kain takes the spatial structure of accommodation prices as given and accepts that this varies with location in a manner dictated by economic rents related to the work access advantages of various sites following households' attempts to minimize work-journey expenses. Location rents, therefore, decrease with increasing distance from workplace. In these circumstances the quantity of accommodation purchased by a household is a function of income, preferences, and accommodation price. Given the household's workplace and transport costs per mile, its residential location must be a function of its space consumption. The location rent function gives the savings per unit of residential space a household can achieve by moving further from its place of work. Assuming that a given sum spent on transport or rent has the same dissatisfaction for a household then Kain argues that the best combination of the two is included in the set which minimizes the combined outlay on rent and transport for each quantity of residential space. Rent expenditures may, however, bring positive satisfaction because of the amenity factor.

Muth considers the total transport expenditures of households, but again the equilibrium location for a household occurs where savings in the quantity of housing purchased there by a short move are balanced by the change in total transport expenditures made.

Such models throw light on the factors influencing residential locations in highly idealized situations, but once the highly restrictive assumptions are relaxed, it becomes impossible to specify the access-transport cost function for any location; thus Kain points out that as workplace distance from the urban centre increases, the relationships predicted in his model deteriorate. The resultant patterns of all these models also rest heavily on the assumed preferences of households.

## Changing Residential Patterns

When one household changes its residential location a chain reaction frequently follows, as the accommodation it vacates may provide an opportunity for another household to improve its standard of housing.

The nature of the supply of new housing will be important in determining which households obtain new houses and, therefore, the number and type of second-hand houses which become available to other households. Areas of recent residential growth illustrate the population's current tastes in housing. The location factor is thus important in the relationship between the existing housing stock and new construction. New houses for the lowest income groups are not economically feasible for private developers in an established urban area. Thus in a free market new residential development primarily takes the form of single houses in the suburbs or luxury apartments in highly central locations for higher income groups and other apartments for middle-income households replacing old, single houses in near central locations. Single-family houses for owner occupation face definite locational constraints because of the low density of development which do not apply to apartments and other forms of residential accommodation.

Changing residential patterns within a single urban area are due to population growth, income changes, and transport improvements. The influence of increasing affluence depends on the income elasticity of demand for housing, transport, and space. Cars and suburban living space appear as complementary superior goods, for increased consumption of one accompanies increased consumption of the other, and the consumption of both increases as *per capita* income rises (Meyer *et al.*, 1966). Rising standards and incomes bring an increased preference for separate accommodation by people sharing accommodation and for better housing by those already in their own home (Greve, 1961) with owner-occupied houses being the most highly valued (Donnison *et al.*, 1961). As urban transport improves, the area of developable land is extended, the range of locational choice is widened, and more sites can be developed according to their amenity values. Most persons prefer to keep a reasonable distance between their workplace and residence, but centrifugal redistribution of population tends to increase the average length of journeys to work and to other urban facilities. Suburban living means increased expenditures on transport for many households, but generally they can afford it although this way of life may leave less money for other things or savings (Gottmann, 1961). Access to workplace will become less important as a locational factor as the working week gets shorter. With more free time, consumers have caused a demand which goes beyond the house (Burby, 1967) as increased leisure time and greater mobility strengthen the pull of amenity and recreational facilities on choice of residential location. The movement to the suburbs is essentially a search for space and privacy (Zimmer and Hawley, 1961), and suburban residential sites are, on average, two to three times as large as near central ones. Newcomers to the urban area, as well as centrifugal urban migrants, choose suburban residences, but the former do so because they are more likely to work locally. Overall improvements in transport and income, which allow a greater indulgence of space preferences, reduce price gradients as central housing prices tend to fall and those in the outer parts to rise.

The redistribution of population within an urban area leaves predominant in the centre the lowest income groups who require the greatest amount of public services. A less central employment pattern might provide more jobs in the outer areas for low-income households and lead to a redistribution of low-income residence.

FILTERING

Those households seeking better housing standards and higher space standards must have recourse to new peripheral housing whose construction price is usually at least equal to the price of existing houses occupied by such households. What happens to the accommodation these households vacate? Housing quality declines with age, and time gradually moves each house down the quality scale. This represents a decline in marketable quality rather than in social quality because with adequate maintenance physical deterioration is unimportant. The initial decline in market value is the result of technological and layout obsolescence, although style may sometimes become dated as well. Former high-income housing is thus vacated and handed down to lower income groups. Thus Lowry (1960) defines filtering as the change in the real value of an existing house which allows new occupants to obtain the house.

Accommodation vacated by households—mainly high-income groups—moving into new houses becomes available to other households. Housing vacated by the highest income groups increases the supply in the second-quality bracket relative to demand, and here it must compete with any new houses of lower standard provided by builders. Given the level of demand for houses in the second-quality bracket, the supply of vacated top-quality houses provides a check on the price of any new second-quality houses. It also means that higher standard accommodation is available at a price equal to existing second-quality housing, and certain households in this group will take advantage of this to improve their housing standard. The accommodation they vacate will stimulate similar changes in the third-quality bracket, and so on down the housing standard scale.

Provided the number of households in successively lower income groups increases the ratio of houses available, new plus vacant, at any given standard to households seeking to move into them from dwellings at the next lower standard will remain favourable for the builder and sustain a buoyant demand for new houses at that standard. At some point the number of households in successively lower income groups will cease to increase; this probably happens about halfway down the income distribution (Economic Commission for Europe, 1966). At this point the supply–demand relationship in that part of the market changes, and effective demand would be satisfied from vacated properties. Vacated housing then forms a price-depressing surplus so the prices of all houses in that quality group fall, and this continues until some of the households in the next lower income group take advantage of the low prices to improve their housing standard. Houses within the existing stock would continue to filter down at the lower quality levels, leaving at the bottom of the quality scale an unoccupied, residual surplus of housing. It is precisely the effectiveness of the filtering process which eventually prevents further new building at the lower levels. This occurs around the middle of the market, and from then on down filtering of vacated properties must be relied upon in the free market to provide improved housing for the lower income groups. The effectiveness of filtering in raising housing standards depends on the speed of value decline compared to quality decline. Where the values of existing houses decline rapidly to give low-income groups housing above an arbitrary minimum standard, the market mechanism could help attain the public goal of adequate accommodation for every household.

The above analysis treats filtering largely from the demand side, but what of the reactions of suppliers of existing houses, particularly landlords in the privately rented sector? If a landlord finds the price consumers are willing to pay falls below his annual operating costs, his response is to disinvest, which usually takes the form of cutting back on maintenance. Where all landlords react similarly, the relative quality of houses will remain the same whilst their absolute quality declines. The consumer would not then have the alternative of better housing at about the same price, although there is a time-lag before the consequences of landlords' actions for quality become obvious to the market. Under-maintenance accelerates housing quality decline, and tenants of second- or lower-quality housing may find their houses deteriorating below what they consider to be the optimum. Therefore competition for better quality will force up price again to a level where maintenance costs are covered, so filtering is shut off as the flow of units from the upper brackets are cut off (Lowry, 1960). In this case, filtering will not raise the general standard of housing. Owner-occupiers may well react differently to landlords and maintain their property even in the face of generally declining house values.

The spatial repercussions of filtering depend on the character and location of the new construction which set off the chain reaction of accommodation changes throughout the urban housing market. Not all the vacated houses will, in fact, be available to lower income groups since, with changing conditions other urban uses may find that former residential sites now represent their optimum locations, and frequently residential buildings are adapted to the needs of light industry, office, and other tertiary activities at little cost. This is likely to be the case with large houses in the more accessible locations. Considering the location of units involved in filtering, it is likely that superior housing to that presently occupied by a household is located further from the urban centre; thus any decline in its price must, *ceteris paribus*, more than offset the increase in commuting costs involved in a move to that location. Otherwise household income must increase to permit the lower income household to increase its combined outlay on rent and commuting costs. This is probably the case. Moreover, with many owner-occupiers being able to sell their present house is a determining factor in their ability to purchase another house. At some point the availability of second-hand housing with poor public transport facilities could slow down—even halt—the filtering process, since there comes a point where the low-income household, dependent upon public transport, cannot afford the private car necessary to the use of that particular housing.

## SLUMS

Neighbourhoods, as well as buildings, become obsolescent with the resultant formation of areas of substandard or slum housing. The older the residential neighbourhood, the greater is the likelihood of this happening and, as the oldest houses are near the urban centre, this is where slums are to be found. Slums house the poor, the chronically unemployed, the unemployable, and immigrants, classes not yet integrated into urban life because of an ability barrier in the case of the first three groups and differences in culture in the case of immigrants. It may be only a matter of time before the latter adjust, therefore "slums of hope" can be distinguished from "slums of despair" (Stokes, 1962), where, in advanced societies, poverty and lack of ability are increasingly correlated. Most economic explanations of the existence of slums are based on factors influencing the supply schedule. Increased use of cars, technological obsolescence of older houses, poor initial layout of central neighbourhoods, and inadequate municipal services bring a decline in demand for good-quality central housing, and, consequently, an increase in the supply of poor-quality housing. Increased supply reduces house prices in the affected areas, causing landlords to reduce maintenance expenditures in the face of declining returns. Physical deterioration is, therefore, the main reason for the existence of substandard housing. The external effects reduce the value of surrounding properties. Slums are frequently concentrated in the privately rented sector of the housing market and may be associated with certain rent-controlled properties. Another basis of slum formation lies in construction practices of building whole neighbourhoods at the same time with almost identical structures: these all wear out together (Lessinger, 1962).

## Government and the Housing Market

Government interference with the functioning of the housing market is commonplace. Accepting the idea that every household is entitled to a minimum standard of housing it was seen that filtering could not be relied upon to ensure a housing standard above this arbitrary minimum for the lowest income groups. An alternative method is the provision of subsidized municipal housing and this, on any scale, interferes with the market that may otherwise have provided second-hand housing for the same families. Such municipal estates are likely to be found in those parts of the urban area where land values are relatively low and access to manufacturing industry is easy (Mann, 1965) or in renewal projects near the urban centre. However, not all low-income households get subsidized accommodation, and in circumstances where demand exceeds supply, the Government may enact rent controls which further interfere with the supply of housing. Even new private enterprise owner-occupied housing may benefit from planning legislation as its bidding power for sites for residences may be artificially bolstered by a reduction in competition for certain locations as a result of zoning. Modernization of older houses may also be influenced by government permissive legislation, such as that on improvement grants.

Government measures influence not only the supply but also the demand for housing. Both volume of demand and its spatial impact may be conditioned by government actions. For example, option mortgage schemes, which allow households with incomes too low to obtain full tax relief on mortgage interest to benefit from concessionary interest rates, can lead to a general increase in the demand for owner-occupied housing. Where improvement grants contribute towards the cost of installing bathrooms, hot-water systems, etc., then modernization of an existing dwelling may be an alternative to a spatial move for a household seeking superior accommodation. This may be a particularly attractive alternative since better housing can be obtained without having to sacrifice social contacts built-up during residence in that area. The latter would, most likely, be severed following any spatial move. As a result, demand for superior housing in alternative locations may be lowered. Also, the turnover of a certain proportion of existing houses will be slowed down and hence their participation in the filtering process reduced.

Rent control also interferes with freedom of choice. Firstly, households occupying controlled premises have a reduced incentive to move to alternative accommodation if, in doing so, they lose the advantage of their controlled tenancy. If alternative accommodation is uncontrolled, its price will be substantially higher and the household's disposable income available for other purposes would be reduced. The relative improvement in housing quality obtainable may not be considered worth the sacrifice of such a large part of the composite good. Households enjoying controlled tenancies therefore tend to stay put, again reducing turnover and participation in filtering. Secondly, households not already occupying controlled property can rarely obtain a controlled tenancy and therefore find their range of choice of accommodation effectively reduced. Municipal housing will have similar consequences for demand.

Planning controls particularly affect the spatial incidence of demand since new residential developments require planning permission. Moreover, in so far as these controls stipulate development densities, then the extent to which household space preferences can be realized by occupying new housing, rests partly in the hands of the planners.

In the immediate future the existing stock of houses in any urban area, its spatial distribution, and opportunities for movement within that stock will largely determine the housing opportunities of the urban population. New housing in any time period will represent only a very small addition to stock, and is available to only limited income groups—the wealthy where ability to pay is the criterion, the poor where subsidized accommodation is allocated on some other basis. However, the quality of the stock depends on the volume and quality of recent building as well as the extent to which older houses are replaced or modernized. Moreover, current building helps determine the rate of future obsolescence and, by gradually increasing the average quality of the housing stock, it increases the present rate of obsolescence.

CHAPTER 7

# Urban Growth: (1) Outward Expansion

## Causes of Urban Change

Urban areas are not unchanging: businesses may expand or decline and population may increase or decrease due to natural causes or migration. As a result the optimum locations of activities and inhabitants at the intra-urban level may be altered. Buildings vacated by one occupant may be adapted for use by new occupants or they may be demolished and replaced by different structures. Equilibrium is never established for an urban area in respect of land prices and uses since the underlying conditions of demand and supply are insufficiently stable to allow one set of adjustments to be completed before further adjustments are needed. This is due, in part, to the nature of urban investment.

It is the function of the urban land market to bring about the adjustments necessitated by the growth or decline of urban activities and populations. For example, if urban growth brings a permanent increase in demand for residential accommodation, housing prices rise in the short-run since supply is inelastic and the existing stock must be used more intensively. Where the price rise is sufficiently great, construction firms will be able to earn super-normal profits. This will encourage an increase in the supply of houses as vacant land is converted to residential use and certain sites are redeveloped for intensive residential use. New intra-urban patterns of land use, use intensity, and land values are, therefore, established.

The causes of such changes, stemming from both economic and non-economic sources, are manifold. Existing economic opportunities, in particular the stage of economic development, are a major determinant of urban growth potential. In population terms urban growth in a nation will reflect the proportion of population urbanized and the rate of natural increase of the urban population. Urbanization generates growth since it incorporates a cumulative and circular growth process. Urban areas offer opportunities for greater specialization, the outcome of which, increased production of goods and services, is equivalent to an increase in real income per head of urban population. Higher incomes increase the size of markets which leads to further specialization and, hence, another increase in income. Urban job opportunities attract additional labour from non-urban areas, and more workers also mean bigger markets. Urban growth also provides the greater surpluses of manufactured goods to trade for the increased supply of foodstuffs needed. Non-economic factors, as noted in Chapter 2, may reinforce economic factors in this growth process and vice versa.

Growth of urban population, whether due to natural increase or the receipt of migrants from rural areas or abroad, also increases market size and, therefore, opportunities for specialization. Inter-urban migration favours the largest urban areas. All those urban areas in Britain with extremes of population change between 1931 and 1958 owed this fact to gain or loss by migration and not to natural causes (Moser and Scott, 1961). Technological change is more rapid in urban areas because problems demanding solution are more commonplace and inventive and innovative capacity are concentrated there. This also works towards the production of more goods and services from a given input of resources as new methods of production are substituted for old. *Per capita* incomes are raised further. Political decisions, especially the choice of urban areas as local or regional administrative centres, can promote the growth of the favoured urban areas. Similar repercussions may follow the siting of new universities, motorways, or other publicly provided facilities.

Growth does not affect all urban areas equally. In a nation showing high rates of urban growth some areas will be increasing in population size and economic wealth faster than others. Some may even be declining, e.g. as their mineral resource base is exhausted. Inter-urban competition will determine the extent to which any particular urban area will grow, stagnate, or decline, with the relative attractiveness of the urban area for new investment being the critical factor.

## Effect on the Demand for and Supply of Urban Land

Urban growth and structure are fundamentally affected by changes in the economic base of an urban area. With growth an urban area may acquire new functions and expand old ones, so altering intra-urban and hinterland relationships, increasing the physical extent of the area, and bringing the internal reorganization of activities. The role of export industry, whether expanding or rationalizing its operations, will determine certain labour, transport, and other factor needs, and will influence opportunities for complementary and service activities. Increasing urban size may attract additional export industry as well as new threshold industries, both of which are new elements to be accommodated in the urban land-use pattern. Changes in the underlying conditions of demand and supply for urban land thus accompany urban growth, with demand changing most rapidly in both volume and quality terms.

Certain changes in intra-urban spatial patterns, such as the outward extension of residential areas or the lateral expansion of the central business district, stem simply from increased population size, independent of higher levels of income or technology which generate increased space demands from a given population. Over a period of time the number and type of firms and households seeking urban sites will change, whilst there are alterations in the locational requirements of existing units due to changes in their characteristics, e.g. the family-life cycle in the case of households. Higher incomes and different tastes bring changes in urban residential patterns. New production methods and the changing availability of factors of production do likewise for productive activities. At the intra-urban level reduced friction of distance has expanded the range of locational choice for urban activities and population by making urban land increasingly homogeneous in access terms for most manufacturing, retail, and residential uses. In adapting to changing circumstances by switching locations within an urban area, an activity is likely to alter the amount of space it consumes to compensate or substitute for rising land prices or transport costs. Sooner or later every urban activity may be forced to consider an alternative location when the building it occupies needs replacing.

### Physical Expression of Urban Growth

Urban areas grow centrifugally with major transport routes having a dominant influence on the directions of physical expansion. This leaves the core as the oldest, least up-to-date part of the urban area. Increased total size of urban area has both intensive and extensive impacts. Existing buildings and facilities are used more intensively. New buildings are constructed, as a rule, in response to demands for accommodations beyond those available in existing buildings. This represents a more intensive use in the case of redevelopment and a more extensive use where the built-up area is extended. An increase in the spread of the built-up area will increase the average length and exposure of all types of movements.

Urban growth necessitates considerable investment in physical plant. As a consequence of investment fluctuations under free-market conditions, besides being a cumulative process, urban growth is also likely to be a cyclical process. Growth for any particular urban area is thus not a continuous process but a succession of jumps which may also be related to the indivisibility of certain basic investments in infrastructure essential for growth (Malisz, 1969). Growth, especially new suburban building, corresponds to the upswing and boom periods of business and, especially, building cycles. Therefore new construction investment, which is the basis of urban structural change, is one of the most volatile elements in the national economy. Allocation of capital investment to different types of construction within a particular city is closely related to investment in the different sectors of the national economy (Bourne, 1967, ch. 5).

Over a period of time, changes in intra-urban activity distribution patterns reflect not only the physical relocation of existing activities but also the differential growth rates amongst the various urban parts. Redistribution of existing activities throughout very large urban areas in response to structural forces (Alonso, 1964) has produced what has been termed the "spread city" (Campbell and Burkhead, 1968, p. 639). For example, the formidable obstacles to the expansion of large manufacturing plants at their existing sites has, in the light of the development of space-extensive technology, reduced the demand for central locations. Where a firm changes its location, the new site must offer sufficient advantages to offset the costs involved in the move, such as the sacrifice of any non-transportable fixed capital. Apart from the relocation of existing units, relative decentralization will occur as a result of the decline of firms in disadvantaged locations and the rise of new firms at more favourable peripheral urban sites.

The physical process of urban growth involves the lateral expansion, infilling, and internal reorganization of the existing built-up area. The costs of land at various locations relative to the costs of building an additional storey set an economic limit to the vertical expansion of an urban area, and pressure of demand beyond a certain point must lead to outward expansion. The existing urban area will be expanded via concentric, axial, and dormitory growth: urban sprawl is thus a form of growth.

Infilling takes place where areas previously bypassed in the urban expansion are now developed. Sites ignored because of some handicap which raised costs of development to prohibitive levels at the time concerned may now be developed as a result of advances in building technology, e.g. use of raft or pile foundationing. The relative location of such sites in the urban area allows transport cost savings which make the incurring of higher development costs worth while. Other sites, previously developed extensively, may be subdivided—as when new houses are built in the large garden of an older house.

The increased demand for buildings accompanying urban growth will be met in the first place from within the existing stock of buildings. Only much later will investment in new construction be generated to meet demands not satisfied by the existing stock. A person or firm requiring a given location must adjust to the buildings which exist there, whether they are altogether suitable for the internal functioning of the activity in question or not. The continual rearrangement of the activities of existing firms and households, the appearance of new firms and households, and the mobility of occupiers means that buildings are frequently used for purposes other than those for which they were designed. Individual buildings may, therefore, go through a succession of different occupiers and uses.

As demands change over time, the stock of buildings may be altered to suit: existing buildings may be modified accordingly and any new buildings will be constructed in locations and to specifications currently demanded. Due to ageing and obsolescence, the replacement of buildings is forever taking place as each site or area is tested or re-tested to establish its highest and best use. Low buildings are replaced by higher ones as more intensive use is made of the most accessible locations. New building in the form of redevelopment has side effects since any displaced activities must seek accommodation elsewhere. Each urban site may experience a series of different buildings.

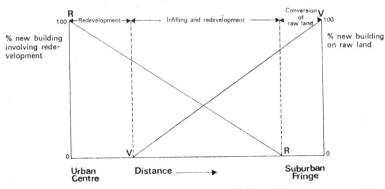

FIG. 7.1. Proportion of new building involving redevelopment and vacant land within an urban area.

The conversion of existing buildings, with or without modification, to new uses and redevelopment, i.e. the demolition and replacement of an existing building, are both part of the same process of internal reorganization.

Given that older buildings are more frequent nearer to the urban centre, the proportion of new construction involving redevelopment declines steadily with increasing distance from the urban centre as line *RR* in Fig. 7.1 shows. Alternatively, the proportion of new building taking place on raw land would increase, as line *VV* shows, with distance from the urban centre. However, viewed in terms of the volume of construction, building activity is greatest at the urban periphery with a second peak representing redevelopment activity in and around the urban centre as in Fig. 7.2.

The physical growth of an urban area involves the antagonistic yet complementary processes of spatial concentration of more activities and people into the area and decentralization at the intra-urban level. Internal reorganization, especially redevelopment, and suburban expansion are part of the same process, and for any activity may serve as investment alternatives.

## Why is Adjustment a Slow Process?

The creation and adaptation of the urban environment is a long-term process and one that is never complete. Moreover, the current pattern of land use in any urban area is strongly shaped by prior developments, for buildings and facilities—once constructed—may dominate subsequent development for generations. The stock of urban buildings and facilities has been built up over considerable periods of time in re-

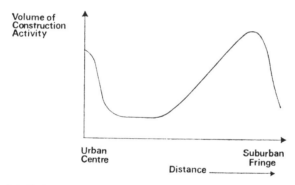

FIG. 7.2  Volume of construction activity in an urban area related to distance from the urban centre.

sponse to repeated demands for space in line with requirements current at each period. An urban area, in this physical sense of buildings and infrastructure, is a static thing, but the activities which comprise the urban area as an economic and social entity are dynamic elements whose requirements for urban locations and buildings change much more rapidly than the great bulk of buildings and facilities can be adapted. The physical structures are sluggish in response due to their durability, so the dynamic activities must adjust themselves to the physical structures as best they can. With new construction equivalent to such a small fraction of the existing stock, the latter dominates the market. Over time the building stock may become increasingly out of phase with current demands for space. In no instance can a well-established urban centre represent as efficient a solution of current needs as might be achieved on a virgin site.

The existing urban spatial structure and building availability act as a constraining framework for change. Changes in any one period of time take place as minor modifications around existing clusters of dominant activities. Each change represents a separate improvement designed, as a rule, on its own merits with the object of making that building or site a more efficient instrument for carrying out the activities taking place there, but with scant regard for wider consequences. Whatever tendencies exist for movement towards optimum locations, this may be severely restrained for any activity by the existence of sunk costs in present locations. Building costs are such a sunk cost, committed in anticipation of long-period returns which cannot be withdrawn. So a building may be occupied by whatever urban activities care to use it. The locational distribution of the building stock is fixed, and as a result buildings cannot escape the characteristics of the environments in which they are located. Current patterns of urban land use thus reflect both continuance and reorganization on the part of urban activities. Any adjustments to changing circumstances are worked out separately by businesses, government authorities, or social groups, each in response to its own set of limitations.

In the development of any urban area, land is automatically divided into profit-making and non-profit uses, and once this division has taken place, it tends to fossilize, so that decisions made in the private sector have to take the pattern of land use and public infrastructure as given. For example, redevelopment by private concerns is most likely to take place within the existing road layout. Few changes can be made in the short run to the non-profit uses. In the long run, minor adjustments, such as road widening, may be the most common form of adjustment since the adaptation of land in urban areas to provide accommodation and space for non-profit uses, especially for movement, requires substantial investment. This has the effect of slowing down the adjustment of urban areas as a whole to changing conditions.

Urban real property is strongly influenced by legal and ownership restrictions, and with each property subject to different controls and agreements, the response can vary widely. In particular the size of the site, which reflects a past optimum, may not represent the present optimum layout. Although the size of land units may be obsolete, because of ownership factors, change cannot readily be accomplished. Also, with new buildings the time that must elapse before the building becomes available for use is considerable because of the time needed to acquire the necessary site, for designing the building and arranging the finance as well as the actual construction process (Lean and Goodall, 1966, p. 315).

Given the durability of buildings, the considerable difficulties in altering the size of site and the provision of non-profit uses, and the time-span for new development, adjustments within an urban area are never completed. The functioning of the urban area as a whole may be less efficient as a result.

## Outward Expansion

The physical expansion of an urban area may involve expansion due to population growth as well as the redistribution of activities within the urban area. Much of what has been termed decentralization is, in fact, just growth. The amount of land needed per unit of time to accommodate the outward expansion of an urban area will depend on the size of the urban area, its rate of growth, the proportion of demand channelled into suburban preferences, and the density of new development. At any one time there are many times more sites with development potential for urban use than are needed. Which of these possible sites will be developed? In the solution to this question the pattern of outward expansion is determined. Of course, the outward expansion of the urban frontier is but one facet of urban change and of the general theory of urban land use. Viewed from general theory it represents a problem in marginal or boundary analysis.

## The Pattern of Outward Expansion

The pattern of outward expansion has frequently been described as sprawl. This represents an observation about the urban fringe at a point in time. Sprawl, lying in advance of the principal lines of growth, is most noticeable when urban areas in general are expanding rapidly and around the fastest-growing urban areas. Expansion involving the initial improvement of vacant land is usually confined to residential and industrial land uses. The first wave of development in any peripheral zone is likely to be patchy, reflecting such factors as differences in access or amenity conditions and variations in the size of development. A major feature of outward expansion under the price mechanism is, therefore, its tendency to discontinuity and this has been termed sprawl (Clawson, 1962), perhaps more precisely leapfrog sprawl, to indicate that areas of undeveloped land separate new developments from each other and from the continuous built-up area. A feature of the growth of large urban areas is the appearance of new settlements budding off from it (Dickinson, 1951). These are dormitory settlements and being dependent on the large urban area for job opportunities and many retail and service facilities they have an excessively high proportion of land in residential use. In addition to sporadic development, expansion follows lines of least resistance—essentially major radial roads—out of the urban area. Ribbon development occurs when land on either side of such a main road, for considerable distances into the countryside, is converted to urban use. Low-density continuous development may be recognized as a further major form of sprawl (Harvey and Clark, 1965).

Potential urban development is a threat to the existence of agriculture in the rural–urban fringe. Indeed, much undeveloped peripheral land may be taken out of farming and allowed to lie idle until such time as it is developed. Such land derives its value from expectations of development. Urban expansion bids up the value of land far beyond agricultural value, but this need not render land immediately derelict for farming. Even where a farmer has sold his land to a new owner, who knows nothing about farming, the latter could lease the land to another farmer and this would contribute some income to set against the costs incurred in holding the land until it is ripe for development. However, successful farming becomes increasingly difficult. In some cases only part of a farm may have been sold for development, leaving a remnant too small to be a viable economic entity with the result that it too becomes derelict. Farming of the type commonly found in the urban periphery may not be wholly compatible with urban expansion. Consequently, as farmland in the area declines, successful farming on the remaining agricultural land becomes more difficult. Urban sprawl may, therefore, bring an increase in the amount of land not used for any economic output at any given time.

## Factors Influencing Expansion Patterns

Sprawl occurs because it is economical in terms of the alternatives available to those firms and households deciding on rural–urban locations. Close-in land is bypassed by new development because of the smaller size of available land parcels and the greater cost of acquiring sites with existing, often unsuitable, structures. Sprawl is largely determined by the scattering of manufacturing plants away from areas already too crowded by such plants and into districts with good transport facilities and within easy reach of one or more large urban areas (Gottmann, 1961, p. 210). The motor-car has provided the essential condition for residential sprawl since it has allowed easier, but not necessarily cheaper, commuting.

Where all landowners seek to maximize the price or rent they can obtain for their land, it would be expected that sites adjacent to the existing built-up area will be developed first because they enjoy access advantages to existing transport facilities and urban services. However, suburban development frequently takes place in the absence of full information on the part of the buyer/developer and, arising out of such uncertainties, as well as the variability of site characteristics and individual preferences, expansion will be more dispersed. The expansion of the urban fringe has been described as a spatial diffusion process (Morrill, 1965) in which the development of new property is, land being homogeneous, essentially random in direction. Development follows an inverse probability distribution as to distance from the urban area: although the chances of development are greatest for sites nearest to the built-up area, this does allow for leapfrogging, i.e. gaps in the development. A direct probability distribution describes the relationship between development and the quality of sites and neighbourhoods. Simulation techniques may be used to trace the process through time.

Under the price system all incremental additions to the urban fringe are speculative ventures. Landowners hold a variety of expectations about the future and demand a variety of rates of return. Where an owner places a higher subjective valuation on his freehold interest than any developer, his land will be bypassed and leapfrog sprawl results. A landowner more distant from the urban area may discount future income at a very high rate, so giving a low subjective valuation, and he may err in prematurely developing his land. It would be expected, however, that the probability of such error would decrease with proximity to the urban area. The more rapid the rate of growth of an urban area and the greater the number of developers operating in the suburban housing market, the greater will be the number of fragmented, randomly located projects. Thus lack of co-ordination of the decision to speculate produces sprawl rather than the speculation itself (Harvey and Clark, 1965). The importance of the ownership factor may be further stressed because institutional factors, especially estate and public landholdings, affect the marketability of land, particularly in the short run. The type of farming practised may influence the farmer's resistance to urban encroachment since a farmer with a high fixed investment in land improvement will try to operate for as long as he can in order to recover as much of his sunk costs as possible. An increase in hobby or weekend farming by urban businessmen may protect some land from development. In other cases, the buyer seeking a particular environment may contribute to sprawl. Thus the character and preferences of the landowner himself are major factors in determining which parcels of fringe land are developed or remain undeveloped (Clawson, 1962).

Suburban topography may not be suitable for continuous urban development. Development is concentrated on those lands most readily and economically available. Site characteristics influence development costs; thus sites with developmental handicaps, such as liability to floods or excessive slope, are avoided and those with positive qualities, such as sandy soils, are preferred. Indeed, many of the physical qualities making land valuable for agriculture also make it valuable for urban use. Suburban development is concentrated in the better farming areas because urban uses are buying accessibility—to roads, public utility services, etc.—and these are more readily available in the better farming areas. Thus agriculture has little success in stemming urban growth.

Lower development densities are possible in the outer parts of the urban area because there is a more than proportionate increase in the supply of land with increasing distance from the urban centre.

Public and government bodies, in partially determining the framework within which private decisions are made, may influence the outward expansion by imbalancing the relative attractiveness of competing areas (Goodall, 1970). For example, if an urban area relies on parking charges to regulate car traffic rather than road tolls, distance travelled is irrelevant and this will favour commuters from the more distant areas. In the supply of public utility services, charges are commonly set at levels providing an adequate revenue from the area-wide operations of the utility with little consideration for the cost of serving individual communities. For example, the charges made for the installation of household telephones and for telephone rental do not depend on the location of the house. Cross-subsidization occurs with near-in consumers supporting those more distant from the utility system centre. The extension of public services, such as sewerage or water supply, may give an impetus to development in a particular suburban sector, although this is unlikely to be sufficient, on its own, to stimulate development. In the case of ribbon development there is an obvious saving to the private developer on road and public utility costs besides the advantages of direct access to a main route. Density regulations laid down by local planning authorities can also contribute to low-density sprawl, and this is probably more important in the United States than in the United Kingdom (Coke and Liebman, 1961).

The rural–urban fringe is a marginal area in the sense that it represents a margin of transferance between alternative types of land use. Land there is indifferently suited to more than one use (Firey, 1951). For instance, assuming the price any user will pay for sites decreases with increasing distance from the urban centre, then, as Fig. 7.3 shows, the rate of fall of offer price is not the same for every user. Residential users would be able to compete sites nearer the urban centre away from alternative agricultural users as indicated by line *RR*, but the value of sites for residential use falls more quickly than the value of sites for agriculture, represented by line *AA*, as distance from the urban centre

**190**  *The Economics of Urban Areas*

increases. Therefore, *RR* must intersect *AA*, and this happens at distance *OX* from the urban centre. At this intersection, sites are equally well suited to residence and agriculture so these two uses will be intermixed in this zone. Each may depreciate the value of the location for the other use, and thus make possible certain temporary land uses, such as residential caravan sites. It should be noted that the

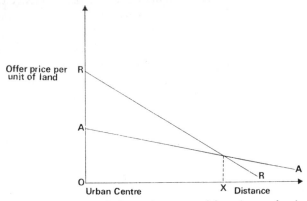

Fig. 7.3. The apparent indeterminateness of the price mechanism at the urban fringe.

apparent indeterminateness of the price mechanism in deciding the use of land at distance *OX* from the centre will, in any particular part of the peripheral zone, be short-lived because the introduction of residences into an agricultural area will bring a degree of determinateness to the future use of sites in that area (Lean and Goodall, 1966, p. 187).

## The Economic Limits to Sprawl

Economic limits to sprawl represent the margin for private development at a point in time, for, with continued urban growth and changing circumstances the position of that margin is altered. New development on sites beyond the existing built-up area will be chosen when this offers a superior alternative to any combination of location and existing or redeveloped property within the built-up area. For an urban area as a whole, outward expansion would be undertaken up to the point where the marginal net benefit from the last unit of suburban development is equal to the marginal net benefit from the last unit of redevelopment and modification within the built-up area.

Each new development in the outward expansion of an urban area needs to be served by transport routes and utility lines. These latter generally follow a corridor out from the urban area and their costs of provision depend in part linearly on the distance from the existing development (Harris, 1967), and in part on the amount of development in that area since this determines the use of indivisible factor units and hence scale economy benefits. A radial corridor of superior facilities, especially transportation, exists where inter-urban traffic is catered for. Urban use is extended outward along this route up to a point where the marginal saving in time costs, compared with sites away from the route, are offset by the marginal increase in distance costs as development is pushed further out along this route. The outer limit of profit for any given use from the urban centre will thus be greater along major radial routes than in the interstitial areas between such routes. Overall, development will be pushed to the point where the marginal cost of travel from the outermost sites to the urban centre is the same in all directions.

Physical features are not uniform, and terrain differences cause variations in the costs of development between areas so that lower site development costs may occur in particular sectors of the urban fringe or on more distant rather than closer-in sites. If for a given urban area site development costs are lower in one general direction than all others, then, *ceteris paribus*, the urban area will expand asymmetrically as in Fig. 7.4a. A linear urban area would appear, Fig. 7.4b, where site development costs are lowest in opposite poles as with the case of urban areas developed in incised valleys, e.g. in the South Wales coalfield. The limit to growth in the favoured area(s) comes when the marginal cost of site development and transport of the last site $M$ developed in the favoured area is equal to the marginal cost of site development and transport of the last site $L$ in the difficult area. Marginal cost in the favoured area increases because the use of more and more distant sites demands greater transport inputs in the use of those sites, and at some point the increasing transport costs will offset the advantage of lower site development costs. At this point sites in less-favoured areas with higher site development costs but lower transport costs become competitive.

If in a given direction site development costs are lower further out than nearer to the existing built-up area, the outward expansion need no longer be contiguous, but smaller settlements may be spawned off as with area *E* in Fig. 7.4c. Development of area *E* is preferred to area *D* because the marginal saving on site development costs more than offsets the higher marginal transport costs from *E* to the urban centre. Thus the marginal cost of site development and transport for all sites

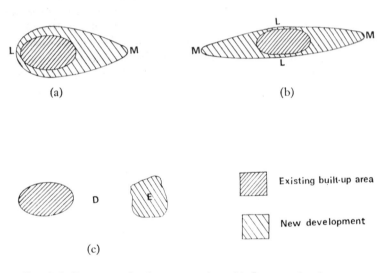

(a)                          (b)

(c)

Existing built-up area

New development

Fɪɢ. 7.4. Patterns of urban expansion. (a) Lowest development costs in one direction only. (b) In two opposing directions. (c) In an area separated from the existing urban area by a zone of higher costs.

in area *E* is less than the similar marginal costs for all sites in *D* because the latter's higher site development costs more than offset its transport cost advantage.

In the case of the speculator who holds onto his land as outward expansion takes place, there is the question of when to develop. The longer the speculator holds out the more distant the urban frontier gets and the greater the transport cost savings that would accrue to a prospective user of the undeveloped location. At some point in time the ageing of surrounding properties would threaten the desirability of the land as a site for development. The speculator sells when the decline in this environmental value per unit of time is equal to the growing increase in distance cost savings over the receding urban periphery (Thompson, 1965a, p. 328).

## The Role of the Developer

The basic process involved in outward expansion is the conversion of agricultural land to a higher order use. This is usually the specialized function of a developer although various other persons or organizations can play a role in the process, ranging from the original landowner, through subsequent landowners to the final consumer of the improved real property. Usually at least the original landowner, a developer, and the consumer of the completed property are parties to the process on any particular site. In discussing reasons for the pattern of outward sprawl, the part played by the preferences of landowners, including speculators, in the release of or the holding back of land for development, has been stressed. What of the roles of other parties in the development process? Peripheral residential development has been represented as an evolutionary sequence of states and decisions (Weiss *et al.*, 1966). At some point in time a person or organization sees agricultural land as potentially of more value in a higher order use: this is the state of urban interest. The second stage, when land is actively considered for development, is indicated by landowners or estate agents offering land for sale and developers and builders advertising for development land in an area. In the third stage, land is programmed for development and will have been purchased by the developer or builder. The timing of the actual development could be uncertain following particular purchase decisions, as with the rapid turnover due to speculation rather than the imminence of development or where the land is held as stock-in-trade by the developer for some considerable time. Active development, the fourth stage, indicated by the developer's decision to proceed, follows the approval of his detailed plans by the local planning authority. In the final stage a consumer buys a completed house and the land has passed into its new use—residence. From start to finish the process may cover as little as 2 years or as much as 10 years, and progress from one stage to another involves an economic decision.

This outlines the normal, free-market procedure where a large proportion of new houses purchased are located in speculatively built residential suburbs. A very small proportion of new house-buyers commission a builder to erect a house designed to their specifications on a site they have obtained for themselves. Therefore the developer or speculative builder appears as a central agent influencing the pattern of outward expansion since his policies largely determine which peripheral land is considered suitable for residential development and the sequence in which such land is developed. Individuals seeking particular sites and erecting their own premises make only a small contribution to the overall pattern of residential expansion, although they assume more importance in the case of manufacturing. A knowledge of how developers select peripheral sites for conversion to residential use is essential to the understanding of outward expansion patterns.

The choice of locations to be developed is an integral part of a developer's overall selection of inputs and outputs in an attempt to maximize his profits. These locational choices can, therefore, be viewed alongside developer decisions in general within a micro-economic framework of profit and production functions (Kaiser, 1968). The chosen locations and their associated site characteristics will not be the only, nor even necessarily the most important, factors determining the developer's profit. The profit-maximizing decision will also depend on the type of firm, scale of operation, entrepreneurial approach and financial backing, and intended market.

Peripheral land is not homogeneous, so location and site characteristics can influence profits because of the effects on the developer's production function. Each site is an input variable with possible differences in physical characteristics and access conditions which influence development costs and act as a constraint on output. Developers are likely to show preference for certain types of locations and sites, thus Chapin and Weiss (1962, p. 434) recognize thirteen land-development variables ranging from physical characteristics of the site, accessibility to major roads, variations in the availability of urban services and the coverage of local government controls, to differences in socio-economic characteristics of areas. Requirements of the customer are but one factor influencing the developer's choice of locations. Given this limitation, whether the customer gets what he wanted also depends on the accuracy of the developer's interpretation of the market. In deciding which sector or sectors of the residential market he will cater for, a developer's evaluation of the market potential is often cursory. Once this is decided his choice of locations for development seldom involves the explicit weighing up of alternatives to find the profit-maximizing location(s) at a given point in time. What is most likely is a sequential evaluation of sites until one is found that meets the requirements, and this is developed. That development will yield the developer a profit but not necessarily as high a profit as that which could have been earned by developing on an alternative site—one which had yet to be included in the developer's search procedure. The outward expansion of residential development is very much an *ad hoc* process, and the relatively unsystematic manner in which many developers approach the production of residential estates suggests that most decisions at this stage of the development process are probably made on the basis of the developer's experience and his general awareness of "what is going on" in the local real property development market (Burby, 1967, pp. 72–73).

The size of a development firm and the scale of its operations are important determinants of its locational activity patterns. In the United States, large-scale developers prefer locations that have public-policy imposed characteristics of available public water and sewage, more restrictive zoning, better access to the location of areas of higher socio-economic rank near to existing development (Kaiser, 1968). It has been suggested that land prices have a positive directional influence which encourages developers to seek sites away from the existing urban area (Tunnard and Pushkarev, 1963, p. 81). However, the large developer also tends to locate further away from the urban area because his scale of operation demands larger sites which can be assembled more easily with increasing distance from existing development. The rapid growth of a peripheral area is closely associated with the development of a few large sites by a few large developers rather than with the piecemeal growth of a multitude of small developments (Craven, 1969). Contrasting developments reflect the size of sites available for development. Small sites have either very few substantial detached houses or a larger number of dwellings at exceptionally high densities. The distinctive form of development taking place on large sites comprises middle density semi-detached or town houses. Changes in the organization of the development industry within an urban region may, therefore, have implications for the nature and pattern of outward residential expansion.

Developers must take some note of customer requirements, for the selling price of completed residential packages will be lower the poorer the social location, the poorer is access to urban facilities. Consumer hesitancy over pioneer locations and inadequate information on opportunities also restrain developers from expanding beyond the particular area with which they are familiar. In seeking to reduce the risks involved in speculative building, developers in the United States have turned to environmental innovations, such as artificial lakes (Burby, 1967), in an attempt to increase the saleability of projects. These innovations may be traded off against unfavourable site characteristics as well as reducing the importance of accessibility and, hence, increasing the developer's range of locational choice.

Therefore, in the pattern of outward expansion, the developer must be viewed as an independent element with considerable scope for initiative even within a framework of comprehensive land use controls, public investment decisions, and requirements of customers.

### Criticisms of Urban Sprawl

Firstly, sprawled or discontinuous suburban development, even at densities comparable to existing settled areas, is more costly and less efficient than a more compact form of urban expansion. Many costs depend on maximum distances or maximum areas, and if these could be reduced by more continuous development, costs per unit and *per capita* would be lower. For example, where telephone subscriber lines are becoming longer the cost of services will rise, *ceteris paribus*, at least relative to what it would be if urban areas were not spreading outward (Meyer, 1962). Small fragmented developments may hinder progress towards optimum units in the provision of local public and utility services. Ribbon development can lead to congestion of radial routes and consequently to higher transport costs.

Secondly, where new development at the periphery is to a lower density than other settled areas, this is more extravagant in its use of land. This, coupled with the bypassing of large areas of usable land in the outward expansion, means the urban area may grow unnecessarily large, and then transport, utility, and local public services may all become less efficient and less economic. Intervening areas of unused land appear to be wasted, and there is a lack of public open space. The speculator appears guilty, in social cost terms, of forcing up transport costs because urban residents have to pass his vacant land and have to bring utility pipes and wires further out. Such cost criticism of sprawl is justified providing (1) sprawl yields the same levels of benefit as alternative forms of settlement, and (2) a true cost comparison is being made.

Costs did not appear prohibitive to the suburban settler at the time sprawl occurred, which would suggest that the level of benefits relative to costs favoured suburban locations rather than alternative locations. However, this considers only the direct costs borne by and the direct benefits accruing to the suburban dweller. Where the suburbanite has purchased in ignorance of the full facts, costs may be higher than anticipated. Also, the level of benefits may be lower than expected in that the suburbanite did not always get what he desired as the provision of houses outstripped that of other facilities. Certain costs may be shifted onto urban society in general, as with charging practices for utilities which are not related to costs of installation and operation at each individual peripheral site. In these cases suburban land uses do not pay the full cost of their locational choice. It could be that the increased costs of providing for and operating low-density developments may be considerably in excess of the benefits of spaciousness derived by owners of large sites, so that the total net social benefit is lower (Thompson, 1965a, p. 325). Besides escaping payment of certain social costs, the suburbanite is not credited with any benefits, such as light or fresh air, which his actions create for neighbours.

In examining the economic costs of sprawl at a given point in time, it is usually argued that costs per person and per dwelling in peripheral development are greater than the corresponding costs in a unit of higher density where development has been completed. If sprawled development represented the completed development, such a cost comparison may have some relevance, although benefits would have been ignored. Otherwise the actual cost per unit or per person should be related, not to the situation at any point in time, but to the number of inhabitants and the number of dwellings eventually developed to take advantage of a given capital facility. Costs of development at the periphery will often be high because there is a need for increased capacity in utility systems, such as sewage disposal. Frequently existing facilities cannot be expanded for financial or technical reasons. Such problems would be faced wherever the increased population was to be accommodated in the urban area. Thus cost per unit and per person early in the development span of an area will obviously be greater than the cost per unit and per person after the area has reached maturity. Areas of sprawl and discontinuous development may eventually be infilled and costs, therefore, reduced on a unit/person basis. Only if the location of sprawled developments on sites precludes their further subdivision will higher costs per unit and per person persist in the long run.

A third major criticism of sprawl is the loss of prime farmland that is entailed. Allowing that it is the best, most intensively farmed, land, such as market gardens and dairy farms, which is most often taken, the protest is as much emotional as rational. Urban expansion must take place somewhere, and to protect prime agricultural land from urban encroachment would mean redirecting the urban expansion to alternative locations on poorer agricultural land. These locations may be sub-optimal from the point of view of urban uses because benefits are lower or costs are higher, or both. Where urban expansion on poor agricultural land would yield the same net benefit as on prime agricultural land, then, from the community's point of view, the expansion should take place on the poorer land. What of other cases where the expansion of the urban area on poor land would yield a lower net benefit than expansion on better agricultural land? A greater agricultural output would be sacrificed if the better land succumbed, and this would need to be replaced by extending the intensive margin of cultivation on the remaining farms and the extensive margin of cultivation by bringing more land into farming or even by increased imports (Wibberley, 1959). Some combination of these actions to replace the lost agricultural output may represent a lower economic cost than the increase in costs or the loss of benefits that would ensue if urban uses were denied that land. In such circumstances there is no economic grounds for protecting agricultural land.

Fourthly, sprawl is criticized because the land speculation which accompanies it is regarded as unproductive, absorbing of capital, manpower, and entrepreneurial skill (Clawson, 1962). Correct speculation, however, performs a worthwhile economic function in the real property market (Denman, 1964, p. 19).

Fifthly, urban sprawl is regarded as unaesthetic and unattractive—an aimless overspill into the countryside (Chapin and Weiss, 1962, p. 448). This is a value judgement. Sprawl is a form of growth, but it is measured and described at a moment in time, usually as a static and unchanging thing. Supporters of a full urban way of life are critical of suburbanites' preference for open space and privacy rather than for frequent and easy interpersonal contact. Where sprawl is viewed over time, an important question may be how long before compaction takes place, in which case the inefficiency in land use which may accompany sprawl lasts only until the open spaces have been infilled. Where sites are multiples of the minimum necessary and the house is located so that the site can be fully subdivided at a later stage, this subdivision will take place when the urban area has grown to a size where the savings in transport costs to a new home-owner by locating on the vacant part of the site is greater than the value of that amount of open space as an amenity to the owner of the site. An expansion pattern which is inefficient in the short run may be more efficient in the long run as the interim period of greater sprawl gives way to lesser ultimate sprawl for an overall net gain when all values are discounted to the present (Thompson, 1965a, p. 328). Thompson (pp. 328-9) also points out that the future may bring very different space needs and land passed over in the initial phase of outward expansion may prove valuable in accommodating these needs. Thus an advantage may accrue from holding some land vacant because of the flexibility this allows for adjustment to future needs. The point where the extra cost to present urban efficiency by keeping another unit of land supply vacant is equal to the probable benefits of having another unit of land use flexibility with which to adjust to changing optima may be determined by marginal analysis.

## The Role of the Planner

It is, perhaps, appropriate to consider the role of the planner in relation to urban sprawl although the general principles of government action are discussed later, in Chapter 12. Accepting sprawl as the most likely form of urban expansion produced by the market and that it represents a net disadvantage for the urban area and the nation, then, the planner must seek to redress the balance. However, increased urban population and economic activities have to be located somewhere.

The essence of the planner's approach is controlled location. In the United Kingdom, where all new urban development requires planning permission, the planner has an effective control over which land will be developed, the purpose for which it will be developed, and the probable timing of that development. Merely to prohibit development in one location by refusing planning permission will not solve the problem of where the activity in question will locate. It is also necessary to give positive indications as to where development will be permitted and encouraged. This can be achieved by zoning and the choice then facing the activity in question is between permitted alternative locations. Indeed, publication of a development plan outlining planners' intentions for the suburban fringe could go some way towards remedying imperfections of knowledge, increasing the certainty of decision taking, and, hence, bring about a more co-ordinated and compact pattern of outward expansion.

To check the outward sprawl of very large urban areas, further measures may be necessary. The designation of a green belt around the existing built-up area is one means of accomplishing this. Development control will be rigorously applied within the green belt in order to exclude non-conforming, basically urban, land uses. Such controls have had marked successes in restricting residential expansion, as in the case of the West Midlands Green Belt (Gregory, 1970, p. 45), but have been less successful in the case of non-residential developments. For example, local authority service developments have not been uncommon in green belts. Surprisingly, green belts have not made a significant contribution to the improvement of the supply of public and private open space for recreational and leisure activities, since many activities in this category have been refused planning permission to develop facilities there (Gregory, 1970, p. 67). In this sense the control has been negative rather than positive.

The presence of a green belt will increase the pressure for more intensive development within the encollared built-up area as well as the demand for building land beyond the green belt. Planners have succeeded in channelling development to urban areas and villages which have been selected for expansion. Where these are within the green-belt development has been permitted to round off the building line or by way of infilling. Development beyond the green belt has, in part, comprised controlled dispersal to new and expanded towns. However, with the continued increase of population in metropolitan urban areas, a review of this policy of permanent restriction is necessary and, in certain cases, land adjacent to the existing built-up area has been released for approved purposes, such as municipal housing. Thus, given a comprehensive system of land-use controls, the pattern of outward urban expansion owes much to planning policies—past and present.

## Outward Expansion and Effects on Internal Structure

As the parts of an urban area are complementary, outward expansion will have repercussions for the internal structure of that urban area. This is in addition to the reorganization within the existing built-up areas caused by pressures of growth in those areas. Outward expansion influences internal structure because that expansion is only part of an urban environment, and peripheral communities must rely on other parts of the urban area for various facilities and opportunities. Variations in the pattern of outward expansion have differential effects on internal structure. Consider the positioning of any lateral expansion of the residential area and the possible effects on land-use patterns within the existing urban area. Where the residential expansion takes the form of equal building all round the periphery, as in Fig. 7.5a, the effect on existing internal structure will be greatest. For example, the level of demand in any part of the expanded area is unlikely to be great enough to support the development of neighbourhood and higher order shopping centres. Their inhabitants have to rely on the existing urban centre, thus bringing greater demands for accommodation in the

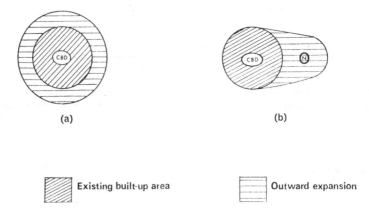

(a)　　　　　　　　　　　　　　　　(b)

| | Existing built-up area | | Outward expansion |
|---|---|---|---|

FIG. 7.5. Outward expansion and internal urban structure. (a) Equal expansion in all directions. (b) Asymmetrical expansion.

central business district, perhaps necessitating the redevelopment of part or all of the existing central business district (Lean, 1969, p. 124). Alternatively, if the residential expansion to house a similar population was concentrated in one direction as in Fig. 7.5b, at least a neighbourhood shopping centre $N$ is likely to develop to serve the demands of the inhabitants, and an industrial estate may be encouraged to locate on that side of the urban area. In this case pressure on the existing central business district will be small and the development of the central business district will be less well marked than in case (a) whilst the importance of subsidiary business centres will be greater (Lean and Goodall, 1966, p. 201). Where the residential development is of sufficient magnitude, then out-of-town regional shopping centres may arise leading to the absolute decline of the central business district.

Where outward expansion in any particular sector has taken place at one and the same time, then improved properties in that area are likely to be similar. Projecting well ahead to long after the time that such development has been swallowed up by general urban expansion the area will wear out *en masse*—a future urban renewal problem? Hence the idea that new communities should be built in stages (Lessinger, 1962). Where piecemeal development has proceeded over a considerable period of time, such problems should not arise to the same extent.

## Outward Expansion and Urban Theory

Theories, such as the concentric and sector ones, are dynamic, for an explanation is offered of patterns of urban growth as well as of internal urban structure at a point in time. These theories emphasize the pressure for growth from the centre, i.e. the expansion of central business district functions. These theories were differentiated according, in one respect, to the nature of the outward expansion they distinguished. Thus concentric zonation outlines the overspill of central business district functions into the zone of transition and then the successive outward displacement-expansion of each zone which gives new outward development where the peripheral zone is expanded. The sector theory emphasizes the growth of high-grade residences outward along the lines of the fastest existing transport routes, toward high ground and areas of natural beauty, and toward the homes of the leaders of the community. Intra-urban location of other types of residence were related to this, and differential growth rates in outward expansion could be accounted for. When the key influence of topography and transport routes was grafted onto these generalizations, a feasible explanation of the outward expansion of any urban area was possible.

Certainly, the old type push from central areas does operate, but outward urban expansion may stem, also, from other sources. For example, the basic idea that immigrants to an urban area gravitate to the poorest, most obsolete housing in the transition zone, is not altogether tenable. Certainly some do, such as the Negro and Puerto Rican immigrants to New York (Handlin, 1959), but British migrants to Australia go straight to the owner-occupied sector in the suburbs of large urban areas (Johnston, 1969), and most of the new suburban dwellers of Megalopolis came from outside the urban areas rather than moving out from the central areas (Gottmann, 1961). Dispersion is likely to be wider than suggested in theory as a result of such instances.

Outward expansion may also be due to structural forces (Alonso, 1964), so that choice of peripheral location is a matter of preference, backed by available funds, rather than of growth *per se*. In so far as public land use controls contribute to the pattern of outward expansion, these are not considered in such theories which deal primarily with free-market situations. Moreover, the role of the developer is neglected in these theories even under free-market conditions. The detailed controls of outward expansion have been only cursorily treated, until recently, from the economic standpoint.

# CHAPTER 8

# Urban Growth: (2) Internal Reorganization

## Internal Reorganization: An Adaptation Process

Changes in the underlying conditions of demand and supply have an immediate impact on the existing urban pattern and stock of buildings. Increased demand generated by growth of population and activities is accommodated within existing urban structures, at least in the short run. Changes in demand, reflecting changes in social standards consequent upon economic progress and growth, must also be largely satisfied within existing supply situations. Improvements in transport, routes, and media, alter the relative locational advantages of sites and prompt changes in use and intensity of use of sites and buildings within the existing built-up area. Technological advance can reduce the relative attractiveness of older buildings for the uses for which they were originally designed. Changes within the existing stock of buildings, redevelopment, and addition to stock by outward expansion, represent complementary adjustments in the process of urban growth. In the absence of government controls it is the normal function of the market mechanism, trying to maximize returns to land-owners and land-users, to bring about these necessary adjustments. Internal reorganization—adjustments to use made of certain existing buildings and replacement of other buildings—is, therefore, representative of the supply–demand mechanism's attempt to achieve an equilibrium between the present and optimum uses of land and building space. Equilibrium is never established since underlying factors are continually changing and buildings have too long a life for all occupiers to be accommodated in structures designed for their individual use.

Most changes in demand are accommodated within the existing stock of buildings as activities alter their locations or the amount of space they use, or some combination of both. Without the improvement or modification of existing buildings and facilities, considerable spatial rearrangements of land uses and locational shifts of population and activities take place in any urban area. Consequent upon the increased demand for accommodation in and around the position of greatest accessibility, the rise in price of accommodation will displace certain activities, especially residence and light industry, from the central area. These are replaced by higher order tertiary uses. The displaced activities then seek locations elsewhere in the urban area and may gravitate to new outward development.

The modification of the basic urban pattern and the standing stock of building represents an adaptation process. The constant switching of location and buildings by activities within the standing stock is facilitated by the wide range of uses to which most buildings are suited. Adaptation is necessary largely because of the nature of urban real property investment. In any urban area, given the durability and immobility of buildings, the supply of real property is fixed in the short run, and change is slow and costly. Once a building has been erected, it is generally uneconomic to replace it with anything other than a building which represents a more intensive use. Where a reduction in site use intensity is demanded, such change is largely impossible. The urban building stock can, over time, become increasingly out of line with current demands for physical space because the rate of replacement of physical structures is considerably slower than that of the activities which use them. All buildings are vulnerable to change of use since the capitalization of structure and facilities which bind a building to a location do not similarly bind a particular user to that location. This also follows from the fact that ownerships and use of buildings can be separated.

The physical modification of a building to suit its new occupant will only be profitable when demand reaches a certain level. Much less frequently is there an economic basis sufficient to justify demolition and replacement. Redevelopment, in the form of vertical expansion, brings higher order uses or more intensive existing uses. This is complementary to the displacement of certain activities and outward expansion. In many British urban areas, central real properties may represent third, fourth, fifth, or even more stages of building although a restricted proportion have been rebuilt this century except in the case of areas which suffered extensive war damage. Occurring via market decisions, redevelopment is a continuous process induced by prospects of private gain, whereby the costs of change are absorbed by the expected productivity of new uses. Viewed over time, for any part of an urban area, a repetitive or cyclical pattern of change may be discerned.

## Economic Life of a Building

An understanding of the concept of the economic life of a building is essential to an appreciation of the decision to redevelop or change the use of an existing building. A continuous cycle of change affects all buildings. Immediately after construction a building can enjoy increasing or sustained value. This is followed by a long period of maintenance and depreciation, perhaps with some modification of the building to accommodate new occupants before, finally, it is demolished and replaced.

A site or building will change hands when a prospective purchaser offers a higher price for its use than the existing occupants. The deal may represent a transfer of ownership where the freehold is purchased or, in the case of rented property, a change of tenant. In the latter case opportunities for change may be restricted to the end of rental agreements or leases. Assume a prospective purchaser of an existing freehold building intends to use it as at present and that there is no prospect of redeveloping to a more profitable use. The price he offers represents the present capital value of the future stream of net benefits he expects to enjoy from the use of that building. Since a building was constructed, changes in the neighbourhood—such as improvements in accessibility—may create an opportunity for redeveloping the site to a higher and better use. In these circumstances the price paid to acquire the site plus the existing building reflects—not the value of the future use of the existing building—but the value of the potential new use to which the site can be put. Thus the capital value or price of the site, cleared of existing buildings and other improvements, depends on the use to which that site can be put in the future. The value of the cleared site to any developer will be equal to the present discounted value of the anticipated earnings from the new building minus the capital construction costs of the new building, the present discounted value of the running and maintenance costs of the new building, and the costs of demolishing the old building. That is,

$$S_N = Y_N - C_N - O_N - D_E, \qquad (8.1)$$

where $S_N$ is the site value in the new use, $Y_N$ the present capital value of the expected earnings of the use in the new building, $C_N$ the costs of constructing the new building, $O_N$ the present value of the costs of operating the new building, and $D_E$ the costs of demolishing the old building and preparing the site.

Alternatively, in terms of the analysis used in Chapter 3, the value of the cleared site will be the sum of money available to purchase the existing interests in the property minus the cost of clearing the site. Cleared-site value represents, therefore, the present value of the net income that can be earned by investing in the improvements necessary to put land to its optimum use (Nourse, 1963), and such site values represent an economic valuation of location. Therefore the economic life of a building may be defined as the period over which the building commands a capital value (price) greater than the capital value of the cleared site (Lean and Goodall, 1966, pp. 179–80). That is, so long as

$$B_E > S_N, \qquad (8.2)$$

where $B_E$ is the present capital value of the existing real property, the building will not be demolished.

This can be shown diagrammatically. Figure 8.1 refers to a particular developed site. Assuming that residential use was the most profitable use when the site was first developed in year $O$, then $CC$ shows the capital value of the developed real property over time, i.e. land and building together. $CC$ decreases with the passage of time because the building is subject to wear and tear in use and, with increasing age, maintenance and repair expenditures may be expected to increase. $SS$ represents the value of the cleared site over time, i.e. the present net income to be earned by developing the land to its optimum use. Assuming there are no changes in underlying conditions of demand and supply, residential use would remain the most profitable use of this site, the capital value of the cleared site would be stable and equal to $OS$, and hence $SS$

horizontal. So long as *CC* lies above *SS*, it is not profitable to demolish the existing building and redevelop because the price or capital value a prospective occupant of the existing building would offer the present owner is greater than the price or capital value any developer would offer for the cleared site and an owner seeking to maximize his returns would sell to the former. In the case outlined, redevelopment would take place as soon after *OR* years as possible because the capital value of the cleared site exceeds that of the existing real property. *OR* years is the economic life of the residential building constructed in year *O*.

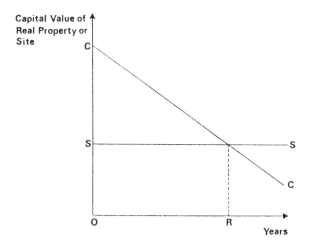

Fig. 8.1. Economic life of a building.

The economic life of something as durable as a building varies widely in practice and ends not because the structure is physically worn out but because of changes in demand, reflecting alterations in accessibility, in environmental merits, in economic, social, and technological standards, and in the materials used and services expected in modern buildings. Since change is continually taking place, any building can only be in line with current standards during the earliest years of its economic life and will become less well adapted to the highest performance of its functions as time passes. All buildings, therefore, become progressively obsolete, although the physical condition of the building itself and its basic equipment is seldom a primary criterion of obsolescence. The physical and economic life spans of a building are not the same, for the economic life of a building is determined primarily by the earning power of that building rather than by its structural durability. The physical and economic lives of a building would only be identical in such cases as sound buildings which are completely destroyed by fire, etc. Sooner or later the decision has to be taken to end the use of a building and redevelop in the most profitable way.

## Economics of Redevelopment

As already suggested, the economics of redevelopment or replacement can be defined by a set of cost-revenue relationships which show the profitability of redevelopment to be a function of the cost of redevelopment relative to the value of the new property created. The rationale for redevelopment depends on the developer's/owner's estimate of anticipated income from the new property compared to the costs of constructing and operating the new building, the costs of removing the existing structure, and the income lost by removing the existing building. Redevelopment will take place where, *ceteris paribus*, anticipated income is greater than the costs of replacement and the original investment lost, that is, if

$$Y_N > C_N + O_N + D_E + B_E \qquad (8.3)$$

redevelopment is profitable ($Y_N$, $C_N$, $O_N$, $D_E$, and $B_E$ are as previously defined). From eqn. (8.1) it can be established that

$$Y_N = S_N + C_N + O_N + D_E. \qquad (8.4)$$

$C_N$, $O_N$, and $D_E$ are common to both eqn. (8.3) and (8.4), thus the significance of $S_N$ and $B_E$, the two terms which are related in eqn. (8.2). If $B_E$ is greater than $S_N$, then

$$Y_N < C_N + O_N + D_E + B_E, \qquad (8.5)$$

redevelopment is not worth while and the existing building has not reached the end of its economic life, whereas if $S_N$ is greater than $B_E$, then

$$Y_N > C_N + O_N + D_E + B_E, \qquad (8.6)$$

and redevelopment will take place.

Redevelopment is usually to a more intensive use which means, in the case of urban sites, higher buildings than previously existed. The limits to the height of buildings are economic. On the demand side there may be limits to the activities which can make use of upper floors. On the supply side the state of building technology at any given time could render certain subsoil conditions unsuitable for tall buildings, whilst there is a progressive rise in building costs as additional storeys are added as well as an increasing proportion of unremunerative space which must be devoted to servicing and maintenance of the building, e.g. lifts, corridors, and heating equipment. Beyond a certain point, where the marginal revenue from an additional storey equals the marginal cost of providing that extra storey, the provision of further storeys will be unprofitable.

What factors influence the likelihood of a particular building being redeveloped? Analysis of economic life suggests that age/condition of a building will be a factor in determining the present value of a real property. The taller a building the more accommodation that is provided, the higher the income produced, the lower the proportion of capital value attributable to the site, and the greater the likelihood that discounted future incomes from the existing use exceed site value. Size of site may also be an important factor in determining future use and ownership, for the ease and cost of acquiring and preparing the site influence the feasibility of redevelopment and, therefore, site value. The potential for economic gain in the redevelopment of a site usually depends on its relative location in an urban area and on neighbourhood factors such as the social and physical qualities and any external economies accruing from proximity to related uses. As with outward expansion, the ownership factor is again significant in determining which sites are redeveloped at any given time, since property-owners respond differently. Even where economically justified redevelopment may be delayed by the poor judgement of land-owners who overvalue the prospects of their property and hold out for unwarranted prices. In other cases, they may anticipate even higher development costs than the increase in revenue, whilst others may hesitate to write off the current market value of their property, some lack the financial means to do so, and yet others are thwarted by diffused ownership where redevelopment on a larger site unit would be the most profitable course of action. Even though they may be forgoing even higher profits, the cost-revenue structure of their existing building allows these owners to continue on a profitable basis for some time.

The replacement of individual buildings, or piecemeal redevelopment, is easier than redevelopment of larger areas since the financial requirements are lower, the problem of relocating any existing occupiers smaller, and the acceptance of current land-ownership patterns avoids long and complex legal problems.

## Change in Use of a Building Prior to Redevelopment

Prior to its demolition, changes in the ownership and use could occur when alternative users were willing to pay higher prices/rents for that real property than existing occupiers. Of particular importance is the case where a change of occupier signifies a change of use, as from residence to office, or a change in use intensity, as when large single-family houses are subdivided into a number of self-contained flats. The original building is not specifically designed for its new use and adjustments, if any, are made by means of internal alterations, leaving the shell of the building intact. This reflects the rapidity with which the demand for various types of accommodation changes with urban growth relative to the slow adjustment of supply in terms of the number and types of buildings. This is a key to the explanation of the zone of transition.

Increased demand for urban accommodation raises the values of existing sites, the more so the greater a site's relative access advantages, since higher order and/or more accommodation would be provided if the site was to be redeveloped immediately. Therefore continued present use of the existing real property incurs increasing opportunity costs. The owner has alternative courses of action to immediate demolition and redevelopment. Firstly, he may be able to raise rents or subdivide further the existing accommodation concurrently with rising opportunity costs. Thus well-located older buildings can maintain fairly high rents, especially where their internal services are modernized and their external appearance altered to accord with what is expected of them. One often gets quite costly front-and-fixture alterations in commercial structures (Rannells, 1956). Secondly, the landlord could practise disinvestment by undermaintaining his property until the revenue stream falls below the prime costs, then demolish the structure. Net disinvestment in real property is both the result of elements affecting the demand for sites and buildings and of developments which tend to reduce the productive capacity of properties such as ageing and obsolescence (Wingo, 1966). Ageing depends on construction, obsolescence on the rate of technical innovation. Such disinvestment, i.e. outlays on repair, maintenance, and modernization, less than those required to maintain a property in its original physical condition or at a stable level of economic productivity, equals urban blight. It is identified with buildings in outmoded locations which are no longer suitable for the original occupants but are not worth redeveloping at present. Such buildings are used by whoever is willing to take them, and they often provide temporary homes for lower order uses during the ripening period whilst the owner awaits that time when redevelopment to a higher order use is profitable. During that period they serve a less-demanding group of activities at rentals able to support their operation. The new occupier has less regard for the physical quality of the building and the successive use of old buildings by group after group of poorer income people accelerates the rate of obsolescence. Often the occupants would be willing to contribute to better maintenance, but they seldom own the building. In socially declining neighbourhoods a landlord is less interested in keeping up property than in making as much profit as possible from it before it becomes completely obsolescent, leaving merchantable value in the site only (Gottmann, 1961, p. 410). The decline of rented dwellings is undoubtedly more rapid than that of owner-occupied.

Therefore for the individual building the process of change falls into a number of stages (Bourne, 1967). Starting from an equilibrium situation where a building is occupied by the user for which it was designed, the first stage is represented by the replacement of the original use by another use but with little or no modification of the structure. The new use represents either a higher-order activity or an increase in intensity of use by the same activity. A second stage brings partial conversion or modification of the building to better accommodate its new occupants. This is most likely where the building occupies a site with considerable access advantages. Rehabilitation would be a profitable course of action for a property-owner where the present capital value of the rehabilitated building plus the present capital value of a new building in $n$ years time is greater than the capital value of the optimum building produced by immediate redevelopment. Finally, the building is demolished and replaced. Not all buildings fulfil this sequence, nor do similar buildings appear at the same stage at the same time. However, these stages do describe the process of adaptation in the structural stock of the urban area in order to accommodate changing demands. It also shows that demolition and replacement stems primarily from external economic pressure for change rather than from obsolescence or physical deterioration.

## Consequences for Economic Life

Changes in the type of user and/or intensity of use of an existing building can either delay or accelerate the redevelopment of the affected building (Lean and Goodall, 1966, pp. 182–4). It was shown in Fig. 8.1 that, *ceteris paribus*, the residential building provided would be redeveloped after $OR$ years. However, it is likely that changes in underlying conditions of demand and supply will have materialized before $OR$ years have elapsed; thus the circumstances on which the cleared site value $SS$ and the value of the real property $CC$ were based will have changed, and these values need to be reassessed. A site near to the central business district may benefit from the increased demand for central sites as the urban area grows and activities spill over from the central area. Where improved or new transport facilities have been provided since the time the building was constructed, this site may enjoy greater accessibility and so be suitable for a higher order use. Thus increased demand brings an upward revaluation of that site's potential since redevelopment would be to a higher-order or more intensive use than at present.

In Fig. 8.2 it is assumed that a transport improvement which increases the accessibility advantages of a particular site is completed in year $N$. The higher capital value prospective developers would pay for the cleared site is shown by $S_2S_2$. Where the transport improvement has been made in response to urban growth, an increased demand for central sites would have been apparent for some time, and the site value would have shown a steady increase throughout the period $ON$ rather than the abrupt upward step in year $N$ postulated in the diagram. However, in year $N$ the capital value of the real property in its continued existing use, i.e. $CC$, is greater than the new, higher, cleared site

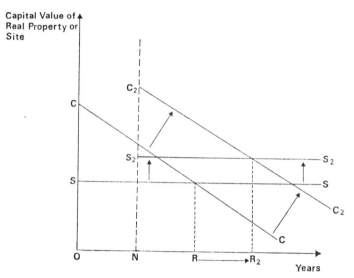

FIG. 8.2. Economic life of a building extended as result of a transport improvement

value, so redevelopment will not take place immediately. The transport improvement will alter not only the cleared site value, but also the value of the existing real property. Uses for whom accessibility is critical to earning power, finding the supply of accommodation fixed at any time, must compete buildings on sites whose accessibility advantages have improved away from uses whose locational decisions were made under different past circumstances. Thus an office user may be prepared to pay a price for the existing residential building on the site in order to obtain accommodation in the area of improved accessibility. $C_2C_2$ shows the price (capital value) the office user would pay at any time to obtain the residential unit for office use. As Fig. 8.2 shows, the residence would be converted to office use in year $N$ because $C_2C_2$ is greater than its value in residence. The latter is assumed to remain

unchanged at *CC*, although desirability as a residence could be altered
by the improvement. Assuming no further changes, the building would
remain in office use until year $R_2$ when redevelopment would be profitable. Redevelopment would take the form of purpose-built office
accommodation. However, the change in use, from residence to offices,
has delayed redevelopment and extended the economic life of the
existing real property by $RR_2$ years. This is likely to happen where the

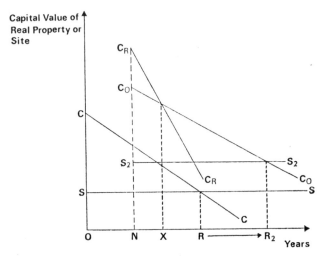

Fig. 8.3. Change in use of building extends its economic life.

proportionate rise in the value of the existing real property is greater
than the proportionate rise in the value of the cleared site and the rate of
decline of the new, higher capital value of the real property is no
greater than that in its original use.

In practice the situation may be more complex with various alternative uses competing for the existing real property. Thus in Fig. 8.3
the existing building continues in residential use after the transport
improvement in year $N$ because its new residential capital value $C_R C_R$
is greater than its value for office use, shown by $C_O C_O$. After the
transport improvement, the building would continue in residential use
until year $X$ when it is converted to office use, and in which use it

remains until redevelopment is economically feasible in year $R_2$. The slower rate of decline of capital value in office use compared to residential use means a greater extension of the economic life of the existing building.

Redevelopment will not be delayed in every case. In certain circumstances redevelopment may be speeded up. Three possible situations may be instanced. Firstly, in Fig. 8.4 the increase in the site potential exceeds any increase in the value of the existing real property, and redevelopment would be immediately profitable since the new cleared site value $S_2S_2$ is greater than the new capital value of continued use of the existing real property $C_2C_2$. Redevelopment, therefore, takes place $NR$ years earlier than when no transport improvement had been effected. This situation is likely where the new structure will contain a

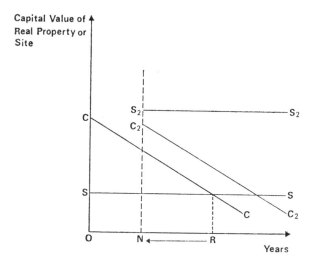

Fig. 8.4. Immediate redevelopment where transport improvement shortens the economic life of a building.

very much greater amount of accommodation than could ever be achieved by subdividing the existing building.

Secondly, where the proportionate rise in site value is greater than the proportionate rise in the capital value of the real property, then redevelopment will be brought forward by $R_2R$ years as shown in

Fig. 8.5. This again reflects the greater scope that accompanies the provision of a new building and that the existing real property may be particularly unsuitable for certain types of uses.

Indeed, thirdly, it is possible that the capital value of the existing real property may fall because the building is not suitable for conversion to alternative uses and its value as a residence may be reduced by

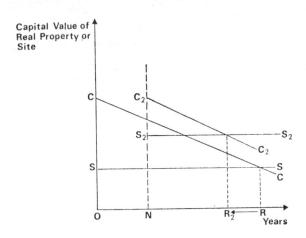

FIG. 8.5. Transport improvement induces change in use of existing building and reduces economic life.

loss of amenity following the completion of the transport improvement. Redevelopment is again brought forward, in Fig. 8.6, by $R_2R$ years.

Similar analysis could be pursued in the case of real properties where changing conditions lead to a reduction in site value. In most cases this would extend the economic life of the existing building.

What determines whether the economic life of any particular building will be shortened or lengthened by changes in underlying conditions? It depends, primarily, on whether or not it is possible to adapt the existing building to a higher order or more intensive use. A majority of existing buildings are capable of being used for alternative purposes. For example, the large houses built for successful Victorian businessmen may be suitable for conversion to offices by trade unions, local government, solicitors, and the like, or to flats, maternity homes, etc., or even to light industrial use. Warehouses may be adapted for industrial use and factories for warehousing; even former churches are suitable for storage. Conversion is less possible, however, with back-to-back terrace-houses and tenements.

## The Building and its Neighbourhood

The use to which any real property is put depends on its relative location within the urban area and the relative qualities of its immediate environment. Buildings and neighbourhoods constantly react upon one another. For example, the greater the proportion of obsolescent buildings in a neighbourhood the less desirable is that district as a location

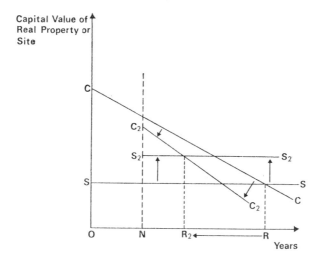

Fig. 8.6. Transport improvement causes fall in value of existing real property and shortens economic life.

for new activities and the more difficult it is to sustain the value of sound buildings or redevelop individual sites. This is a "neighbourhood effect". Obsolescence spreads throughout a neighbourhood accelerating the displacement of people and activities. Improvement or redevelopment of a real property depends on the rejuvenation of the whole neighbourhood. Changes in the use of individual buildings have a parallel at the neighbourhood level in what human ecologists have labelled the invasion-succession concept (Chapin, 1965, pp. 21–27).

With increased demand accompanying urban growth, more intensive uses outbid existing uses for the locational advantages of an area and each land use zone expands into the area of less intensive use immediately surrounding it. Speculation precedes invasion by the more intensive uses, often creating artificial land values which contribute to the physical and social deterioration of the threatened areas. Where existing buildings are taken over by new uses they tend to deteriorate faster, and this has an effect on adjacent property whose use has not changed. With housing the process represents the spatial equivalent of the filtering process: occupation is usually by an inferior population group prepared to live at higher densities than the previous occupants, and their presence accelerates the exodus of the present population bringing a decline in real property values. The first of the new group purchasing in a neighbourhood may bid price up since they must outbid existing users. Where successful, their presence will depreciate the value of surrounding real properties and the long-run effect is, therefore, one of price fall as the neighbourhood declines. An alternative line of reasoning (Scheitinger, 1964), suggests that the residential movement of minority racial groups results in a reduction in demand for residential property in the path of such movement, therefore a fall in price in the short run. Once minority settlement commences in that path, pressure of demand from minority group buyers brings recovery.

In large urban areas there are sufficient wealthy residents and enough attractions to business activities down-town to allow some sectors to remain well defended. Obsolescence and decline in housing may appear more rapid in smaller urban areas.

Neighbourhoods as a whole, like individual buildings, exhibit a cyclical pattern of change. Five stages in the process of neighbourhood evolution have been recognized (Hoover and Vernon, 1959, ch. 8). In the first, rural land is converted to residential use with development in the form of single-family houses. Many neighbourhoods then experience a long period of quiescence before the second stage—further building, particularly multi-family structures—takes place. Increased demand has raised the value of land and made higher densities more profitable. The third stage sees the down-grading and conversion of existing buildings. Demand conditions have changed, there being a new set of consumers. With the more intensive use this brings of existing structures, population and density increases and the area soon becomes a slum. For some neighbourhoods, as suggested above, this stage may never materialize. The fourth stage, one of thinning out, is characteristic of slum areas decades after they have been turned over to slum use. There is a decrease in demand for accommodation, with only the aged, heads of families staying put. Population and density declines. Earnings from slum property fall until the fifth stage, demolition and renewal takes place. Renewal takes time since sites of old tenements have to be painstakingly assembled by private developers or depends on local government initiative. Private redevelopment in the form of luxury flats attracts those residents who are able to pay adequate rents and who are willing to live in high-rise structures because they value locations with convenient access to the urban centre. In contrast, re-development sponsored by local government will include accommodation at subsidized rents for lower income groups.

Such neighbourhood changes have repercussions for other land uses. By way of example take the third stage of the cycle just described. The population change is anticipated. The normal replacement of retail and service establishments which fail or close ceases, vacancy rates rise and commercial property owners reduce maintenance expenditures because of the uncertainty regarding future use (Berry, 1967, p. 123). During the period of population turnover, demand for the higher order goods and services falls off drastically. The more flexible shops switch price lines whilst the smaller specialist units go out of business. There follows a stabilizing phase as the neighbourhood settles down in its new lower *per capita* income character. However, the gap in maintenance expenditures means it is virtually impossible to restore the previously sound building conditions from the economic earnings now possible; thus rents drop further. In time the more viable establishments from commercial ribbons move in to fill vacancies.

Urban blight appears from stage three onward. As a concept, blight involves a degree of subjectivity regarding the non-acceptance of obsolescent buildings and neighbourhoods as well as the more factual aspects of real property depreciation. Functional and social depreciation have been recognized (Breger, 1967). The former follows a decline in a building's capacity to render a service or from a decline in the demand for the service rendered, both of which depend on changes in supply/demand conditions and are reflected in a loss of earnings. Social depreciation is equated with a loss of prestige, consequent upon rising social values, or the progressive over-utilization of property due to imperfections of the market. A loss of productivity leads to blight because property-owners react by disinvesting. Wingo (1966) equates blight with disinvestment and emphasizes its causes as changes which reduce a building's productive capacity on the supply side, such as age and obsolescence, and falling demand which reduces income expectations with the consequent drying up of capital replacement investment. Blight is, therefore, a response to change.

Disinvestment by undermaintenance can lead to intolerable structural condition but such disrepair is usually evident only in the advanced stages of functional depreciation by which time non-maintenance has succeeded undermaintenance. Besides undermaintenance many landlords are ignorant of or indifferent to the state of their property and are unwilling to take action to improve it. This disinterest is often a function of age of landlord or the fact that the landlord inherited property, the responsibility of which is to be shed at an early opportunity (Greve, 1961; Cullingworth, 1961). Deterioration may also be enhanced by the effects of rent control during inflationary periods. All urban property may be subject to functional depreciation because of its immobility. The negative characteristics of blighted neighbourhoods seldom represent a simple aggregate of defects in individual properties, for often important service facilities are lacking in these neighbourhoods.

Therefore the causal factors in urban blight commonly stem from economic progress and urban growth. The conflict between fixed real estate resources and highly mobile social and economic demands underlies many of the basic maladjustments in the spatial structure of modern urban areas. Adjustments such as blight are palliatives, suboptimal changes from the community view. Blight is a diseconomy of urban growth, and the misallocation of resources could be such that it becomes a major policy issue for local government.

Blighted neighbourhoods correspond to the zone of transition. This zone performs an important function in an urban area since it provides cheap housing for poor in-migrants. That is it attracts residents who have no choice but to live there. Moreover, its decay is also attributable to the anticipated expansion of the central business district. Land is held for speculative purposes, further improvement, or even reasonable maintenance of the existing property is not justified. The neglect of improvement or rehabilitation does allow the building to be occupied by miscellaneous temporary uses during the ripening period. Why spend money on the present building when the larger gain was to come from the land itself, not from the present use? This could be a normal function of the market mechanism trying to maximize returns to owners. Indeed, it has been argued (Davis, 1960) that, given time, the urban land market would, in the absence of externalities, right the blighted area.

Externalities do exist. One property owner on his own would get no benefit from improving or redeveloping his property; it needs the simultaneous development of the whole neighbourhood. Thus rebuilding may be profitable on a large scale of a whole area but not of any individual building taken by itself. In such circumstances an owner will only gain from investing in his property if his neighbour follows suit. The neighbour is better off not to follow suit because he will benefit from the first owner's action. Neighbouring property-owners are interdependent, but neighbours are trapped by the uncertainties of each other's behaviour into a position where the optimum strategy for each acting independently produces a lower return than the case in which each was constrained to follow a strategy that would maximize the yield to the group. A coalition is only possible where each understands the pay-off possible to the others as well as to himself. This interdependence trap is a central phenomenon of urban blight and illustrates the problem that must be faced in its solution (Wingo, 1966). The private developer's dilemma is that, because of the unattractive environment in the area to be redeveloped, should he create his own environment to ensure the project's profitability? This requires increasingly large areas of land, in a sector where property ownership is extremely fragmented, if redevelopment is to be effectively shielded from the surrounding environment. The costs of buying up slum property, clearing the land, and putting up new structures may be greater than the value of the new structures; thus it is unprofitable for private enterprise (Nourse, 1966). Indeed, slum housing could well be the most profitable use of the land (Pennance and Gray, 1968), for the slum is an organic part of a complex urban society which serves important social and economic functions within the urban area as a whole.

Piecemeal redevelopment only improves the efficiency of an urban area in carrying out its functions in so far as one building is replaced by a more modern one. The layout of the urban area, its roads, public utilities, etc., can just as easily become obsolescent, and this is the case in the transition zone. There comes a time when the urban infrastructure needs redeveloping, and this is a further factor favouring the comprehensive redevelopment of large sectors of the transition zone. Indeed, the scope may be far beyond individual private firms' resources and require public initiative.

The revitalization of the zone of transition may be an intractable problem. The zone possesses neither the advantages of central business district locations nor the conditions for a widely desirable pattern of residence. The principal demand for non-residential space was met in the nineteenth and early twentieth centuries by outward expansion from the central business district and the displacement of surrounding residents. Urban growth today differs from the manner of 50 years ago (Griffin and Preston, 1966), so the zone of transition is no longer a fluid environment where business and industry expand concentrically via land use invasion and succession. The period of rapid central business district expansion has passed. The consequences for the transition zone are a slowing down of invasion-succession leading to stagnation in certain parts of the zone and, therefore, a shift away from concentric outward expansion. Basically this means a reduced demand for land near the centre. Decentralization has reached a new level of maturity which has not been appreciated by zone landowners who still hope to sell at inflated prices, which only accentuates movement to the suburbs. Few one- or two-storey buildings can afford central sites. At the same time the demand for multi-storey apartments or other intensive uses is not great enough to cover all the zone; thus sectors of general inactivity and stagnation are not uncommon. People can afford to move out more easily than industry, and homes have become obsolete more rapidly than factories. Near central locations have lost their advantages as places to live and work. Central areas were formerly of such importance that replacement costs were justified and areas were rebuilt, but now the spatial differential has left a legacy of deteriorating land and buildings in many areas of the transition zone for which there appears to be little re-use potential.

## Redevelopment as a Spatial Process

The amount of private redevelopment taking place in any urban area at any time is largely determined exogenously to the economy of that urban area (Bourne, 1967, ch. 5). Investment in redevelopment is closely related to national investment in the various sectors of the economy and shows a similar tendency to fluctuate over time. Variations in the availability of funds to different types of building mean that certain types of new construction exhibit greater volatility than others. Over time, redevelopment activity may show cyclical fluctuations reflective of national economic trends. In spatial terms new construction activity must be viewed as a whole, extending from redevelopment at the urban centre to new development at the urban fringe. Theories of urban structure suggest that redevelopment as a proportion of property in a ring at any given distance from the urban centre decreases as ring distance from the centre increases since older buildings are found nearest the centre. Thus redevelopment activity is greatest in and around the position of greatest accessibility. As renewal is completed, the ring of greatest redevelopment activity moves outward into successively more distant rings: this would be the expected pattern since building age in urban areas shows a concentric zonation. Large suburban nuclei may be redeveloped in part as the urban area grows, and the increased demand can only be met by providing higher buildings in positions of local accessibility.

In practice redevelopment does not fit into the simplified pattern deduced from urban structural theory for, at any time, redevelopment is highly localized in space and affects only particular types of property since changing location factors steer other uses to new intra-urban locations. Even where the pattern of redevelopment is treated over a considerable period of time, it still shows considerable variability and does not fit the simplified constructs. However, changes in factors influencing intra-urban location and investment decisions are reflected in the redevelopment pattern. Redevelopment shows a definite concentration or clustering within an urban area and provides mainly new office or apartment accommodation at the intensive level or parking and commercial motor-use at the opposite end of the intensity scale, but little else.

Activities considering redevelopment as a means of obtaining a location and a structure best suited to their needs have a wide choice of location. The selection of a site for redevelopment is based on the cumulative assessment of the relative attractions of alternative parcels of land. Variations in intra-urban redevelopment patterns will reflect the character and distribution of activities, the character and distribution of the existing stock of buildings, the quality of the environment, the relative access to urban population and hence distance from the urban centre, and the size and cost of individual land parcels. It has already been pointed out that near the urban centre activities considered suitable as occupants of redeveloped property generate insufficient demand to cover the whole blighted area. Such activities provide a basis for redevelopment only if the unit involved is sufficiently large to generate its own environment. The developer, especially where his commitment is speculative, appears as an independent agent and his actions in choosing a site for redevelopment can be important. Developers seek out large plots where ownership consolidation has already taken place, with vacant land acting as a strong positive factor in attracting and orienting redevelopment to particular locations. Economic pressure for redevelopment builds up in certain broadly defined parts of the urban area and as shown in Toronto (Bourne, 1967, ch. 6), sharp variations in redevelopment between urban sectors are apparent. Greatest activity, where redevelopment is left to private enterprise, is in the better quality/higher income sectors, since these provide attractive environments for apartments and offices. Once initial planning regulations and community resistance have been overcome, developers concentrate on that sector although the nodes of redevelopment within that sector may change drastically with time. This concentration raises costs of land in the initial area and they rise rapidly until there is no longer any absolute advantage over other areas, construction continues until redevelopment to the maximum potential is completed. Other redevelopment patterns may be generated where local authorities promote slum clearance.

Therefore, the replacement of existing stock does not fit readily into existing theories of urban spatial structure. The process of structural change in the standing stock of buildings in an urban area represents a long-run adjustment to supply and demand forces. From the dynamic viewpoint the historical theories of urban structure and growth, which emphasize age and obsolescence, suggest that the replacement process should be concomitant with land use succession and the spatial pattern would be readily apparent, for the rate and magnitude of such structural change would be greatest at the margins of each expanding zone. A wave-like progression of new building outward from the centre following the original pattern of growth would be expected. This, as suggested, does not seem to be the case for, even in the sequent occupance of existing buildings, there has been a shift from concentric expansion–zonation to one of uneven and interrupted expansion (Griffin and Preston, 1966) due to better transport, artificially high central land values, trends in business operations, and a changed attitude toward the urban centre. More and more activities have migrated to outlying locations.

## Planning and Redevelopment

Much of the foregoing analysis suggests that, because of the "neighbourhood effect", the extent and character of the internal reorganization brought about by market forces represents sub-optimal adjustment to the changed conditions. This is particularly so in the case of redevelopment. Planning intervention is, therefore, necessary if a superior end-product is to be achieved. A system of planning permissions cannot compel development to take place, and thus the limits of such an approach to the physical reconstruction of large areas of obsolescent buildings and badly laid out development should be obvious. The initiative must rest with the planner, and publicly organized schemes of redevelopment are called for.

What do planners seek to achieve in the field of urban renewal?

Urban renewal allows planners to take a comprehensive approach to the substitution of new social capital for old. Sectors of an urban area differ in the extent to which they need treatment, therefore the phasing of action by planners will have a marked influence on the spatial pattern of redevelopment. Also, the average size of plots being redeveloped will rise because of the emphasis on the comprehensive, rather than piecemeal, approach. Some areas may respond to rehabilitation, others are ripe for slum clearance under the Housing Acts: yet this still leaves extensive "twilight areas" to be treated as comprehensive development areas under Town and Country Planning Acts. A basic requirement of planning in this context is a wide power of compulsory purchase. The use of such powers to obtain control of land in areas scheduled for comprehensive redevelopment will lead to the displacement of persons and activities and so generate intra-urban movement and overspill, part of which will be directly catered for by the planning authorities.

What are planners to do with the area obtained? One objective—the removal of slums, etc.—would already have been achieved, but the more important objective—the purpose of rebuilding—remains. Urban planners must have a clear-cut objective, otherwise the scheme could degenerate into a mere real property transaction with the cleared land being sold to the highest private bidder (Senior, 1966, p. 99). However, the urban planners can determine what they want to build, how it should be built, and where, within the project, any building will be located. Where the land is sold or leased to private developers, precise obligations will be stipulated, and this represents a powerful, positive development tool. But private developers will only be interested in the planned buildings if there is a market for them. For any other type of building the local authority will have to act as developer and, as most schemes contain some developments of a non-profit nature, a local authority–developer partnership may be appropriate.

## The Overall Pattern of Change

Urban growth brings increased demand for accommodation within the urban area. As a consequence of such pressure certain existing activities may relocate as their present sites are bid away by more intensive uses or new customers appear at different intra-urban locations. In addition other changes, firstly, in demand (such as changing preferences) and, secondly, in supply (such as changing production and transport technologies) promote further adjustments. In the dynamic sense it may be argued that urban growth increases location costs throughout the urban region unless transport improvements take place at a rate which more than offsets them. More activities generally mean an increased demand for movement and interaction, and expanded flow rates in an urban system nearly always cause marked changes in the anatomy of that system (Meier, 1962, p. 136).

Growth will, therefore, be reflected in changing spatial patterns of activity locations, land-use intensity, and land values. Distance between activities in an urban area is a function of urban size rather than another variable such as age or location of the urban area *per se* (Loewenstein, 1963). Intra-urban location patterns are characterized by increasing specialization as urban size increases since more activities of a given type will be seeking similar locations, external economy benefits pull complementary firms and activities together, and new activities with higher threshold limits and particular location requirements appear. Specialization takes place in both type of service provided and in the location of those services within the urban area. The process of adaptation is selective. For example, the central business district first loses its dominance in food and industrial activities, followed by general retailing and department store functions. The rate of change in each category with increasing city size reflects more the differential growth rate of new activities in the suburbs rather than migration from the city centre. Increasing specialization within the central business district produces a "dead heart" in the centre for residential population is excluded as the area becomes subdivided into subcores. Indeed, the central business district itself may "shift" from time to time (Murray, 1970), partly to maintain a central location relative to population and partly in response to traffic congestion.

The greater demand for accommodation makes higher buildings profitable and raises land values. Land use intensities and land values show the greatest increase in the position of greatest accessibility, i.e. the central business district, with other above average increases in limited sectors of the transition zone and in and around poles of local accessibility. The proportion of persons housed in multi-family dwellings increases with increasing urban size. Land values within the already built-up area may shift as a result of certain changes in underlying conditions as when a transport improvement increases the accessibility of a particular sector. Moreover, any transport improvement which effects a saving in transport costs could mean more money available to pay for the land.

In the growth of any urban area the original districts of specialization may disappear to be replaced by other districts and specializations. The shifts are not entirely haphazard since several types of district tend to follow very similar and definite life cycles (Wendt, 1956, ch. 5). Theoretical explanations of these shifts emphasize the time factor. Historical theories of urban growth explain residential redistribution in terms of housing near the urban centre becoming increasingly unsuitable for high-income families as the urban area grows. This encourages the rich to build new homes on the periphery. The inevitable effects of age and deterioration are implicit in such generalizations although the concept of ageing of structures, sequent occupance by income groups, and population growth are dynamic elements of such theories. Population growth is critical since the number of low-income families must increase to demand houses vacated by the richer or movement will cease as indicated in the discussion of filtering in Chapter 6. Redistribution of population may equally be due to structural forces, such as changing preferences (Alonso, 1965, ch. 6). Recent trends, however, suggest that growth forces are focused on a number of alternate centres as urban areas become larger and more dispersed, thus exposing a limitation of theories assuming a single centre. However, these theories could be adapted to include a random element which, for example, might account for the different sales policies followed by different types of landowner. When one group is a large owner of property in an area and has a low record of sales activity among its holdings it is likely, on San Francisco's experience (Monsen, 1961), to be relatively inactive as to new construction or redevelopment.

## Problems Associated with Urban Growth

Under conditions where buildings had very short lives, the actual shape and internal structure of an urban area would be close to its equilibrium pattern. But this is not the case, and urban areas never attain equilibrium. The very successful urban area has always grown beyond its immediate political bounds. Adjustments to changing supply and demand conditions are not without difficulties and, on occasions, they may give rise to problems which are more serious than "growing pains". Many such problems are intensified as urban size increases. However, the normative assumption has been that urban growth is the channel through which desirable changes may be achieved (Thompson, 1965a, Introduction).

Poorer urban immigrants still gravitate to the urban core, for here is the cheapest housing on offer. With the redistribution of population that has taken place within urban areas, those persons remaining at the urban centre are predominantly of low income. This could lead to the impoverishment of the central area since the urban service requirements of such slum communities are high, whereas their contributions are low. Slums create costs for the community by way of declining property values, increased fire and police protection costs, and higher public health and welfare costs. Redevelopment is not profitable for private enterprise; hence the initiative for slum clearance rests with public authorities and such redevelopment must be subsidized (Ullman, 1962). Slum clearance displaces families who have to be rehoused elsewhere and, if left to their own devices, these families move into areas adjacent to the one vacated so accelerating the creation of the next set of slums.

Urban growth is dependent on an increase in the communications rate or contacts between persons and businesses but overloading of the channels of communication causes disorganization (Meier, 1962, p. 2). Most obvious is the traffic and parking problem, for many urban contacts are very dependent on the use of motor vehicles. However, the provision of roads and other facilities comprising the urban infrastructure is removed from the influence of the price mechanism, and changes in supply, i.e. new investment, are not necessarily geared to changes in demand but to the availability of public money. This is especially true where no direct price is charged for the use of facilities, as in the case of roads. Disorganization, stemming from such overloading of communication facilities, can encourage intra-urban relocation and add to the problem of revitalization of the urban centre as more and more activities seek non-central locations. This may increase further the pressure on urban movement systems. Indeed, one effect of the increased specialization of land use which accompanies urban growth is the further separation of residence and workplace which throws a further burden on roads and public transport at peak hour flows because journey to work lengths have been increased.

Absolute size may be a brake on urban growth (Thompson, 1965a, p. 24) because as an urban area's population grows and its density and physical extent increase a point may be reached where unit costs of public services rise or the quality of those services drops. In particular the form of outward expansion may be critical for it has been suggested (Schechter, 1961) that certain patterns of outward development have led to increased costs of providing everyday services and performing everyday functions.

The problems can be multiplied. Where local political boundaries are outdated questions of responsibility for and financing of public services loom large, especially where a rural authority has to cope with outward expansion. The formation of a conurbation by coalescence of adjacent, growing urban areas may mean an urban entity is subdivided between several urban authorities. Overhaul of local government thus becomes necessary. Environmental deterioration, increased atmospheric pollution, greater incidence of suicides, increased cost of motor accidents, etc., also count against urban growth.

In spite of these disadvantages urban areas continue to grow, the largest areas showing some of the fastest rates of growth. This would suggest that the disadvantages of growth and increased size do not, as yet, outweigh the advantages. Large urban areas have been leaders in a wide range of public and social services, they provide a wider range of facilities in education, medicine, etc., and usually maintain standards of institutional facilities unsurpassed by smaller areas. However, the advantages of size may be "internalized" by private persons and firms whereas the disadvantages are more likely to be "externalities", often of a type which are difficult to quantify and express in money terms. The question of urban size will be returned to in Chapter 11.

# CHAPTER 9

# The Level of Urban Economic Activity

## Urban Growth versus Fluctuations in Urban Economic Activity

Economic forces provide the principle explanation of short-run changes and of long-run growth in the fortunes of urban areas. The physical manifestations of growth, discussed in the two previous chapters, are the result of changes in the type and volume of activities which form the economic base of any urban area. Urban economic theory seeks not only an explanation, but also attempts to determine the extent of fluctuations and growth of the urban economy. The production and distribution of goods and services create employment and income-earning opportunities which attract people. The distribution of growth between urban areas and the way in which urban areas are differentially affected by unemployment are but two dimensions of the pattern of economic growth and change. An urban area cannot be considered in isolation, for it is part of an all-embracing system in which relative considerations are paramount. Each urban area's past economic performance, present economic position, and future economic potential will reflect what share of the regional and national total of goods and services it produces in each line of economic activity relative to that of other urban areas. Economic activities in any urban area are affected by those in other urban areas in the immediate region and are ultimately linked to the national economy as a whole.

How and why do urban areas grow economically? Why do some urban areas grow more rapidly and at the expense of other urban areas? Why are some urban areas more susceptible to fluctuations in their levels of economic activity? One approach suggests that urban areas exist, suffer fluctuations in their levels of economic activity, and grow because of economic activities whose locations are determined exogenously to the urban area by that area's comparative advantage in regional, national, and even international economic systems. Thus the economic basis of any urban area is that it exports goods. Where an urban area attains a high degree of specialization in the production of goods and services it supplies to outsiders, it cannot be self-sufficient. This export trade sector represents a significant proportion of total economic activity for any urban area. The smaller the urban area the greater is the importance of exports and the higher is the level of imports to satisfy the requirements of its inhabitants. Larger urban areas can trade within themselves and produce rather more of their requirements, saving transport costs on goods that would otherwise have to be brought from elsewhere. Specialization in economic activity offers an urban area the prospect of maximum growth but, equally, it may pose the threat of temporary or severe recession, even of stagnation and decline.

Urban growth and short-term fluctuations in urban economic activity may, therefore, be viewed as the response of economic activities within an urban area in supplying more goods and services following an increase in demand from outside the urban area. The demand emphasis indicates the short-run time concern of this approach. An associated idea suggests a balance between population of an urban area, its economic resources and its volume of export production. Urban economic functions are assumed to be in equilibrium or constantly trying to regain equilibrium lost through a change in one of its functions. The mechanism through which this equilibrium is regained, is, however, largely neglected (Czamanski, 1965). Confusion exists for fluctuations in urban economic activity over relatively short periods of time have not been adequately distinguished from long-run, structural or secular trends. As Fig. 9.1 shows, cyclical fluctuations in economic activity are possible about a secular growth trend, where the latter represents a moving average of the level of economic activity. The explanation of fluctuations in the level of economic activity of an urban area is different from an explanation of the phenomenon of urban growth. Macro-economics is designed to explain the former, with the emphasis being laid on aggregate demand. For example, an increase in the demand for exports from a given urban area would be emphasized and the repercussions of that increase for the internal functioning of that urban area may be quantified in the form of a conventional economic multiplier. However, it must be stressed that such multiplier analysis is essentially short-run analysis. As one moves from urban cyclical fluctuations to urban growth and development, so emphasis

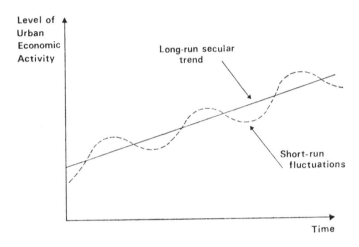

Fig. 9.1. Comparison of short- and long-term levels of urban economic activity.

must be shifted from multiplier analysis, in income or employment terms, to a concern for comparative costs relative to competing urban areas. Growth analysis deals with the rate at which the upper limits of supply are changed over time and recognizes that growth, in enlarging an urban area, restructures the urban economy. This allows for change in the type of urban export activity following new inventions, innovations, and their linked investment decisions. This will be discussed further in the next chapter. Here attention will be concentrated on the determinants of the level of urban economic activity at any given time and on short-run fluctuations in that level.

The basic measures of the economic performance of an individual urban area are regarded as level of *per capita* income, equitableness of the income distribution and growth and stability of that income flow over time (Thompson, 1965a, Introduction). Urban growth is assumed to bring desirable changes in the level, distribution, and stability of that income. Thus growth may become a strategy to be pursued by urban governments. The future course of an urban area's economy rests only partially in the hands of its government but even partial control of its destiny rests on an understanding of the growth process. Often outside factors dictate the major economic problems facing an urban area, and frequently these problems accompany what may be regarded as undesirable growth rates. Relatively high levels of unemployment and poverty follow where an urban area's growth is too slow, whilst too fast a rate of growth brings congestion of facilities consequent upon capital shortages. Indeed, the urban system appears biased toward growth for restorative measures are used, for example, where unemployment exceeds a certain level, in order to maintain momentum (Meier, 1962, p. 142). Therefore it is how much of the current increment of national growth an urban area is able to attract that determines whether it is doing relatively well or relatively badly.

## Determinants of the Level of Urban Output

Given a full employment level of aggregate demand, the level of output of any urban economy is limited by the quantity and productivity of the resources available to it. At a lower level of aggregate demand the level of economic activity within an urban area would, in the short run, depend on the ability of its export firms to compete with outside suppliers of the products concerned, i.e. on its share of national product markets. The higher the proportion of old, obsolescent plants, the lower will be the level of economic activity in such circumstances. In the short run, import of capital goods and materials could be used to supplement intra-urban supplies, and, therefore, permit more efficient resource combinations than would be possible in the absence of such imports (Crosson, 1960). Inter-urban trade is thus a mechanism by which certain limits to production may be partially pushed back.

An increase in the level of urban economic activity in the short run is explained more by the growth rate of its export industries than any other single factor. Growth of export activities depends on factors outside the urban area which induce changes in the demand for export products, such as population increases, preference changes, or appearance of more competitive sources of supply.

The longer the time span the greater is the relative importance of factors. The physical ability of an urban economy to expand its level of output depends on its ability to increase its stock of natural resources, human resources, and accumulated capital. Where there is no inmigration of capital or labour or no discovery of new resources, growth of urban output will depend on natural increase of urban population. Capacity for a higher level of output must be differentiated from an actual higher level (Lane, 1966) for the latter depends also, for example, on the attitude of local entrepreneurs to invention and innovation. Development will alter the quantity and quality of the stock of local urban resources. Thus the very essence of long-run change in urban output levels is the transition from one export activity to another.

Various attempts have been made to explain urban economic fluctuations and urban economic growth. Prominent among such attempts have been purported growth models which are based on the sectoring of the urban economy. Base multiplier and input–output models have been most commonly used. The common element in such approaches is that growth can be initiated by exogenous and/or endogenous factors and that a change in one part of the urban economy will induce change elsewhere. These linked changes represent measurable quantities; thus the extent of the changes consequent upon an initial stimulus can be predicted.

## Economic Base Theory

Economic base theory emphasizes that parts of an urban area's economic activities are dependent on demands from outside that urban area. That part is termed the exogenous sector and comprises the base or export activities. Such export activities would be expected to have location quotients greater than one since the area must have more than its proportionate share of that industry. According to the theory export industries provide the reason for the existence and growth of an urban area. The growth of an urban area is the response of its export industries to increased demand for their products from outside. Certainly the current growth rate of an urban area is explained more by export sector growth than any other single factor. Export activities provide a means of payment for goods and services an urban area cannot produce for itself. Some export industry is necessary in every urban area to pay for the foodstuffs that must be imported. Export activities also support service activities, the latter forming the endogenous sector of the urban economy. Service activities will exhibit a certain similarity between urban areas whereas export activities may show striking differences.

The exogenous and endogenous sectors are distinguished spatially in terms of the location of their demand areas. Export activities obviously supply goods and services to points outside the confines of the urban area or to persons coming to that urban area from outside, whilst service activities satisfy a market entirely within the urban area. The level of economic activity within an urban area is the sum of the levels of activity in these two sectors, i.e.

$$T = E + S, \tag{9.1}$$

where $T$ is the level of employment (income) in the urban area, $E$ the level of employment (income) in export sector, and $S$ the level of employment (income) in service sector. The level of activity in the export sector depends, at least in the short run, on factors over which the urban area has no control, such as the demand for its exports, the amount of investment from outside, and the propensity of its residents to commute outside the urban area to work. Such export activities cause income to flow into an urban area. The urban households spend part of this income within the urban area, and the generation of employment that results from the satisfying of intra-urban demand identifies the endogenous or service sector. Since the level of activity in the endogenous sector depends on the level of demand generated via the exogenous sector, then the latter is the one which initiates change in the level of an urban area's economic activity. Therefore

$$S = kT, \tag{9.2}$$

where $k$ is a constant equal to that proportion of total economic activity representing service activity. A cause-and-effect relationship is postulated between export and service activity. Thus

$$T = kT + E; \tag{9.3}$$

hence
$$T = (1 - k)^{-1} E, \tag{9.4}$$

which indicates that the level of urban economic activity is determined by the export sector. If export jobs are lost service employment would decrease as the level of demand within the urban economy drops, unemployment would increase, and, in time, emigration would lead to a fall in urban population. Should, however, a service firm close down, the theory argues that a replacement would automatically spring up to take its place since there has been no change in the level of demand. An increase in the level of export activity would, therefore, be expected to generate additional service activity because the level of demand will have increased and more people will be attracted to the urban area. Changes in export activities bring sympathetic changes in service activities—an automatic but not necessarily instantaneous response.

Viewed in this way exports are the point of contact between the urban and the national economy. Export activities import national disturbances and transmit them to the urban economy through their production and employment responses. Fluctuations in the level of urban economic activity are, therefore, seen by the theory as reactions to exogenous forces, in particular the local business cycle may be clearly traced to the instability of external demand. In this sense base theory is a limited application of Keynesian ideas.

Exports are of decreasing relative importance as size of urban area increases. Thus the volume of urban economic activity generated in the service sector increases with urban size, i.e. the larger the urban area the more self-sufficient it is. Alternatively, the smaller is the urban area the greater is the importance of exports as a source of fluctuation in its level of economic activity. Exports are not of the same relative importance in all urban areas of the same size. The ratio of export to service activity varies depending on (1) the nature of the export activity, (2) the location of the urban area, (3) the age of the urban area, and (4) the effect of local business cycles (Andrews, 1955). For example, motor-vehicle production generates more service activity than pulp and paper making, a dormitory urban area has an abnormally low service element due to its competitive position in relation to the major urban area, whilst the service element increases as an urban area ages and matures or during the downswing of a local business cycle.

A base multiplier, in employment or income terms, can be computed which relates changes in exports, the principle exogenous factor, to the derivative change in the level of urban service activity. New industry has a multiplier effect both in the form of new demand created by the establishments themselves and by the purchasing power of their labour force. By means of a series of ratios the extent of urban growth or decline can be determined. In its simplistic form ratios are estab-lished by considering crude employment figures. Urban economic activities must be allocated to either export or service categories. Where an activity supplies markets both within and outside an urban area its employment is subdivided between export and service categories according to the proportion of that activity's sales made in each market. Ratios are established between export and service employment and, therefore, between export and total employment and knowing the proportion of working to urban population between export employ-ment and urban population. For example, if in an urban area of 80,000 population 1 person in 4 is in employment and that, for every 1 person employed in export activity $1\frac{1}{2}$ persons are employed in the service sector, then the series of ratios would be:

|  |  |
|---|---|
| Export: service employment | 1: 1·5 |
| Therefore Export: total employment | 1: 2·5 |
| Total employment: urban population | 1: 4 |
| Therefore Export employment: urban population | 1:10 |

The export-service ratio is assumed to be "normal" or constant for that area, and so long as it remains unaltered the level of economic activity will be in equilibrium. An increased demand for the urban area's exports disturbs the equilibrium and sets in motion adjustments designed to restore equilibrium. Assume an increased demand for exports creates 1000 additional jobs in the urban area of 80,000, then the equilibrium situation shown in stage 1 of Table 9.1 no longer holds, and a state of disequilibrium, stage 2, exists. Urban population will have increased by 4000 as a result of the influx of 1000 export workers and their families. According to the export-service ratio at stage 2,

TABLE 9.1 URBAN GROWTH FOLLOWING INCREASED EXPORTS

| | 1 Equilibrium | | 2 Disequilibrium | | 3 Equilibrium restored | |
|---|---|---|---|---|---|---|
| | Number | Ratio to export | Number | Ratio | Number | Ratio |
| Export workers | 8 000 | 1 | 9 000 | 1 | 9 000 | 1 |
| Service workers | 12 000 | 1·5 | 12 000 | 1·33 | 13 500 | 1·5 |
| Total workers | 20 000 | 2·5 | 21 000 | 2·33 | 22 500 | 2·5 |
| Urban population | 80 000 | 10 | 84 000 | 9·33 | 90 000 | 10 |

service activities are now under-represented and they will expand until the 1/1·5 ratio is re-established. The restored equilibrium situation is shown in stage 3, where the urban population has risen by a further 6000 due to an extra 1500 service workers and their families. These ratios provide a short-cut method of arriving at the new equilibrium situation, i.e. they provide a "multiplier" by which the original change in export employment must be multiplied to find the change in service employment and urban population. For example, again assuming the above ratios, if 500 export jobs are lost, service employment will decline by 750 and urban population by 5000 by the time equilibrium is restored. Therefore, if the service proportion in the export-service ratio increases one expects, eventually, a decrease in the level of urban economic activity and hence in urban population. A decrease in the service proportion reflects an increase in export activity which raises the level of economic activity and brings an increase in urban population. This illustrates the mechanical application of economic base theory to urban growth. Its apparent advantages are that it is quick and simple. Its crudity is understood and accepted as the price to be paid for the speed and simplicity it embodies (Murdock, 1962).

Base theory has been criticized both for its mechanical application and its conceptualization. The latter is obviously the most significant.

The use of a constant or "normal" set of ratios and hence multipliers for any urban area is questionable. Since service sector reaction is lagged, can one be certain that historically determined ratios are "normal" for that urban area? Moreover, why should the ratios stay the same as change takes place? *Ceteris paribus*, reasoning cannot hold in dynamic circumstances, and it would appear more likely that the ratios actually change with the growth or decline they are supposed to estimate (Gillies and Grigsby, 1956). There is an increase in the relative importance of service activity as urban areas grow in size. This is to be expected, for as an urban area's population increases, so does the size of the urban market, and this stimulates the production of items formerly imported. Thus with increasing size an urban area crosses successive thresholds at which it becomes profitable to establish further service industries within that area. In fairness it should be pointed out that there is nothing in the basic formulation of the theory that sets fixed ratios and rules out growth-inducing changes in the service element so long as the growth effects of such changes are small relative to the growth induced by expansion of export activities. It must also be admitted that the service element can change independently, as in time of national crisis such as war, or as a result of changes in consumer tastes and levels of income. As real income rises a smaller proportion is spent on necessities and more is spent locally on houses and services (Hoyt, 1961).

An urban area may have several exports, each growing at different rates and each generating varying amounts of service activity. Base analysis in the form of an export-service ratio represents an averaging procedure which masks differences between export industries. Changes at the margin need not be the same as the average represented by the ratio. Although the simplistic numerical application of the theory may be suspect, it need not detract from the value of the underlying proposition that changes in the level of urban activity depend upon changes in export activities. But would refinement of the numerical application be worth while?

A major criticism is the undue importance attached to export industries in determining the level of economic activity in an urban area. For instance, in larger spatial units such as nations, exports are not the major determinant of the level of economic activity. But what is true for a part need not be true for the whole. Although at the global scale exports do not determine the world level of economic activity this does not invalidate the proposition that the level of economic activity in each urban area is largely determined by its exports. The opportunity for increased specialization is a major force in urbanization and as specialization depends on the extent of the market exports from a particular urban area represent one way of enlarging the market. The value of base theory has been to draw attention to this factor.

Specialization also means interdependence. Besides relying on other urban areas to purchase its exports, a given urban area must depend on other urban areas to supply the goods and services it cannot produce for itself. Even export industries may need to import some resource inputs. Payment for imports must result in a money outflow from an urban area which ought to be balanced against the export industry income inflow. Should an urban area's increased export earnings all be spent on imports there would be no increase in demand for the products of its service sector. Thus the larger the proportion of any increase in income which is spent on imports the smaller will be the multiplier effect on service activity. Therefore, it is as important to measure the imported and locally produced shares of total local consumption as it is to measure the exported and locally consumed shares of total local production. Purchase of imports from other urban areas will have a trade multiplier feedback (ignored by this theory) since the higher an urban area's imports the higher the level of income generated in other urban areas and, given their propensities to import, the higher their level of imports and the greater the opportunities for export from the original urban area.

The position of service activity needs careful scrutiny. Replacing imports by local production would effect the same transformation in an urban area's "balance of payments" as an equivalent value increase in exports. Increased production in export or service sectors has the same effect on local growth. Base theory allows insufficient scope for internal, i.e. service sector, growth sequences. Although the fortunes of some service activities may be tied to those of export industries, this is not true for all service activities, for some people live by "taking in each other's washing" (Blumenfeld, 1955). Maybe an urban population cannot all live by taking in each other's washing, but if no one does so, employment and income-earning opportunities are forgone (Ferguson, 1960). Independent change in service industry may follow from changes in consumer tastes or production technology. Furthermore, the export–service relationship is not one way, for the efficiency of the local service sector may be critical to an urban area's export industries which engage in interregional competition. Could not a viable local service sector provide a framework for the production of exports and, therefore, a positive locational factor in attracting new and/or additional export activity? Champions of the service sector (Blumenfeld, 1955), indeed, argue that the service sector is really "basic", for this is enduring whilst export manufacturing is transitory when a long-run view is taken. Replacement export firms can be born on the basis of a viable service sector.

Discussion of the role of service activities reveals that base theory makes no distinction on the time factor. Indeed, continuous identification of exports with the antonomous variable determining urban economic activity has led to wrong conclusions about urban growth (Tiebout, 1956b). Exports are critical in the cyclical sensitivity of an urban area, representing a carrier by which changes in the level of national economic activity are diffused. In economics, multiplier analysis is usually short run, offering an explanation of fluctuations in the level of economic activity. Export industries may be the dynamic factor in determining the short-run level of urban economic activity because they may be—depending on the elasticity of demand for exports—a chief source of instability. The base approach is, therefore, legitimate in the analysis of urban business cycles during which short period of time the industrial structure of an urban area is stable (Thompson, 1965a, ch. 1). But base theory is not the growth theory it was once purported to be, for, in the long run, lines of causation are reversed and the ability to attract new export activities will depend on an urban area's comparative costs in the performance of those activities. Such costs must reflect the efficiency of the local service sector. Base theory, therefore, explains short-run fluctuations in the level of urban activity but not urban growth. This is especially obvious when it is noted that base theory, in focusing on the magnitude of change within an urban area, gives no indication as to when and why a change in the export activities of a given urban area will take place. Given the magnitude of export changes, base theory indicates the subsequent adjustments: it tells what will happen if the export base changes—not what that export change will be. Thus factors such as the natural population growth of an urban area which promote growth are not discussed.

Base theory does not distinguish adequately between income and employment flows. At any given time the equilibrium level of economic activity in an urban area may employ all or only a proportion of that area's factors of production. Assuming full employment conditions at the national level an increased demand for the exports of a given urban area need not generate greater employment in that urban area, only higher wages, at least in the short-run. If local resources are fully employed and no new resources can flow into the urban area more exports can be produced only at the expense of a lower output in the service sector. This is illustrated in Fig. 9.2, where curve $XY$ represents the production possibilities curve for a given urban area at its full employment level of activity. *OX* represents the maximum output of the service sector if all resources were allocated to services, and *OY* the maximum export sector output where all resources are devoted to export production. Curve *XY* thus represents all possible combinations of service and export outputs where all available urban factors are fully employed. Its shape is determined by the principle of diminishing returns. Point *R* represents an output of *OK* exports and *OL* services. If the demand for exports rises to *OM*, this can be met, as point *S* shows, by reducing the output of the service sector to *ON*. Export

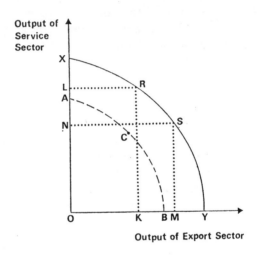

Fig. 9.2. Urban production possibilities curve.

industries compete resources away from the service sector, e.g. by paying higher wages for labour, but there is no change in the total level of urban economic activity. Only if unemployed resources were available in the economy would it be possible to expand both the output of service and export sectors in the short run. This would be the case if the level of urban economic activity was on a lower production possibilities curve such as point *C* on curve *AB*. In the long run a greater combined output would depend on such factors as augmentation of factor supply and technological advance, factors which do not figure in base theory. Therefore, to understand the process of urban growth, it is necessary to start where base theory leaves off, i.e. to explain when and why export activities change.

## Urban Income Analysis

The integration of base theory with the mainstream of economic theory (Tiebout, 1956 b and c,) emphasizes a Keynesian approach to the determinants of short-term fluctuations in the level of urban economic activity. The major problem associated with a Keynesian approach at the urban level is the lack of statistics. However, the functioning of the urban economy can be examined to provide a more exact multiplier statement. Figure 9.3 represents a simplified urban economy in which the urban activities have been divided into four basic sectors—export, service, local government, and households, plus a fifth sector—an urban banking system. The money-flow interrelationships between these sectors and their connections with the extra-urban economy are shown by flow arrows. The extra-urban connections are ways in which money may leak from or be injected into the urban economy. The diagram shows the basic circular flow of money within an urban area as urban households spend part of their incomes on goods and services produced within the area whilst receiving income from hiring the factors of production they own to the productive activities in the urban area.

For any given period, the values of goods and services produced within the area equal the money income paid out to the factors of production which have contributed to that output. Of the income paid out by urban industry, irrespective of whether export or service sector, part may be (1) paid to factors of production owned by persons living outside the urban area, e.g. share capital in industry or workers commuting from another urban area; (2) retained in the form of undistributed profits by producing firms which they hold within the banking system; and (3) the remainder will be paid to factors owned by households within the urban area. A proportion of urban household income will be siphoned off by national government taxation of incomes, and some households will choose to place all or part of their income in the banking system. Additional income may be earned by urban

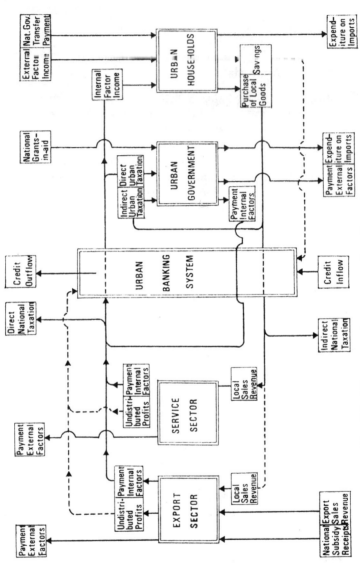

Fig. 9.3. Diagrammatic representation of an urban economy.

households owning factors of production hired to producers located outside that area or because they receive national government transfer payments.

Urban households dispose of their incomes in three ways, expenditure on goods and services produced within the area, spending on imports, and savings, the latter being channelled into the banking system. Urban local government acts as both producer and consumer, supplying services to urban households and purchasing goods and services from producers both within and outside the urban area. It also brings about redistributional effects since a major source of local government revenue is some form of local taxation, such as rates. The urban banking system is important, not so much in its role of providing jobs for urban residents, but as the supplier of credit, adding flexibility to the supply of funds available to an urban area not only in terms of the pyramid of credit that can be built on deposits from within the urban area but also because of the inflow (and outflow) of credit through linkages with the national banking system.

The money inflow to an urban area derives from outsiders' spending on exports, earnings of externally employed factors, receipts of national government transfer payments, subsidies and grants-in-aid, and any credit inflow. The effect on the urban economy of any increase in this money inflow will depend on the proportion of the additional money which is spent within the urban area, i.e. on the marginal propensity to consume internally produced goods and services. The multiplier in this case would be 1/1-marginal propensity to consume internally produced goods. Alternatively the leakage of money from the urban area could be considered. Expenditure on imports, payment for the services of externally owned factors, national government taxation, savings, and any credit outflow will generate economic activity elsewhere. Although in the national economy the multiplier is largely determined by the savings leak, in the case of an urban economy it is the reciprocal of the rate at which money leaks from the urban area which is important, and this is largely determined by the marginal propensity to import. The multiplier thus becomes 1/marginal propensity to import. The more elastic is the demand for imports the higher is the cyclical marginal propensity to import and, therefore, the lower the local multiplier. The equilibrium level of urban economic activity will be where the rate of money inflow (largely export earnings) equals the rate of money out-flow (largely import spending) (Thompson, 1965a, ch. 4).

This multiplier indicates the extent of change in urban income consequent upon an initial increase (or decrease) in the money inflow into an urban area. It remains for the increased (or decreased) income to be translated into employment, population, and land-use terms. Such factors are wage differentials, increased productivity due to improved capital equipment, mean family size, and man/land ratios must be taken into account in the calculation. The multiplier effect increases in absolute terms as urban size increases, but there is no difference in relative terms, for as an urban areas grows it becomes more self-sufficient, i.e. the propensity to import falls, giving a positive multiplier effect, but the propensity to export falls, decreasing the multiplier effect so that the product of the two remains unchanged (Thompson, 1965a, p. 144).

## Urban Input–Output Analysis

Base theory pointed to the advantages of sectoralization of the urban economy as a means to understanding the functioning of the urban economy. Keynesian analysis suggests that certain criticisms of base analysis might be overcome by a more detailed sectoralization of the urban economy. General interdependence techniques, such as aggregative urban social accounting and urban input–output analysis, achieve this. Both deal with economic flows over short time spans. Input-output analysis only will be illustrated here. It is a technique that can be used to detail the production and distribution characteristics of urban economic activities and, when a spatial dimension is included, the nature of their spatial interrelationships.

The construction of an input–output table may be illustrated by dividing the urban economy into manufacturing, tertiary, and household sectors, and by aggregating external dealings into an export–import sector. In practice the sectoralization of an urban economy can be as detailed as available statistics allow. Table 9.2 represents such a table. The sectors are arranged in the same order horizontally (at the top) and vertically (at the left). Reading horizontally the table shows how the output of every sector or urban activity is distributed, i.e.

TABLE 9.2 INPUT–OUTPUT MATRIX FOR URBAN AREA (£m)

| Sector producing \ Sector purchasing | Urban economy | | | | Exports | Total urban output |
|---|---|---|---|---|---|---|
| | Manufacturing | Tertiary | Household | | | |
| Manufacturing | 0·2 | 0·1 | 0·1 | | 1·0 | 1·4 |
| Tertiary | 0·4 | 0·2 | 0·6 | | 0·1 | 1·3 |
| Household | 0·6 | 0·5 | 0·2 | | 0·1 | 1·4 |
| Imports | 0·2 | 0·5 | 0·5 | | * | 1·2 |
| Total urban inputs | 1·4 | 1·3 | 1·4 | | 1·2 | 5·3 |

* Cell left vacant because inter-area transactions between other urban areas and regions are external to the urban area under study.

which of the other sectors are its customers, with the final entry in the row representing the value of the gross output of the sector. Receipts or sales figures thus allow the table to be completed row-wise. Reading vertically, the input–output table shows the sources of inputs of every sector, with the final entry in a column representing the total cost of inputs in that sector. Expenditure or purchasing figures enable the table to be completed column-wise. Whichever way the table is completed the result must be the same: this identity must follow since every sale is at the same time a purchase. The table may also be adapted to distinguish capital transactions from current transactions. Its utility as a descriptive device is, therefore, immediately obvious.

The input–output technique also lends itself to impact analysis, i.e. tracing the effects of change, in this case on the various sectors of the urban economy. To enable its use for predictive purposes production (or inter-industry) coefficients must be calculated for activities wholly internal to the urban area and trade (or input) coefficients for activities with external relations. These coefficients are obtained, for example, in the case of the manufacturing sector, by dividing the total value of manufacturing sector output, namely £1·4m, into each of the inputs listed in the manufacturing sector column. As a result a coefficient is obtained which states the £-worth of inputs from each sector necessary to produce £1 of manufactures. Table 9.3 shows the coefficients obtained from the information contained in Table 9.2.

To use these coefficients for predicting the amount of growth it must be assumed that they represent constant relationships. This is questionable because scale economies, technological advance, and changes in the relative prices of inputs and outputs would alter these coefficients over time. However, the coefficients could be adjusted by extrapolation where determining factors exhibit regular patterns of change, but this may not be possible for factors such as technological advance. Thus assuming that the export demand for manufactures increased by 10 per cent, i.e. £100,000, then, using column 1 of Table 9.3, the input requirements necessary to produce that amount of additional manufactures can be calculated. By multiplying each coefficient in column 1 by £100,000, the input requirement from each sector can be found. For example, £29,000 of inputs would be required from the tertiary sector. But to produce the first-round requirement of manufactures

TABLE 9.3  COEFFICIENT TABLE: DIRECT INPUTS/£ OUTPUT

| Sector producing \ Sector purchasing | Urban economy | | | Exports |
|---|---|---|---|---|
| | *Manufacturing* | *Tertiary* | *Households* | |
| Manufacturing | 0·14 | 0·08 | 0·07 | 0·84 |
| Tertiary | 0·29 | 0·16 | 0·43 | 0·08 |
| Households | 0·43 | 0·38 | 0·14 | 0·08 |
| Imports | 0·14 | 0·38 | 0·36 | — |
| Total | 1·00 | 1·00 | 1·00 | 1·00 |

requires extra services and the inputs necessary to produce these extra tertiary outputs can be calculated by multiplying each figure in column 2 by £29,000. This represents a second-round input requirement, which applies also to the other sectors and such second-round inputs will require further inputs. Thus the second-round is followed by a third, the third demands a fourth, and so on. The reiterative procedure goes on *ad infinitum*, but with successive rounds the additional input requirements become smaller and smaller. The total effect on the level of urban economic activity is found by summing the round by round requirements and because successive rounds get smaller, the sum can be approximated with some accuracy. This result could also be derived, by a short-cut, from an inverse matrix derived from the coefficient table (Isard, 1960, p. 332).

## Linear Programming

Refinement of calculation cannot overshadow the fact that although input–output analysis, from the point of view of urban levels of economic activity, adds considerable sophistication to the description of complex urban economies and to the multiplier analysis of the effects of change, it gets no nearer an explanation of why that change takes place. The latter is the basic factor if the urban growth process is to be understood. Such techniques then, ranging from the simplistic base theory to sophisticated input–output analyses, are basically equilibrium-biased studies in that they view change as a disturbance to the system and seek to trace through the steps in the re-establishment of an equilibrium situation. But is the equilibrium position so attained an optimum one? Keynes (1936) demonstrated that equilibrium was more likely to occur at a level of economic activity other than the full employment one. On economic and social grounds full employment may be regarded as the optimum level of national economic activity. Similar considerations would apply to the urban economy.

For example, in terms of the export–service division what is the optimum allocation of resources to the export sector *vis-à-vis* the service sector? An urban area has limited resources, and the problem is to put them to their best use. Here techniques such as linear programming are called upon. In general the objective of linear programming is to maximize or minimize some linear function, subject to certain linear inequalities (Isard, 1960, p. 414). That is, it is a method based on a series of linear equations which intersect each other and the intersection points can be used to calculate the optimum solution. What is to be maximized or minimized? The choice of goal represents a value judgement. Assume that the urban community wishes to distribute its available resources so as to maximize total urban income. A simple example will illustrate the technique. Assume there is a largely self-sufficient urban area which wants to allocate its limited amounts of labour, capital and raw materials between the production of goods and the production of services so as to maximize total urban income. To generate £1 of income each activity requires inputs of each of the resources and these can be listed in a requirements table, such as Table 9.4.

The principles involved may be illustrated by the graphical solution of this simple two-activity situation, although a more general mathematical formulation is necessary for the solution of more complex activity situations. For each resource or input resource limitation lines are constructed which indicate the various combinations of production levels of goods and services which just use up the total amount of that resource. These lines, based on the information in Table 9.4, are shown in Figure 9.4. Consider Fig. 9.4a. At one extreme, *L*, £5000 worth of

TABLE 9.4  RESOURCE REQUIREMENTS/£ OF INCOME

| Resources \ Resource unit requirements | Goods | Services | Total urban resources ('000) |
|---|---|---|---|
| Raw materials | 0·6 | 0·2 | 3·0 |
| Labour | 0·5 | 1·0 | 5·0 |
| Capital | 1·9 | 1·25 | 10·0 |

goods could be produced if all the raw materials were channelled into that sector. At the other extreme *M*, £15,000 worth of services could be produced if all the raw materials are used in that sector. Below and to the left of *LM* exists an infinite number of possibilities that use less than 3000 units of raw materials, but any point within the shaded area

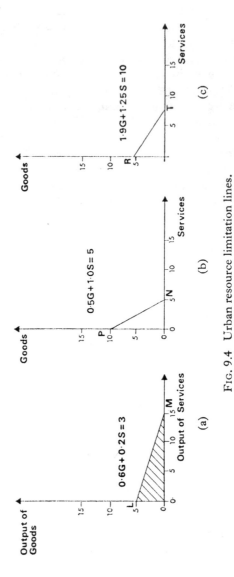

Fig. 9.4 Urban resource limitation lines.

$OLM$ represents an inefficient combination of output levels so far as the material limitation is concerned since all points on line $LM$ correspond to a higher level of output of both activities. Figure 9.4b shows the resource limitation line for labour and Fig. 9.4c for capital.

A solution requires that all three resources are jointly considered. Thus in Fig. 9.5 the individual resource limitation lines for raw

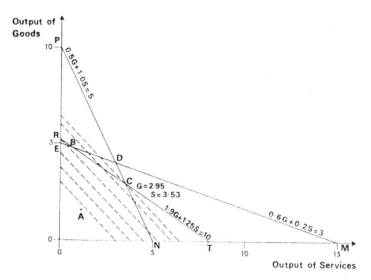

Fig. 9.5. Combined effective resource limitation line.

materials, labour, and capital are superimposed. In this case the combined effective resource limitation line $EBCN$ is convex to the origin and all efficient solutions lie on this curve. Within the hull are feasible but inefficient solutions, such as point $A$, while outside it lie impossible situations. Therefore the maximum level of production of goods is £5000 because the raw material limitation is the first to become effective in the case of goods. Service's maximum level of output is also £5000 corresponding to the level at which its first resource limitation, labour, becomes effective.

Which of the points on $EBCN$ yields the highest income? Because inputs were specified in terms of a level that generates £1 of income iso-income lines can be drawn, the value of which increase as such lines move further away from the origin. Therefore the combination of goods and services which yields the highest income is at $C$, which is that point on *EBCN* which lies on the highest iso-income line. This is the optimal solution, where £2950 of goods and £3530 of services are produced in the time period concerned. Where more than two activities are concerned and additional areas are considered, alternative means of solution, dependent upon more formal mathematical principles (the iterative or simplex method usually being adopted), are called upon (Isard, 1960, pp. 419–31; Yeomans, 1968, pp. 347–50).

This technique thus allows an optimum solution to the question of the level of operation of urban economic activity to be deduced for any given criterion and time period, but again the method makes certain assumptions regarding, e.g., production coefficients, which restrict its long-run applicability.

## Gravity Models

Further insight into the level of urban economic activity obtaining at any time may be derived from gravity, potential, and similar spatial interaction models. The level of economic activity in a given urban area depends on the internal and external relationships. Gravity or interaction models can be used in the analysis of the external relationships of an urban area. Such gravity relationships at an aggregate level describe, of course, both the inflow or import relationships which work to hold down the level of activity in a given urban area and the outflow or export relationships which promote a higher level of activity within that area. These elements may be isolated but in both instances such models suggest that the relationship, for any given urban area, reflects the size and distance away of other urban areas. The competitive element in the urban system is thus recognized and emphasized.

The gravity approach draws heavily on physical analogies in attempting an explanation of the frequency and intensity of interaction between urban areas. The economic flow between two urban areas is hypothesized to be positively related to the "mass" at each point and negatively related to the "friction" operating on movement or contact between those points (Meyer, 1963). In its simplest form this interaction is proportional to the population size of the urban units involved and is in inverse proportion of a certain power of the intervening distance between the urban areas. Thus the volume of economic interaction between urban area $A$ and urban area $B$ would be

$$E = \frac{P_A P_B}{d_{AB}^x}, \tag{9.5}$$

where $E$ represents the volume of economic interaction, $P_A$ the population of urban area $A$, and $P_B$ of urban area $B$ (hence $P_A \times P_B$ equals the total possible number of contacts that could be made), $d_{AB}$ the distance between the two urban areas and exponent $x$ a measure of friction or distance elasticity of demand (Boudeville, 1966, p. 42). The larger the urban populations, the shorter the distance between these urban areas and the easier transport between them the greater will be the volume of economic interaction between these two urban areas and, therefore, the higher will be the aggregate level of urban economic activity.

In terms of the export relationships of urban area $A$ with $B$, i.e. interactions originating in $A$ and terminating in $B$, it would be expected that these represent some proportion of the total relationship and would reflect the relative importance of $B$ to $A$. If this proportion is denoted by the constant $k$ the formula becomes

$$E_{AB} = k \frac{P_A P_B}{d_{AB}^x}, \tag{9.6}$$

where $E_{AB}$ denotes exports from $A$ to $B$. The level of economic activity in $A$ will be higher the greater are its exports to $B$ and these will be higher the larger are the two urban areas, the shorter the distance or easier the movement between them and the greater the value of $k$.

As illustrated here, population has been taken as representative of mass, but this is obviously not wholly suitable for the accurate determination of economic quantities. Mass would probably be better measured, from an economic viewpoint, in terms of purchasing power, income levels, sales figures, employment, or other similar terms. Likewise air-line distance is an inadequate measure of space friction and time–cost–distance measures are better substituted. There are also problems in the practical use of the technique arising from the need

for weightings to be applied to the masses involved, e.g. scale economies become increasingly important as urban size increases and the
urban areas with the largest populations may need "weighting" so that
the importance of such scale economies is recognized. Similar problems are involved in the selection of the exponent by which the friction
element is to be raised, and it is likely that this exponent will vary for
different activities (Isard, 1960, p. 509). Further, it may be questioned
whether the interrelationship of mass and friction is of the straightforward linear nature postulated in the above formula for it is equally
possible to fit quadratic functions to sets of interaction data (Isard,
1960, p. 510).

The gravity model is easily expanded to account for the economic
relationships between a given urban area and all other urban areas.
Thus in population terms, for urban area $A$ the general formula may be
written as

$$E_A = k \frac{P_A P_1}{d_{A_1}^x} + k \frac{P_A P_2}{d_{A_2}^x} + k \frac{P_A P_3}{d_{A_3}^x} \ldots k \frac{P_A P_n}{d_{A_n}^x}, \quad (9.7)$$

where $E_A$ represents exports from $A$ to all other urban areas and 1, 2,
3, . . . , $n$ represent those other urban areas. Equation (9.7) may be
rewritten as

$$E_A = k \sum_{B=1}^{n} \frac{P_A P_n}{d_{A_n}^x}. \quad (9.8)$$

On a per unit of mass basis this may be expressed as

$$\frac{E_A}{P_A} = {_A}V = k \sum_{B=1}^{n} \frac{P_n}{d_{A_n}^x}. \quad (9.9)$$

Equation (9.9) is the basis of potential models, and ${_A}V$ represents the
economic potential at $A$. Analysis of the potentials of various urban
areas may justify the location of certain economic activities in particular urban areas, e.g. a comparison of urban areas on the basis of their
overall sales potential could reveal an optimum urban area for a market
oriented economic activity.

The greater the degree of urbanization (reflected in the number and
size of urban areas) and the smaller the economic distance between

urban areas the greater will be the level of economic activity in urban area *A*. Further refinement can account for any intervening opportunities between any pair of urban areas (Stouffer, 1940).

Such an approach assumes that urban areas are competitive, but this is not always so and, as pointed out in Chapter 2, urban areas may be complementary. Complementarity of urban areas would, of course, alter the economic contacts of a given urban area within a particular set of urban areas, and the extent to which it is a factor modifying gravity-type relationships needs further investigation (Kariel, 1963).

Therefore the level of economic activity in any urban area is, in the short run, largely a function of demand conditions, and here demand for the exports of an urban area can exhibit particular importance. However, the short-run level of activity may or may not be an equilibrium level, nor may it make the best use of resources currently available. The factors discussed in this chapter are thus especially relevant to the level attained by any urban economy in the short run and the stability of that level. Little or no light is shed on the long-run growth of urban areas.

CHAPTER 10

# Urban Economic Growth

## The Nature of Urban Economic Growth

In the long run, factors other than the fortunes of an urban area's current export activities play the vital role in initiating urban growth and promoting change. Changes in the level of exports from an urban area are certainly the major determinant of short-run fluctuations in the level of economic activity in that urban area. Also certain urban areas, largely single basic industry areas, owe their long-run growth to changes in the volume of that basic industry located there. Such changes come about either by the physical expansion of existing productive units or by the addition of new units. But even these urban areas have to keep abreast of technological and market changes in order to maintain a position of comparative advantage. For most urban areas, however, growth is not tied so closely to the fortunes of a single export industry or group of activities but reflects the extent to which new export activities are acquired. New export activities may be acquired, first, alongside the original ones but may, in time, eventually replace the original export industries as the latter decline. The growth of an urban area in the long run, therefore, takes place because of the acquisition of new or substitute economic activities. Urban areas which are unsuccessful in the competition to obtain new economic activities will, therefore, stagnate, even decline, if their existing industries disappear.

An understanding of urban growth, therefore, begins where the analyses of the previous chapter left off, namely with an investigation of the circumstances which lead to the growth of existing industry and with the determination of the locations of units of new economic activity. There are two factors in urban economic growth, the permissive and the implemental (Lane, 1966). The former represents the physical ability or capacity of an urban area to grow in terms of, for example, resource availability. An analysis of the conditions leading to the in-migration of labour and capital and of factors influencing the natural growth of population and labour force of an urban area are important. Implemental factors must, however, be present for actual growth to take place. These are positive or stimulating conditions relating, for example, to the level of product demand, the cost conditions of production, and, especially, the attitude of entrepreneurs.

Growth rates differ between urban areas. On the one hand, urban areas with rapid growth rates are characterized by high levels of labour force participation or high activity rates and hence low unemployment rates; they show a high incidence of overtime working and, as a result, residents enjoy high *per capita* average earnings. Slow growing urban areas, on the other hand, have lower activity rates, higher unemployment rates, and experience out-migration of those with ability and ambition and, therefore, show a more unequal distribution of income at a relatively lower average *per capita* level. Within the overall economic system urban growth is largely of an individual nature, for the continued long-run growth of any urban area depends on its capacity to invent, innovate, or otherwise acquire new export activities. Thus Thompson (Perloff and Wingo, 1968, p. 9) sees the economic base of the large metropolitan urban area as: "the creativity of its universities and research parks; the sophistication of its engineering firms and financial institutions, the persuasiveness of its public relations and advertising agencies, the flexibility of its transport networks and utility systems, and all other dimensions of the infrastructure that facilitate quick and orderly transfer from old dying bases to new growing ones." The growth of only a few urban areas in an urban system to metropolitan size suggests that initial advantage is extremely important to the growth of any urban area in a competitive system. It is a matter of the right timing—to start later than or to begin on a smaller scale than neighbouring urban areas is to court disaster since it can bring a relative competitive disadvantage which is the more difficult to overcome.

Large scale and urban growth go hand in hand. The economic rationale of urban areas and urban growth lies in the external economies provided by and in urban areas. Increased scale of production in manufacturing creates opportunities for scale increases in both private and public service sectors. Increases in scale are not without their problems, but the atmosphere in a large and growing urban area is conducive to problem-solving to a much greater extent than that in a stagnating or declining urban area. Urban size reflecting on the scale of operations may have a significant bearing on the comparative costs/ relative profits of operating a given economic activity in a particular urban area.

Changes taking place during one period of urban growth are related to those occurring during preceding and subsequent periods. Urban economic growth is an interrelated process with each stage of growth being a function of previous stages.

GROWTH STABILITY

Urban growth rates vary not only between areas but also for the same urban area over time. As part of a larger economic system a given urban area will find that its rate of growth varies according to its relative competitive position within that system and, as a consequence, that fluctuations in economic fortunes at the aggregate level may be transmitted to all the parts of the system. Overall some urban areas exhibit more stable growth rates than others. What factors contribute to urban growth rate stability?

Firstly, the extent to which urban areas mirror national business cycles. Individual urban areas may show relative fluctuations of greater or lesser magnitude than the national ones depending upon the mix of economic activities present in those urban areas. If the urban area is an exact microcosm of the national economy the same relative changes would be expected at the urban as at the national level. But urban areas are never exact replicas of the national industry mix. Should an urban area have greater than its relative share of industries producing commodities whose demand is price inelastic then it is likely that that urban area suffers less of a setback in times of deflation or recession and hence its growth rate may be more stable. It must be noted that the point at issue here is the stability of the growth rate, not its magnitude, and circumstances leading to stability need not also lead to the highest rate of growth over time. Alternatively, an urban area concentrating on the

production of producer durable goods will suffer a greater relative setback during deflationary conditions than the nation as a whole since
the accelerator effect magnifies the drop in consumer demand on the
demand for producer goods.

Secondly, the growth prospects of urban areas' export activities
differ. Considering the structure and organizational characteristics of
urban business, then businesses in an urban area with a concentration
of older plants, i.e. marginal productive facilities, will be forced to cut
back more or close down first in a recession and will recover later when
price has risen to a high enough level to cover their higher costs. This
reasoning may also apply to small concerns and to branch plants producing complete products. The future extent of the market for urban
outputs will differ according to industry. It will depend on the nature
of the output—the quality of the commodity, its durability, its use
whether by producers or consumers, and whether it represents a final
or intermediate commodity in the production sequence—and upon the
price and availability of substitutes. In terms of income elasticity of
demand urban areas producing goods with an income elasticity of
demand greater than one have time on their side since the demand for
their output will increase more than proportionately to increases in
income.

Thirdly, urban areas show differing degrees of success in substituting new economic activities for their declining ones. Urban areas
which achieve this substitution prior to the death of declining firms will
show more stable rates of growth than those areas which exhibit a
time lapse before replacements are found for closed firms.

Overall it may be argued that growth produces growth stability, i.e.
that the growth rate becomes more stable with increasing urban size.
Why? Increased urban size brings a greater industrial mix or diversifica-
tion but whether or not it brings cyclical stability depends on the
cyclical fluctuations of the new industries compared to the existing
ones. Continued growth, however, would eventually produce a replica-
tion of national fluctuations. Thus it would appear that the more
heterogeneous the industry mix the more stable the urban growth rate.
Conversely, industrial specialization, which can yield the prize of
maximization of growth rates, can bring the threat of local stagnation
and decline. The larger the urban economy, therefore, the more

diversified its industry mix, the more stable its growth rate and the more it resembles the national economy in both growth rate and growth stability (Thompson, 1965b). However, all urban areas cannot be large, and of the smaller areas not all can possess sufficient plants in stable industries to allow them stable growth rates. Moreover, the growth of large urban areas may be slow because of the lower marginal propensity to consume associated with increased income at the higher level of *per capita* income enjoyed in such areas. Hence there is a need for a proportionately larger volume of investment to stimulate growth than in a smaller area.

## Changing Urban Supply Capacity

In the long run the ability to push back limits to the supply of goods and services imposed by the availability of factors of production is the principal factor in the growth of an urban area. An increase in an urban area's ability to supply goods and services must depend on an increase in the amount of resources available or on improvement in the productive efficiency of existing resources. Most usually it is the result of both. The natural increase of urban population, and hence of the urban labour force, demands expanding employment opportunities if a full employment level of urban economic activity is to be maintained. This is all the more important where technological advance is reducing employment opportunities in existing urban plants. New firms must be acquired, and here the role of the entrepreneur must be emphasized. Certain resources, such as labour and capital funds, will in time follow economic opportunity wherever it is created, but the choice of location, a vital part of the investment decision, rests with the entrepreneur. He expects to reap profits from the results of his action. Similar reasoning applies to technological advance, for the decision to innovate, i.e. give commercial status to an invention, also rests on entrepreneurial decisions. Entrepreneurship and innovation must be the volatile factors in urban growth with successful entrepreneurship and innovation creating the conditions which call forth the necessary supply of other resources.

The size an urban area has already achieved could well be the critical factor in determining the rate and character of its future growth. Large size ensures growth at a near average rate because such urban areas include new fast-growing, middle-aged, slow-growing, and old declining industries. Initial advantage is a key to why some urban areas are larger than others. Moreover, the historical growth of an area may greatly influence its future growth pattern. For example, inherited traits become especially important with reference to the local labour force.

Entrepreneurship looms at the heart of comparative urban growth in an open economic system because of its significance in the decision-taking context. An entrepreneur will invest in new or expanded plant at an urban location because he anticipates a profit from that action. Entrepreneurs must make decisions on the basis of the information currently available to them and it is likely that the spatial field of information is smaller the smaller is the size of firm concerned and the smaller the urban area in which the proprietor/entrepreneur resides. Such small firms may be ephemeral, being dependent upon the wishes of their sole proprietor and thus are likely to die with him. In this case the choice of location will be largely determined by the area in which the entrepreneur lives. Increasing size of firm brings stability to the entrepreneurial situation, and in many cases leads to institutionalization of entrepreneurship via public joint stock companies and boards of directors. Large businesses are more likely to choose locations in large urban areas, and this calls forth ancillary professional services. Where these companies are multi-plant concerns, their routine productive and perhaps administrative operations may be found in smaller urban areas. In such cases that plant may dominate the employment situation in a small urban area whose growth will become dependent upon that branch plant. Moreover, decisions regarding the future of that plant will be largely external to the urban area in which it is located. Persons with entrepreneurial ability but lacking capital funds can find employment in a managerial capacity with large companies, and they tend to gravitate to large urban areas.

Thompson (1965b, p. 455) advances the idea of cycles of local entrepreneurial vigour with increased activity corresponding to periods of crisis in an urban area's growth. Entrepreneurs appear showing a willingness to experiment and try new ideas, and are more aggressive when most needed; thus every crisis produces its saviour. But does it? Small urban areas will not always spawn the entrepreneurial genius at the right time. Many small urban areas cannot drag themselves out of the mire, and so their growth pattern may be erratic depending on when the entrepreneurial genius appears and whether he stays in that small urban area or gravitates to a larger one where he will find more lucrative opportunities. The large urban area will be more likely to have the needed entrepreneurial saviour at hand when the occasion demands.

How are interurban differences in entrepreneurship to be assessed? Here the propensity to innovate in both output and production fields is relevant, and this may well be reflected in firms' willingness to invest in research, to introduce new equipment, etc. However measured—by the geographical distribution of patents issued, by the geographical location of new private investment in industry, etc.—it would appear that the larger the urban area the more numerous the innovators (Ullman, 1958). Innovation at any time is not distributed randomly over the whole economic system (Schumpeter, 1939), and the geographical dimension shows that innovations are non-randomly distributed in space (Pred, 1966, ch. 3), being concentrated in urban areas, especially the large and growing ones. Why? The frequency of innovations in any location is a function of the supply of inventions and of capital funds and the demand for innovations and information regarding existing technological advances. Both inventions and innovations concentrate in urban areas which are growing rapidly. Rapid growth promotes invention and innovation since new equipment can be added without having to scrap the out-dated plant. Where growth is slow, new equipment may be obtained only when the existing plant needs to be replaced. Invention feeds upon itself in large urban areas where there is a tendency for individual industrial inventions to fall into an orderly sequence stemming from the fact that solution-awareness as well as problem-awareness can set the inventive process in motion (Pred, 1966). Each new invention has the possibility of stimulating further inventions in the same productive process because it creates technological disequilibrium between the stages of production and promotes new mechanical devices to serve in other production processes. The process may well be cumulative. Moreover, the atmosphere in a growing urban area facilitates risk taking: entrepreneurs are more willing to shoulder risks in these circumstances and lenders more willing to loan capital funds to finance projects.

If innovation is concentrated in growing and large urban areas, new products and new industries would first appear in such areas. These urban areas provide the necessary skills needed in the early stages of production, and high wages are justifiably paid. With technological advance the product and its processes are routinized and the skill requirement is reduced. Then the high wage rates of the innovating area may appear excessive and so the industry or parts of it filter down or relocate in less industrially sophisticated urban areas, basically the smaller ones, where cheaper labour is now up to the lower occupational demand. Thus Thompson's (1968a, p. 56) filter-down theory of industrial spatial diffusion within an urban system is largely a redistribution of existing industry from innovating areas, and the growth of small urban areas comes about as a result. This is in contrast to the view that changes in industrial distribution patterns come about as the result of functions new to the economy (Madden, 1956).

It would appear, however, that there is an interplay between urban growth and innovation. Innovation, aggressive and successful entrepreneurship, expanding industry, and growth of an urban area go together. Equally a low *per capita* level of inventiveness, conservative and cautious entrepreneurs, largely static industry, and little or slow growth of an urban area, appear likely bedfellows.

## Circular and Cumulative Causation

Urban growth feeds upon itself and may, therefore, be viewed as an interrelated process in which each stage in the development of an urban area is a function of the previous stages (Pred, 1966). The cumulative causation hypothesis (Myrdal 1956, 1957 a, b) thus appears a useful and relevant concept in analysing the spatial concentration of economic growth in urban areas. Consider the probable effects of injecting two or more large plants in a given industry into an existing urban area. New demands will be associated with the needs of the plants themselves— for labour, raw material inputs, and services—and with the requirements of the workers for food, housing, clothing, etc. It is likely that such competitive plants are drawn together in horizontal agglomeration by external economies, in particular, perhaps, by a large local pool of specialized and skilled labour created by their own combined demand. The existence of this urban labour pool may attract further plants in that industry and the job opportunities there will attract immigrants, both skilled and unskilled, to supplement the supply of labour. The spatial clustering of these firms attracts common suppliers and linked industries where the combined demands of these firms surpass the threshold for local production. Vertical agglomeration follows, including perhaps vertical integration with existing firms, as the latter expand backward and forward along the production sequence, as the urban area is chosen as a location by firms supplying equipment to the first industry, or using its byproducts in the manufacture of other goods. The external economies available at that location are multiplied several-fold.

The multiplier effect associated with the original influx and the appearance of linked industry enhances the likelihood of invention and innovation. The technological advance which ensues promotes further the array of scale economies, internal and external, available in that urban area. The locational attraction of these economies increases functionally rather than linearly. Technological advance may often promote the vertical disintegration of an industry but the successive stages of production and/or byproduct industries can still demand locational proximity. The changes taking place will be reflected in alterations to the urban area's population and occupational structure and also in the attainment of further local thresholds for industrial production. The appearance of linked firms and new industries creates a demand for more and better local business services. As these appear and increase in number and efficiency they steadily replace the reliance on similar services previously imported into the urban area. However, such services need access to yet more specialized, say financial, services from elsewhere.

Anyway, the addition of extra firms augments local income and a secondary circular process follows from the enrichment of the urban consumption sector. Capital and enterprise is attracted to meet the expanding internal demand: the tertiary sector and the production of goods for immediate local consumption is expanded, adding further to the general economies available in the urban area. The construction industry will be called upon to add to the stock of urban buildings. Moreover, higher urban income will be reflected in an increased flow of funds to urban government via local taxation and a large proportion of these funds will be spent inproving the urban infrastructure. That action may be decisive in attracting further new industry to the area.

The sequence of reaction is, therefore, circular, each subsequent action reinforcing those before. The multiplier effect will vary from industry to industry since industries attract or support differing amounts of linked activities or face differing income elasticities of demand. It will also vary from place to place and from time to time within a single industry depending in the first case, for example, on the relative isolation of the urban area and in the second case, on the rate of technological progress. The natural increase of urban population provides a further opportunity for developments, as it adds to the demand for goods and, in time, augments the supply of labour. The absolute increase in wages and buying power over time which accompanies economic growth further accelerates the process. The process is illustrated in Fig. 10.1, where a much simplified application of circular and

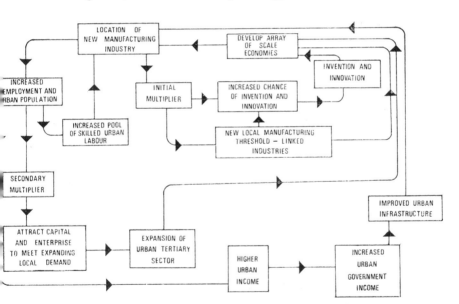

FIG. 10.1. Circular and cumulative causation applied to economic growth of urban area.

cumulative causation to urban growth is represented. The essential circularity of the process is evident although a number of subsets are included to indicate the complexities involved in real life.

If urban areas were non-competitive and had a perfectly elastic supply of resources, the circular and cumulative growth process in each urban area would continue indefinitely, at an irregular pace, until impeded by certain diseconomies. For example, when the urban area has grown too large in terms of the physical area occupied, problems of internal communication and transport would arise, such as increasing journey lengths and, because of traffic congestion, increasing journey times. Probably a more effective brake on the growth of a given urban area is any competitive advantage possessed by neighbouring, concomitantly growing urban areas. Initial advantage, entrepreneurial and resource factors, and infrastructural base are some of the reasons why activities may find the comparative costs of operation more favourable in other urban areas. Indeed, the growth of an urban area may have a "backwash" effect on neighbouring, less economically developed urban areas in the sense that spatial flows of labour, capital, and other resources develop to support the largest urban area. Neighbouring urban areas lose their skilled workers and much of their locally generated capital. At the same time goods originating in the large urban area may flood the markets in neighbouring urban areas, perhaps putting out of business their local industries and certainly inhibiting the further development of those industries in these other urban areas. Hence the growth of one urban area may frustrate the growth of other urban areas.

However, the growth of an urban area may also have centrifugal or "spread" effects. Its growth may stimulate demand for raw materials which must be produced in other urban areas, so promoting their growth. If the spread effects are more significant than the backwash effects, this will generate a process of cumulative causation in other urban areas. This is most likely the more advanced the national economy.

## Location Theory and Relative Profitability

The analysis so far has assumed the existence of manufacturing activity in an urban area or has assumed, at least, that manufacturing will be injected into an urban area. Granted the value of such analyses in tracing the chain of repercussions linked to the expansion or contraction and injection of industry for an urban area, little attention was given to the stimulus or origin of manufacturing change. What industries and how much of each exist or will develop in an urban area remain critical but unanswered questions. Location theory indicates the factors which are likely to bring about differences in the relative profitability of operating in each of the urban areas competing for the economic activities in question.

An urban area attracts a share of the investment in new, including expanding, plant on the basis of its locational advantages, the latter reflecting in the profit levels of operating such plant in that urban area. Growth of an urban area will then depend on its investment opportunities relative to those in other urban areas. Two viewpoints are possible here—the firm's and the urban area's. The individual firm is seeking a location in an urban area which will maximize its profits. The urban area, with its limited resource availability, seeks to compare firms and industries on the basis of their relative profitability. It seeks those firms and industries which yield the highest levels of profit from operating at locations within that urban area since, *ceteris paribus*, such firms are likely to generate the highest levels of urban income. Thus a firm for which urban area $A$ would appear to offer the profit-maximizing location may not be able to obtain resources or sites in urban area $A$ because that area is an even more profitable location for other firms and industries which can, therefore, command the available resources and sites in urban area $A$. Hence, depending on its spatial margin of profitability, that firm finds that its profit-maximizing location is in an alternative urban area. Likewise an urban area may not attract that firm or industry which could make the highest profit at that location because such firms or industries are able to make even higher profits elsewhere. Therefore the emphasis is placed on relative profitability for, in economic systems operating under the profit motive, optimum locations must always exert an attraction.

However, it must be remembered that it is only in a market economy which is competitive throughout that there is a compulsion to achieve optimum locations by the threat of elimination of activities not located optimally. For a monopolist there is no such compulsion (Beckmann,

1968, p. 9), although he must pay a price for any sub-optimal location. This illustrates that actual locations may differ from those considered optimal under a perfectly competitive economic system and this renders more difficult the evaluation of real-life locational choice. It is assumed, however, that some degree of optimizing behaviour under-lies any locational decision.

Location theory suggests that an urban area's attraction for economic activity depends on (1) its access at competitive costs to inputs, and (2) its access at competitive costs to markets for its outputs. Different urban areas will incur different levels of cost in performing these tasks be-cause spatial immobilities and inelasticities retard or prevent cost and price equalization throughout space. By emphasizing, for example, geographical immobility of labour the urban labour market becomes autonomous and the local balance of supply and demand is critical in setting the urban wage rate (Thompson, 1965a, ch. 2). A comparative cost study will summarize an urban area's relative locational advantages for each firm or industry. From a basis of established or anticipated markets, known production functions and a given spatial distribution of inputs a comparative cost study for a given firm can establish the point of lowest total cost of production and delivery of products to markets. From a systematic listing of cost differentials between urban areas that urban area with the lowest total cost will be apparent and this urban area would be chosen as the most profitable location for that firm. Such analysis can also be employed to ascertain the effect of changes, such as the discovery of a new source of an input or a new method of production, on the optimum location. Incorporated into the analysis will be a consideration of whether the feasible size of plant differs between urban areas since locations tapping larger markets may yield opportunities for scale economies which more than offset any increases in the costs of input assembly. The comparative cost ap-proach can thus determine the relative profitability of a location for a unit of economic activity and this will be of immense value in the in-vestment decision faced by that unit.

The approach is not without its limitations for the price–cost structure and the magnitude of the market are taken as given. Where the firm or industry is small and has little or no influence on demand, prices, and costs, this is probably justifiable, but it is less warranted where the firm or industry has a marked influence on these factors. For such firms and industries different locations may, for example, provide varying opportunities in respect of turnover because of differences in selling price and/or number of purchasers. Moreover, the analysis is presented in partial equilibrium terms for the actions of other firms, etc., other than the one under study, are taken as static. Input–output or similar analysis would be needed to supplement the comparative cost approach in order to determine the multiplier effects of a location decision on the chosen urban area. For a given change in an activity the kind of growth or decline that follows will depend on the extent to which the new activity is closely tied to, or is independent of, the associated processes that precede and follow it.

Furthermore, consideration of the interaction of economic and non-economic factors may be necessary. Comparative cost analysis may well show a location in a particular urban area to be favourable for a firm in cost–profit terms but the firm's attempts to develop that site may be resisted, even aborted, due to non-economic factors such as community attitudes, political organization, and cultural patterns. Development and growth will proceed more readily where the optimum economic sites are spatially associated with, for instance, favourable community attitudes. Measurement of these non-economic factors is subjective but can be attempted by scaling and latent structure techniques (Isard, 1960, pp. 281–93).

## New Investment

Possible investment in a new or expanded plant at one location must be weighed against anticipated returns from investment at other locations and often against other types of investment opportunities. Hence new investment is a critical element in the economic growth of an urban area. Such investment decisions represent increments in or additions to the stock of capital goods and are determined at the margin. The market mechanism directing investment funds between urban areas operates in the same way as for the national economy (Czamanski, 1965), with priority in the allocation of funds being determined by the anticipated rate of return or relative profitability of the capital sum to be invested. Investment funds may be relatively mobile between urban areas in a developed economy as well as between types of investment. As a significant proportion of new investment is financed by borrowed funds, the opportunity cost element of the decision from the firm's and especially the lender's points of view looms large.

New industrial investment in an urban area may stem from two sources—the birth of new, independent units of activity, and the expansion of existing plants. In the latter case the expansion may or may not be spatially separated from the location of the existing establish-

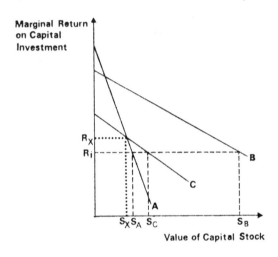

FIG. 10.2. Relative investment opportunities in urban areas.

ment. Indeed, it is often cheaper, though not necessarily more profitable, to expand capacity at the existing site than to construct a new plant on another site. Very often problems are encountered in obtaining land adjacent to the existing plant and expansion there is not feasible. Suppose the investment schedules for investing in, say, retailing in three urban areas are as shown in Fig. 10.2. These schedules will reflect the various factors influencing the level of retail investment; thus for each urban area the marginal rate of return per unit of capital funds is plotted against the total value of the capital stock, i.e. shops. Assume a level of return $R_i$ at which investment is just profitable, that the level is the same for each urban area, and that the rate is independent of the capital stock in each urban area. Then urban area $A$ will support shops/retail floor space to a capital value of $S_A$, urban area $B$ will support $S_B$, and urban area $C$, $S_C$.

Suppose, at any given time, the capital value of the retail stock in urban area $B$ is $S_B$ but in both $A$ and $C$ it is only $S_X$. This would imply a marginal rate of return in both $A$ and $C$ of $R_X$. $R_X$ is greater than $R_i$, therefore it is profitable to add to shopping capacity in urban areas $A$ and $C$ but not in $B$. Thus it is quite possible for an urban area to have favourable conditions for the production of a given commodity or service but not show any growth because opportunities for new investment are less favourable in that area relative to other urban areas. The figure also illustrates that growth prospects are not equal for urban areas $A$ and $C$, for there will be a greater increase in shopping capacity in $C$. In both cases investment is pushed to a point where the marginal rate of return has fallen to a level where no further investment is profitable and, under the circumstances postulated, the same rate holds for investment in $A$ and $C$.

Investment schedules are not static and will shift differently for the urban areas depending on changes in businessmen's opinions regarding the future which, in turn, reflect invention and innovation, population change, changes in consumer tastes, and the like.

In summary it may be stated, therefore, that an urban area will attract those activities and that number of units of those activities for which it offers optimal, i.e. profit-maximizing locations. These activities will be, from the urban area's view, ones for which it has a natural or economic advantage as reflected in their having the greatest ratio of relative advantage or least ratio of relative disadvantage. Profit levels and relative advantage levels rarely remain constant since many factors —transport improvements, institutional changes, etc.—promote change, and new investment will respond in time as the status and prospects of each urban area are altered.

## Government and Relative Urban Advantage

In any mixed economy, government action will have a considerable influence on the relative opportunities for inter-urban development. In particular, there will be a close limit to the extent to which the Government can allow a large and/or specialized urban area to stagnate or decline. Government measures are introduced to facilitate an urban area's transition from one industrial base to another. However, many such measures are permissive in the sense that benefit only follows where the affected urban authorities take the initiative to improve their infrastructure with grants-in-aid. Any new industry subsequently attracted to such an urban area will also qualify for aid in cash and kind.

Why should industry voluntarily locate in a stagnating or declining urban area? Normally industry would gravitate to alternative urban areas which exhibit greater relative advantages. New industry is only likely to locate in stagnating or declining urban areas if (1) the size of the inducement outweighed any relative disadvantage of the location, and (2) it was prevented, by other government controls, from developing at otherwise more attractive locations. Legislation to check the growth of the more successful urban areas is, therefore, a necessary counterpart of any policy to aid disadvantage urban areas. Thus in this and many other ways, government action may influence and alter the relative opportunities for inter-urban development.

### The Stages of Urban Growth

Urban areas are both the instrument and the symbol of economic growth and development and discussion so far in this chapter has emphasized the role of urban areas in initiating, promoting, and fostering economic growth. Attention may also be focused on the success or otherwise of a particular urban area by viewing the stages in urban growth which are expressive of the economic characteristics expected to accompany that same growth process.

Thompson (1965a, ch. 1) recognizes five stages in the urban growth sequence. Most existing urban areas had their roots in villages where rural occupations and customs were preserved and the economic emphasis was on self-sufficient subsistence with little or no investment and trade. Increased population and the diminishing returns witnessed in agriculture partly forced the turn to industrialization and, with concomitant improvements in the field of transport, increased trade, investment, and local specialization were made possible. Thus the primary stage of urban existence has been the recognition of an export specialism, i.e. production for a market spatially distributed beyond the confines of the immediate urban area. An urban area would attract, because of its relative economic advantages of material availability, labour supply, market accessibility, etc., the production of a certain commodity. This initial advantage would be capitalized on. Very often the local urban economy would be in the shadow of a single dominant industry, even of one firm. At this stage an urban area frequently lacks sufficient income to provide a substantial share of its own needed investment capital and must, therefore, rely on outside sources. Such external capital is invested primarily in existing export industry (North, 1955).

Development and growth of the urban area proceeds by widening the economic base, so developing an export complex which represents the second stage of growth. The concentration of the industry leads to the development of a labour pool which serves to attract other firms in that industry as well as common suppliers. The latter promote vertical agglomeration and add to local exports indirectly by increasing the proportion of the industry's turnover that remains within the urban area. Local "value added" thus represents a higher proportion of selling price. Byproduct firms appear, and other firms reliant upon that type of labour or associated technical processes are also attracted. The multiplier effect shows itself in the form of linked firms and industries, and the range of local production for export is consequently broadened.

The third stage witnesses the urban area's economic maturation as the excessive dependence on its export economy and hence, on imports of all other requirements, is lessened. Certain imports are replaced by local production. Growth has a multiplier effect in terms of local consumption industries as well as linked export industries. The latter demand more and better local services, and as these increase in number the service sector develops. The growing local market pulls one activity after another across the threshold of economic local production. Thus a broadening export base is accompanied by a tendency for greater self-sufficiency as the urban area grows in size. First, activities with only modest scale economies and high transport costs and then larger scale economies and lower transport costs locate in the urban area. The more isolated an urban area the more it is forced into attempting to become self-sufficient at low levels of output in many goods and services, but such relatively high unit costs of production impose penalties in terms of the proportion of income it consumes.

Growth increases the range of functions an urban area performs. Where growth is achieved relatively faster than neighbouring centres, that urban area may move up the functional hierarchy and export a growing range of services to smaller nearby urban areas. The extent of growth may be sufficient to attract branch plants of outside firms. In this fourth stage an urban area, therefore, becomes a node connecting and controlling neighbouring urban areas. Should the urban area develop this tertiary specialization further, then it may embrace the nation for a narrow group of services. It will then have reached the fifth and last of Thompson's stages, that of technical-professional virtuosity. The urban area has then achieved national eminence in some special skill or economic function. Indeed, this stage could, for certain urban areas, precede its emergence as a regional metropolis, and in a few restricted cases it may be possible to create an urban area at this level, as with national capitals like Canberra.

Thompson's stages of urban growth emphasize the addition of new economic functions with increasing urban size. Certainly urban areas take on new functions as they grow but the process is not a simple one. Such changes take place at the margin and would be reflected, in one instance, in increases and decreases in urban employment opportunities (Stanback and Knight, 1970). Net employment change masks the extent to which changes are taking place. The growth process affects the competitive position of a firm or industry. As an urban area grows not only the number and type of functions performed alter but also the level of wages, productivity, taxes, and availability of amenities. This allows some industries to expand, new industries to emerge. But other industries may outgrow the urban area in which they are located, or are themselves outgrown by that urban area. Employment opportunities in these industrial sectors will decline. Such decreases must be offset against employment increases elsewhere in the urban area. As the spinning-off of some export-type industry to lower order urban areas is to be expected with growth then, in employment terms, the rate of expansion may decrease with increasing urban size. The largest urban areas must, therefore, be continually innovating new economic activities which they can sell/export to smaller urban areas. Otherwise large urban areas will fail to maintain their relative position.

## Limits to Urban Growth

At the aggregate or national level the limits to urban growth will be set largely by the rate of population increase and the proportion of the nation's population that can be maintained in urban areas by home agriculture and imported foodstuffs. Given the rate of technological advance and of transport improvements, this limit is flexible for any nation and adjusts with time as required. More significant because more immediately operative, are the limits to the growth of a particular urban area.

Growth of the individual urban area, as pointed out above, depends on relative opportunities, for investment in particular compared to neighbouring and competing urban areas. If prospects are worse than in competing centres, then growth will be inhibited. Existing conditions, attitudes, availability of resources, surplus capacity, etc., will reflect on and influence such prospects. Thus the progress of an urban area from the stage of export specialization to that of developed export complex may be postponed because initial conditions may not be sufficiently favourable to build the specialized labour pool and call forth the necessary supply of other resources which would draw complementary firms to that area. It could even be that an existing firm or industry enjoys certain scale economies which are important relative to the size of the market and which, therefore, reduce opportunities for other firms. Growth is hindered where competitive conditions impede the entry of competitors. Also large investment in plant and equipment, i.e. fixed costs, which gives substantially lower unit costs at large outputs, will hinder the development of firms in that industry elsewhere.

Similarly, the movement from export complex to economic maturation may be thwarted because the growth of export industry is slowed down. For example, if the export industry does not enjoy as large internal scale economies as expected, it will not be able to compete as effectively in interregional competition with other urban areas, and the area's drawing power for complementary firms will be limited. As a result the local market does not expand to a size sufficient to induce the creation of local service firms, and these services will continue to be obtained from outside the urban area. An inefficient local service sector, reflected in high prices, may also inhibit growth and encourage export firms to continue to rely on the availability of those services at lower prices from alternative urban centres. Momentum in the export complex may be lost, due to a decline in the external demand for products of that area's export industries. Consequently the urban economy may stagnate, even suffer recession and depression, where the decline in demand is secular. Out-migration, a traditional economist's response to the solution of this situation, is exceedingly sluggish where unemployment is chronic. In depressed urban areas the local government's revenue drops alarmingly whereas its welfare costs soar. In certain areas imaginative schemes are produced by local administrators and businessmen to promote the area's industrial rejuvenation: but many towns never meet this challenge. The ability to substitute one export activity for another depends on such factors as labour force skills, local business services, and market potential. Ghost towns are a most dramatic indication that such substitution is not always possible and that absolute decline is not without precedence.

Beyond the third stage of Thompson's classification, opportunities for urban areas to grow are exceedingly limited: only a few urban areas can attain supremacy in the urban hierarchy and fill positions where they control the functioning of urban areas at lower levels in the hierarchy. Inter-urban competition will determine the urban areas which fill these élite positions. Initial advantage and early large size are powerful weapons in achieving and maintaining an urban area's rank in the hierarchy. However, problems of urban organization increase probably more than proportionately with increases in sheer urban size and management may appear as a factor severely limiting urban growth (Thompson, 1965a, p. 24). The supply of managerial and entrepreneurial ability of the calibre demanded to deal with the organizational problems of the regional and national metropolises is highly limited, and the urban areas concerned must compete with the many multi-product, multi-unit joint-stock companies for the available talent—very often unsuccessfully. Thus the level of urban technology, together with the quality of urban management, in part determines urban size in the short run. The growth of a particular urban area may hesitate or stagnate at any stage in the growth process, although already having attained large size is as good a guarantee as any of continued growth prospects of at least average rate.

Overall the growth of a particular urban area reflects its comparative advantages for the performance of economic activities and in the attraction of entrepreneurial and inventive–innovative capacities. In economically advanced societies, in the absence of government action to the contrary, the advantage must seemingly lie with already large urban areas, although it is accepted that imperfections of knowledge may allow random opportunities at alternative urban locations. Any increase in the degree of knowledge pertaining to decision taking would tend to increase the likelihood of economic development and expansion within the vicinity of major urban areas. Hence the idea of a ratchet mechanism (Thompson, 1965b, p. 442) in urban growth, i.e. the attainment of a minimum size above which growth is virtually guaranteed and decline is impossible.

# CHAPTER 11

# The Size and Spacing of Urban Areas

## The Space Economy

Urban areas come into existence as products of and focal points in the economic life of a community that has reached a certain stage of economic development. Even if the earth's surface were perfectly uniform, urban areas would still appear because of the economic advantages associated with an urban way of life. Indeed, the macro-location of economic activities and population in economically advanced societies tends towards an ever-increasing concentration in a limited number of very large urban areas or metropolitan regions (Clark, 1968, ch. 8). The economic system, of which urban areas are an integral part, is also a space economy, and just as the growth of an individual urban area reflects relative economic opportunities compared to neighbouring and competing urban areas, so the spatial distribution of urban areas also reflects an economic rationale.

The spatial distribution of urban areas reflects man's efforts to achieve an ordered adjustment to the distance factor. Observed distributional patterns have been brought about because society demands the maximum productivity from every location consistent with the maximization of the amount of spatial interaction at the minimum cost. Thus, given the natural disposition of minerals and the state of technology, the space–size distribution of urban areas is such as to secure all output at minimum cost to society's limited stock of resources (Lampard, 1955). All locations have some degree of accessibility, some more than others, and locational decisions are taken to minimize the frictional effects of distance. Those decisions, therefore, reflect the relative access advantages of different locations. Economic space may thus be viewed as a field of forces in which poles or vectors of economic forces arise. Urban areas are found where such poles occur. This focal or agglomerative tendency of persons and economic activities is enhanced by opportunities to benefit from scale economies.

The foregoing suggests that the factors accounting for the spatial distribution of urban areas cannot be treated as independent variables but represent the interaction of forces indigenous to the economic system itself. Three interrelated sets of reasons have an influence on urban spatial distributions: urban areas appear at strategic locations in the transport network, or as the outcome of local concentrations of specialized activities, or as central places meeting the service needs of a rural hinterland. The first case produces an essentially linear pattern, the second is characterized by clusters of specialist manufacturing and/or mining centres, and the last by a regular distribution of central places. In practice, elements of the three patterns will be combined and the relationship between size and spacing of urban areas will thus appear more irregular but will not, however, be arbitrary.

Urban areas are spatially separated from one another although they are inevitably linked through participation in the economic system. Any attempt to explain the spatial distribution in economic terms must have regard to two components: a horizontal one and a vertical one. On the horizontal plane it must be recognized that the larger the urban area the greater the distance separating that area from another urban area of similar size. Also, large urban areas seldom appear isolated but are almost always surrounded, at varying distances, by smaller urban centres, varying in size, with which they are economically and socially intertwined. The vertical component recognizes that with decreasing size of urban area the number of urban areas increases. This size continuum, ranging from a small number of very large urban areas to large numbers of very small urban areas, is essentially hierarchical in its organizational character. Functional specialization between urban areas creates a need for a control hierarchy, even for urban areas specializing in manufacturing.

## Determinants of Size of an Urban Area

### SIZE OF MARKET

The size of an individual urban area depends on the number and type of economic activities choosing to locate in that area and the extent to which specialization is possible within all or some of those activities. Given the level of technological knowledge, specialization depends, in the short-run, on the size of the market for the product. Size of market in turn depends on productivity. The demand of consumers living outside a given urban area for commodities produced in that area will depend on the delivered price at which each commodity can be obtained from that urban area relative to the delivered price at which they are available from competing urban areas. Consumers will, *ceteris paribus*, purchase from that urban area which offers them the commodity at the lowest delivered price. Delivered price reflects cost of production at the urban location and costs of transport from the urban area to the consumer's location. Hence the transport cost element of delivered price increases with increasing distance of the consumer from the given urban area. A point must be reached for any good or service where it becomes more expensive to obtain it from the given urban area than from elsewhere. Thus in Fig. 11.1 it would be cheaper for a consumer residing at $R$ to purchase the given commodity from the industry located in urban area $X$ since he can obtain it for a delivered price of $P_1$. This compares with a next lowest delivered price of $P_2$ if he was to buy from the competing industry in urban area $A$. Hence consumers between $X$ and $L$ will find it cheaper to buy from $X$ and consumers beyond $L$ from $A$. Delivered price from $A$ and $X$ is the same at $L$, and this equals the market boundary between the two competing urban areas. Similar reasoning applies to delivered price at $M$ in the case of competition between $X$ and $B$. Such market limits will be different for the various goods and services produced in an urban area and need not be equi-distant in all directions for a given commodity as there is no unique correlation between distance and cost of transport. Transhipment costs may raise delivered prices in one direction, whereas low back-haul rates lower them in another direction. Exactly the same principles apply to outsiders coming to an urban area to obtain services for the limits to the extent of the market will still reflect production costs and transport costs. The consumer visits that urban area which is able to provide him with the requisite service at the lowest total cost.

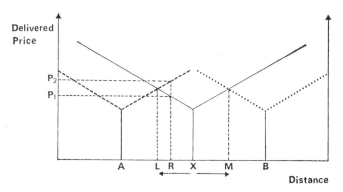

FIG. 11.1.   Determination of market boundaries for a good produced in several urban areas. Height of vertical lines at *A*, *X*, and *B* represents production costs at those sites.

Here, then, is justification for not concentrating all economic activities in a single urban area. Customers in a particular geographical location may be supplied with a given commodity at a lower delivered price from a small urban area than from a competing, larger urban area. This is not to deny that the larger the urban area the greater the likelihood that it benefits from lower production costs associated with greater specialization. It indicates, however, that such advantages are more than offset by transport costs when supplying that commodity to certain potential customers. No matter how large an urban area there must be limiting points to its market beyond which other urban areas have a relative price advantage in supplying that good or service. Therefore, the size of an urban area depends on the size of the market for the products of its economic activities.

For any given commodity there may be alternative factor combinations which yield given levels of output. Moreover, as pointed out in Chapter 2, certain minimum levels of output must be attained before certain specialized and indivisible factor units are employed. Size of market is, therefore, critical in determining whether, at any given time, a particular factor combination yields the minimum, i.e. the threshold or normal profit level necessary to induce the use of that combination. As thresholds reach higher and higher levels, the possibilities of entering the market or expanding existing facilities are confined to a smaller and smaller number of urban areas. Indeed, manufacturing functions may shift from small to large urban areas, becoming more geographically concentrated and leaving in the smallest urban areas only those activities which reap no scale economy benefits and which can be satisfied with the market level offered in such areas.

Individual urban areas have to meet competition from other urban areas in the space economy. It would appear that the larger the urban area the larger the local market and, therefore, the greater that urban area's competitive advantage.

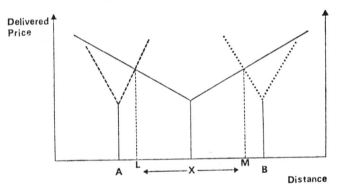

Fig. 11.2. Effect of differences in transport costs on size of market and size of urban area.

Cost of production and size of market are thus interrelated because size of market is a main determinant of levels of specialization. Advantages of specialization can only be reaped, in the spatial context, by incurring additional transport costs. Given the same cost of production for the various commodities in all urban areas, then that urban area with the cheapest transport facilities will have the largest market area for the goods it produces. This would be true of urban area $X$ in Fig.

11.2. Urban area $X$ will, therefore, be larger than urban areas $A$ and $B$. If transport costs were the same for all urban areas, then that urban area with the lowest production costs would be the largest, e.g. urban area $C$ in Fig. 11.3.

Moreover, urban areas possessing relative transport advantages find these reinforced by relative production cost advantages because better accessibility increases their markets which in turn allows them to benefit from greater scale economies. Technical innovations, yielding lower

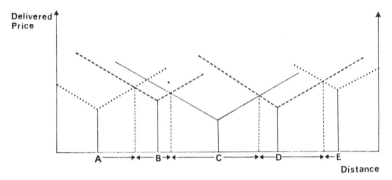

Fig. 11.3. Effect of differences in production costs on size of market and size of urban area.

per unit production costs, also favour the growth of an industry in those urban areas where efficient production is already established and deters development in non-producing and inefficient locations. Specialization makes for higher productivity over time and also tends to concentrate productive activities within the spatial system. Even so, the decreasing costs associated with large outputs in any particular urban area are subject to diminishing returns and will, at any given time, be offset by rising transport costs to increasingly distant markets. Given freedom of entry to the industry, other competitors will begin production in urban areas beyond the range of effective competition from the first urban area.

The size of an urban area is thus a function of the number of economic activities that locate within it, hence of the number and size of firms within each industry—all of which are dependent on the size of the market and the state of technological knowledge. Urban functions, urban size, and relative locational advantages are positively correlated for urban areas with relative locational advantages have better balanced economies, i.e. they perform more functions. Such urban areas, therefore, have larger populations and cover larger areas.

SCALE ECONOMIES

As already suggested, the advantages of concentrating production, for some goods and services, in one or a few urban areas more than outweigh the additional transport costs involved in reaching customers furthest from the place of production. Immense factories, reflecting these production advantages for single or joint products, draw large populations to their vicinities, thus creating and supporting, almost single-handed, urban areas of some size. Successive stages in production are also drawn together in space because of advantages of concentration as well as the desire to avoid high transport costs on intermediate products. This gives rise to industrial complexes which form the basis of large urban areas and conurbations. Indeed, conventional production theory might lead one to believe that economies of scale and mobility of factors of production would eventually bring all economic activities together in one great urban centre (Haig, 1926). This has not, of course, happened, and the persistence of small urban areas indicates that transport costs to scattered markets cannot immediately be offset in every case by economies in plant operation.

The advantages of the spatial concentration of production would appear to be threefold, stemming from (1) the growth of single large firms reaping internal economies of scale, (2) the congregation of firms engaged in a given industry in a particular urban area which affords opportunities to benefit from external economies of scale once the accumulation of firms has reached a certain size, (3) the coacervation of firms in different industries in the same urban area which generates general urban agglomeration economies.

*Internal Economies*

Internal economies of scale have varying significance for the production of goods and services. Every activity has some minimum sized market that its internal scale economies require for profitable production and distribution. Certain products may be tied to localized markets for reasons such as bulk and perishability, and such productive activities are likely to be found in all urban areas. At the other end of the scale, where internal economies are dominant and the goods produced are distributed nationally, then all urban markets could be served from one location by a single plant. Then, if one producer has pre-empted the national market, the excellence of sites in other areas for that same production will avail nothing. Therefore internal scale economy advantages preclude the presence of every economic activity in every urban area and, hence, urban areas of different size must develop.

Given the same relationship between unit output and supported population for all activities, then that urban area attracting the greatest number of national market activities, and having its full complement of lesser activities, will be the largest urban area in population terms. Next largest will be the urban area with the second largest number of such activities, and so on down the scale to urban areas with fewer such national activities to urban areas supplying only regional markets, down to urban areas supplying only local markets.

## External Economies

Similar reasoning can be applied to the case of external economies although this time the effects are dependent on the size of the industry rather than the size of the individual firm. External scale advantages were explained in Chapter 2. As with internal economies, they also differ in significance for industries depending on such factors as the average size of firm in an industry or the nature of the commodity. For example, where inter-firm commodity comparison is important, clustering in space extends the size of the market.

Where external scale economies in an industry are nationally dominant, the firms in that industry will cluster in a particular urban area or group of adjacent urban areas. That urban area or urban cluster which attracts the largest number of such industries plus national market-oriented single industry/firms will be the largest urban area and so on down the scale to urban areas which cannot offer external scale economy opportunities.

*Urban Agglomeration Economics*

The analysis could be repeated for urban agglomeration economies which draw together firms in different industries. Larger urban areas have a clear and sizeable advantage in such areas as cheap and flexible transport and utility systems, better research and development facilities, a more skilled and varied labour force, and better facilities for educating and retraining workers. All of these are economies to be captured by private firms as lower private costs. Newer industries, and especially small firms, are, therefore, drawn to large urban areas, and so great metropolitan centres are created. Moreover, in the capital will be found all those activities whose scale requirements exceed the scale of the economy. Manufacturing on a grand scale must, therefore, be limited to a few urban areas or urban clusters. Furthermore, the advantages of production concentration in a few large urban areas is enhanced by freight-charging practices discriminating against finished goods and by the easy transmission of motive power which accompanied the development of electricity.

Therefore, in any space economy, there will develop a size continuum of urban areas based on productive economic activity. The form of this continuum will reflect the relative importance for all economic activities of these various scale economies. Its form will be most regular where different economic activities are affected differently by these scale economies: it will be most step-like the more common are groups of economic activities which are similarly affected by the various types of scale economy.

## Urban Size Distributions

Empirical evidence confirming a relatively regular relationship between size and number of urban areas has led to attempts to define the number–size ratio in precise terms. There are relatively fewer large urban areas than middle-sized ones; middle-sized urban areas in turn are less numerous than small urban areas. The relationship between urban size and number of urban areas has been formalized in the rank–size rule (Zipf, 1949) and is given by the formula

$$P_r = P_1 (r)^{-1}, \qquad (11.1)$$

where $P_1$ is the population of the largest or first-ranking urban area in size and $P_r$ is the population of the urban area of rank $r$. Accepting the rank–size rule as an accurate relationship, it would be expected that the third largest urban area would have a population about one-third that of the largest urban area. This is, of course, an empirically based finding, not a theoretical or logical construct (Stewart, 1958), and it must be allowed that there is a range of behaviour over time as well as through space. Plotted on double-log paper, the rank–size rule appears as a straight line, e.g. see Fig. 11.4 where the size of the largest urban area is assumed to be 4 million.

Such rank–size regularity applies throughout the world for national space economies which attain both a high level of economic development and urbanization for large countries and for countries such as India and China which, in addition to being large, have a long urban tradition (Berry, 1961). In other cases a marked gap may appear between the largest urban area (or areas) and the smaller urban area distribution. This is classed as a primate distribution, and one possible example is shown for comparative purposes in Fig. 11.4. Primate distributions characterize urban development in small national space economies, with a short history of urbanization and a simple economic and political pattern. A primate distribution, therefore, represents the impact of a few strong forces. The suggestion that many distributions with some degree of primacy take on a more rank–size form as level of economic development and degree of urbanization increase is not fully supported (Berry, 1960, 1961).

Increasing complexity of a space economy, as suggested above, will bring many more factors to bear on urban size and results in the urban size distribution moving closer to the rank–size pattern. The stability of the rank–size relationship over space and time suggests that it can be viewed as a steady-state phenomenon (Simon, 1955), i.e. a dynamic equilibrium condition dependent on a host of small random forces. The size of an urban area is positively correlated with the number of economic activities which locate within it. Urban areas are increasingly the centre of market-oriented activities which are affected differently by the various scale economies and other factors. Urban areas of different size must emerge and some statistical regularity associated with urban size is not unexpected.

## Optimum Size of Urban Area

It has been supposed that there is some optimum or maximum size of urban area beyond which growth stops because that area has become highly inefficient and undesirable as a place for living and carrying on economic activities. The ill effects of urban growth—traffic congestion,

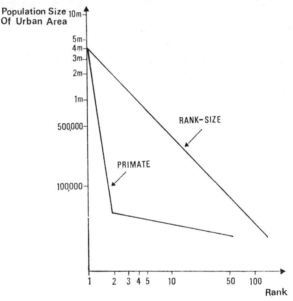

Fig. 11.4  Urban size distributions.

pollution, environmental deterioration, etc.—have been much publicized, but if such a maximum size exists, these ill effects have not been sufficient to prevent the further growth of large urban areas. Continued growth of large urban areas suggests that the benefits of growth more than outweigh the extra economic costs accompanying that growth. The limit may not, in fact, have been surpassed.

Is there an optimum or best size for an urban area? Optimality and urban function should be considered together. The answer, therefore, depends upon the criterion. Any criterion will contain two elements: a normative element where a valuation or judgement is placed on a particular situation, and an empirical element which reveals the relationship between urban size and the variable in question. Various criteria for optimum size of urban area are possible having regard to (1) the physical layout of the urban area in terms of, perhaps, journey-to-work or access to open country, (2) the health of the urban population where facilities for treatment or the risk/incidence of certain diseases and disorders may be considered, (3) the economic efficiency of the functioning of the urban area which will reflect the efficiency of municipal government, the diversity of the economic base, and other factors, and (4) community participation which can be measured in numerous ways to evaluate the quality of the urban way of life as well as to other evidence. There can be no general optimum, and optimum size of urban area will differ according to the criterion. Furthermore, conflicting evidence may be available in the case of an apparently simple criterion. For example, in terms of the risk of ill health, large urban areas have a decided advantage in the early years of a person's life but, as long-term environmental effects of living in large urban areas become apparent, so the advantage is surrendered to smaller-sized urban areas (Lillibridge, 1952). There is no obvious way in which all the conflicting evidence can be balanced, compromised, or weighted to yield the optimum. Indeed, such a search is unrealistic, and necessarily involves heavy reliance on personal value judgements, so producing wide variations in answers. For example, on the basis of subjective estimates Howard (1898) considered 30,000 to be the optimum size, whilst Le Corbusier (1947) preferred 3 million.

Economic efficiency is widely accepted as a socially desirable goal. Considered from an economic point of view, the optimum size for an urban area would be that population and organization of land use which, given available resources and technological and social conditions, maximizes net product and utilities per head of population (Lean and Goodall, 1966, p. 213). This criterion has two implications. Firstly, there is an optimum population for the most efficient performance of productive activities and social relationships. Any increase of population beyond this level creates difficulties out of all proportion to the benefits received. Secondly, there is an optimum area beyond which further growth hinders rather than promotes the efficient execution of an urban area's functions. However, the horizontal or vertical distribution of an urban population of a given size will depend on the physical nature of the site; thus location can have a bearing on the optimality question. Economic criteria regarding optimum populations are especially applicable to closed economies with a given amount of resources and no outside trading links. This renders their application to urban areas which are open economies the more difficult.

What evidence is there regarding the relationship between urban size and economic efficiency? The economic advantages of large urban size are basically the same as the economic advantages of urbanization and should, therefore, be reflected in a higher output per head of population as urban size increases. Income per worker and income per family are positively correlated with increasing urban size (Mattila and Thompson, 1968) due to greater specialization and complementarity. The larger an urban area the larger is the local market, and this encourages more competing firms to come into being with the result that costs are lowered, profit margins squeezed, and invention stimulated (Thompson, 1965b, p. 471). Large urban areas probably have an advantage in the supply of public services, but this is an advantage which, with the exception of a few activities such as the supply of electricity, rests more on quality of service than on cost. Ignoring quality and scope of service then, in terms of scale economies urban areas between 100,000 and 300,000 population might be most efficient as *per capita* cost studies of municipal services show. A survey of seventy-two English urban areas (Baker, 1910) revealed that an urban size of around 90,000 population produced the lowest *per capita* expenditures on municipal services. Urban areas of 100,000 to 250,000 were found to be cheapest to govern in the late inter-war period, with giant urban areas and those with populations under 70,000 appearing, in general, disproportionately costly to govern (Barnett House Survey Committee, 1938). Supporting evidence on the optimum level of technological operation of government services confirmed the size range 100,000 to 250,000 (Phillips, 1942). American evidence (Duncan, 1951; Lillibridge, 1952; Thompson, 1965a) also points to a size range of 100,000–300,000 as economically most desirable. Other economic studies, such as the diversity of the urban economic base or the adequacy of the range of tertiary services, indicate a size range of 100,000–

200,000 as optimal (Clark, 1945). However, it has been suggested that many private firms find their maximum profits when located in urban areas of 200,000–1,000,000 population (Neutze, 1965).

Urban areas frequently exceed the figures quoted above. The ill effects of large size have been noted but are, apparently, not of sufficient magnitude to stem the growth of very large urban areas, for, under the free working of the price mechanism concentration would continue until opposing forces of higher costs balanced the advantages of concentration. Diminishing returns to concentration must set some limits to any particular urban agglomeration just as they limit the economies derivable, at any time, from the use of an individual site. The larger is an urban area the longer are the journeys necessary to take advantage of the greater opportunities afforded by specialization and complementarity. Thus vehicle-miles *per capita* increase with urban size. Moreover, traffic flows in different directions are more likely to cross the larger the urban area so causing delays. Indeed, congestion is a means of economizing within urban areas as the traveller trades his time for lower costs (Thompson, 1965a, ch. 9). Besides the higher *per capita* vehicle operating costs, the *per capita* cost of an adequate road system will be higher the larger the urban area. Furthermore, where the urban layout was designed at some considerable time in the past, diseconomies will set in earlier.

Absolute size could act as a brake on growth for, after a critical size, the increase in costs of providing public services may be disproportionately large due to congestion, density, and administrative problems. With the growth of population the density and physical extent of an urban area increase, and a point is reached where the unit costs of public services rise or the quality of those services drops. The level at which this happens is a function of the current level of urban technology. Long-run diseconomies may be related to the increasing distance over which additional water supplies must be brought as urban size increases or to quantitative thresholds that may be reached, in, for example, the capacity of a sewage trunk that makes it impossible to extend a collector system (Kozlowski and Hughes, 1967; Hughes and Kozlowski, 1968). Indeed, the most significant threshold may be associated with the urban transport system, for around a population of 400,000 the strains imposed on that system are such as to demand consideration of a public mass transit system (Malisz, 1969). Urban threshold theory, dealing with such quantitative thresholds, gives little help, however, in determining the optimum economic size for an urban area. In practice urban managerial efficiency may be a principal diseconomy of increasing urban size (Thompson, 1965a, p. 24), especially where the growth of an urban area involves a number of separate and largely independent local governments.

From the consumer's point of view it might be suggested that the economic advantage of living in large urban areas is illusory because higher costs of living negate any income advantage. However, although rents and certain commodity prices are higher than in small urban areas, it must be remembered that the range and quality of goods and services available to urban residents is also a function of urban size. Here, larger urban areas have a marked advantage.

Foremost amongst the diseconomies experienced in large urban areas may be the environmental ones such as air and water pollution and neighbourhood deterioration. Firms and individuals may pass off certain costs on society in the form of externalities. These costs are not fully reflected in nor do they influence the decision of the firm or individual undertaking the offending action. Thus if a locational decision makes the urban area chosen less profitable or attractive for firms or families already located there, then the locating firm in making its decision will not take into account such costs (Neutze, 1965). Its decision is, therefore, not based on the full social costs of its action. Such costs are more important the larger the urban area. Moreover, the fact that they are largely ignored in private decisions means that factor prices may be biased in favour of large urban areas and understate the true marginal cost of production there. Such external diseconomies of urban size can also be associated with the inability to cover in one local government unit all the major costs and benefits of a public service (Thompson, 1965a, ch. 7). Concern, however, has now reached such a level that attempts to internalize these costs may be expected (Tsuru, 1963) and the increasing sophistication of cost–benefit analysis will allow this.

Economic evidence on urban size is, therefore, not clear cut. There is certainly no single economic optimum size to which all urban areas tend because different urban areas perform different economic functions. Urban size depends upon the functions performed by an urban area, and these functions may be interrelated with location. It may be possible to indicate an optimum size for a given urban area with specific functions and locational characteristics. For example, an urban area performing functions for the immediate countryside will have a smaller optimum size than an urban area which also serves as a regional administrative centre. Instead of a single optimum, a range of sizes related to the functions performed should be contemplated. Furthermore, as each urban area performs several functions and each function has its own optimum level of performance, no absolute value can be placed on the optimum for a particular urban area. Instead a compromise result is achieved which is best expressed as a range of population with the maximum and minimum being based on the greatest efficiency of all functions performed by the particular urban area (Shindman, 1955). The greater the number of functions performed the greater will be the optimum range for any urban area.

## Determinants of Spacing of Urban Areas

Urban areas will be spaced throughout productive territory, and their spacing will be governed by size and function. A national, even international, system of urban areas will develop as a result of interurban competition. The larger an urban area the greater the possibilities of internal specialization and, therefore, the lower are its production costs, relative to those in other urban areas, for a higher proportion of the goods and services it produces. Assume one urban area can supply to another urban area a given distance away half the goods and services it produces at lower costs than the second urban area can produce them for itself. If the size of the second urban area is doubled then the first urban area would now be able to supply less than half of the goods and services it produces to the second urban area at lower costs than that area could produce them for itself. The existence of a large urban area, therefore, inhibits the production of some goods, basically those where scale economies are significant and transport costs low, in smaller urban areas, so limiting the growth of the latter. The corollary is that the larger the urban area the greater the distance before another urban area can produce the same range of goods and services at equal costs and, therefore, grow to a comparable size (Lean and Goodall, 1966, p. 216). Within the distance separating these two large urban areas the growth of another urban area to comparable size is limited by their competitive advantage. Between them, smaller urban areas develop to produce those commodities in which the larger urban areas have little production cost advantage and for which transport costs are high. Still smaller urban areas develop between these for similar reasons. Small urban areas are, therefore, more likely to develop near to each other than near to large urban areas.

Therefore, where market factors determine the locations of economic activities, a definite and regular space–size ordering of urban areas can be recognized. Each urban area has associated with it a specific spatial spread of hinterland, and a hierarchy, based on a nesting principle, is built up where higher order urban areas perform all the functions of lower order places as well as their distinctive higher order functions. Urban population size must increase with order. Such is the theoretical base of the central place system to be analysed below.

Although size of central urban place and market orientation do exert a nodal influence and to some extent hierarchical force (Pred, 1966) on the urban space system, there is also a tendency for comparative cost advantages of sites to determine both the location and growth of firms in resource-oriented industries and the intensive exploitation of break-of-bulk/transhipment transport sites. Specialized activities based on physical resources often produce clusters of urban areas. In addition, the location of different activities may coincide in some instances even though they derive no advantage from such proximity, i.e. chance agglomeration. When these elements are combined, the overall urban space system will probably exhibit a tendency towards a random pattern as nearest-neighbour analysis suggests (King, 1961).

## Urban Areas as Manufacturing Centres

Industries with high product transport costs and small-scale economies must be located close to their markets. Assuming an isotropic surface and a perfectly competitive situation, a regular hexagonal pattern of market areas will evolve for each such industry. Each firm will be located at the centre of its market area in order to minimize transport costs on product distribution. Such a pattern is illustrated in Fig. 11.5a. Assuming marginal cost pricing, delivered price will increase with distance from the firm and market boundaries will be located where the

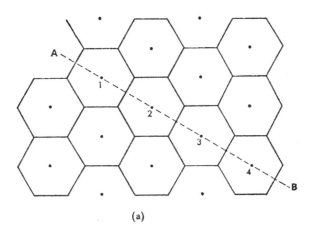

(a)

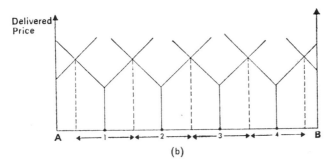

(b)

FIG. 11.5. Locations and market areas of competitive, market-oriented firms on an isotropic surface.

delivered price from two or three firms is identical: Fig. 11.5b illustrates this for the cross-section *AB*. Given perfect competition, the equilibrium set of prices (mirrored in each market area) allows each firm to earn only normal profit. A lower set of prices is not possible because of fixed production and transport cost functions. A higher set of prices would mean that more distant customers are lost to competitors and new entrants are encouraged to enter the industry. This will continue until all abnormal profits have been competed away. This solution, therefore, gives the maximum number of identical sized firms (and urban areas supported by those firms) at the same distances apart.

Industries benefit at different levels from scale economies. Where the products of two or more industries are unrelated, each industry will locate independently in a hexagonal market area pattern of its own. From the superimposition of two such patterns in Fig. 11.6 it can be

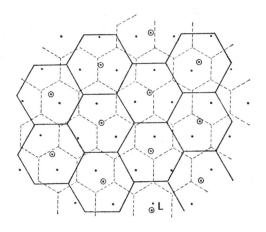

⊙ Location of firms in Industry **A**
• Location of firms in Industry **B**

FIG. 11.6. Superimposition of locations and market areas of firms in two unrelated industries where internal scale economies are of differing significance for the industries.

seen that urban areas of two different sizes arise: firms in industry $A$, which benefit from larger internal scale economies than firms in industry $B$, consequently support larger urban areas. Urban areas of each size are regularly spaced with regard to each other, but the smaller urban areas, supported by firms in industry $B$, are more closely spaced than the larger urban areas supported by firms in industry $A$. However, urban areas of one-size group are not the same distance away from their nearest neighbour in the other size group, in fact, in case $L$ locations virtually coincide. As more unrelated industries are introduced, the more irregular the spatial pattern becomes and the greater the probability of the locations of two firms coinciding.

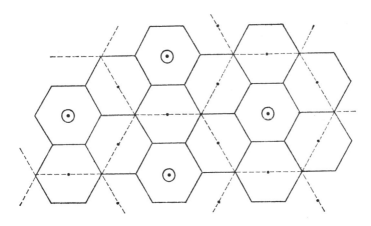

○ Locations of firms in Industry **A**

• Locations of firms in Industry **B**

FIG. 11.7. Possible location pattern where firms in two industries are interlinked.

Where there is a definite linkage between industries there will be a tendency for firms in those industries to locate together, providing the number of firms in each industry is not too dissimilar (Beckmann, 1968, p. 72). If internal economies of scale are twice as important in an industry, which supplies inputs to another industry, than in the receiving industry, then one firm in the first industry will, at its optimum size, supply inputs for two firms in the second industry. Where total transport costs are proportional to distance, a firm in the first industry may locate at any point on the straight line between two firms in the second industry and serve them with equal efficiency. In practice, transport costs are less than proportional to distance, so it would be most profitable to locate the supplying firm alongside one firm in the second industry and ship to the other. Such a location may increase the market because, in equilibrium, six receiving firms are located as closely as the nearest-neighbour firm in the second industry. A possible location pattern for two industries which are spatially linked is shown in Fig. 11.7. Conversely, where the number of suppliers is larger they cluster around receiving firms.

Footloose industries, being largely impervious to transport cost considerations, could serve extensive non-local markets by expanding almost indefinitely at the original location (at least until any diseconomies set in). Many firms in the same industry may, therefore, cluster where external and urban scale economy advantages are significant. These situations will give rise to exceptionally large urban areas or closely spaced clusters of similar sized urban areas. Thus an urban spatial system such as Fig. 11.8 illustrates the elements most likely to be

• Largest Urban Area

• Large Urban Area

· Small Urban Area

Fig. 11.8. Composite urban spatial pattern.

found in practice—a regular size–space system based on market functions, a linear pattern related to transport routes, and urban clusters based on external scale economies, particularly at resource-oriented locations. The problem is thus a combinatorial one which is far more complex than the application of certain elementary economic principles might suggest (Bos, 1965).

## Urban Areas as Tertiary Centres

The links between urban–industrial space systems have not been so thoroughly investigated as the relationship between tertiary activities and urban size and spacing. Any regularity in urban size/spacing has been explained, especially via central place theory (Christaller, 1933). It must be emphasized, however, that central place principles represent a complete statement of urban location only when urban areas function exclusively as retail and service centres for surrounding regions. Every urban area has associated with it a specific spatial tributary area. At the smallest size, or lowest order, a certain amount of productive land is necessary to support an urban area performing services for the surrounding agricultural area. Such urban areas perform the first steps in the distribution process of outgoing basic commodities and the final stage in the process of distributing products for consumption. It is the latter which provides the essential principle of central place theory, namely the consumer orientation of retail facilities. The pattern of urban areas which would develop on an isotropic surface in order to retail a given commodity would parallel the regular hexagonal market area and urban location pattern of Fig. 11.5a. Ideally, tributary areas would be circular, i.e. equidistant in all directions. Tangent circles leave unserved areas (Fig. 11.9a). Overlapping circles bring competition, and a market boundary is established which bisects the area of overlap, so giving regular hexagons (Fig. 11.9b). A certain level of population or purchasing power per unit area is needed to make it profitable to retail the given commodity, and as the retail units are competitive they will be spaced evenly throughout the market area. Each retail unit would be located so as to supply its own threshold market area most efficiently. Under perfectly competitive conditions each shop will, in equilibrium, earn only normal profit since it will be located so as to minimize either distance costs if the commodity is delivered or customer movement if the customer comes to the shop. Accepting consumer orientation as the determining principle of retail location, Fig. 11.5a would represent an urban spatial system based on minimization of customer movement. Under the perfectly competitive conditions assumed, it gives the maximum number of identical scale, retailers offering the given commodity at identical prices in hexagonal market areas of identical minimum size and no surplus profits (Berry, 1967, p. 63).

A larger threshold market area will be needed to support the profitable operation of a shop selling a second commodity which is purchased less frequently than the original one. It would, therefore, be supplied

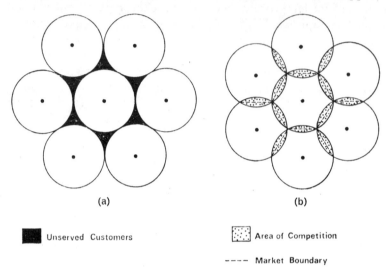

(a)                                                          (b)

■ Unserved Customers          ⬚ Area of Competition

- - - - Market Boundary

Fɪɢ. 11.9. Determination of hexagonal, retail market areas.

from a second set of higher order urban areas. The vertical organization of the system depends on the idea that higher order urban areas supply all the goods of lower order urban areas as well as the high-order goods and services which set them above the low-order places. To obtain high-order goods, low-order places must nest in the market areas of higher order urban areas. The resultant pattern is illustrated in Fig. 11.10. High-order urban areas, therefore, offer a greater range of goods and services, have more establishments and larger populations, serve larger market areas, have larger market area populations, and do a greater volume of business than low-order urban areas. They are, thus, found to be more widely spaced. A general range of functions and a population size range will be typically associated with each level in the hierarchy. For every order above the lowest, the market area of a centre at any given level in the hierarchy will contain the market areas of a finite number of lower order urban areas. The marketing principle thus gives the maximum number of urban areas. Seven orders in the hierarchy are normally recognized, namely consumption, retail, wholesale, transhipment, exchange, control, and leadership (Philbrick, 1957).

In practice the regularity of spacing of central places is proportional to the simplicity and uniformity of the land area. The theoretical ideal outlined is most nearly approached in poor, thinly settled relatively homogeneous and self-contained agricultural areas where urban functions are confined to performing services for the surrounding countryside. The uniformity of the central place pattern will, therefore, be distorted by physical factors such as topography and soil conditions,

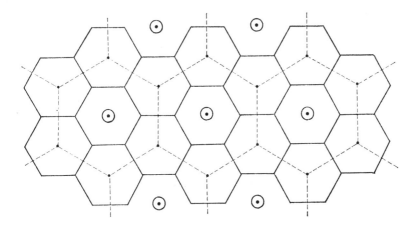

• Urban areas selling low-order goods
⊙ Urban areas selling low and higher order goods

Fig. 11.10. Location of urban areas according to the market principle.

and by socio-economic factors, such as differences in farming practice, population densities, and consumer purchasing powers. For example, if purchasing power and population density per unit area decrease, the range needed to encompass a given threshold increases and urban areas of that order will become more widely spaced. Alternatively, urban areas are more closely spaced the more dense the population and the higher *per capita* purchasing power. Adjustments may be necessary in respect of the functions performed at any given level of the hierarchy. The decrease in market area size with increasing rural population density is slower than the rate of population density increase, so that the total market area population increases. Therefore, functions with the

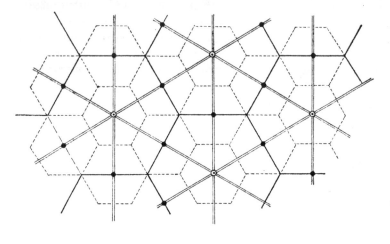

═══ Main Transport Routes

FIG. 11.11.  Location of urban areas and transport routes according to the transport principle.

lowest threshold requirements at any given level of the hierarchy find it profitable to move down to the next lowest level.

Major modifications of this theoretical pattern are necessary for other reasons. If a criterion other than minimization of customer movement is adopted, then a modified spatial pattern is to be expected. For example, if more attention were given to the transport costs a spatial pattern based on a transport principle would be likely to evolve, and a pattern like Fig. 11.11 would result. This produces a hierarchy which maximizes the number of urban areas located on main transport routes as an urban area of a given order is located midway between two urban areas of the next highest order. Both marketing and transport principles mean that the market areas of lower order urban areas lie only partially in the market areas of the next higher order urban area. This may cause difficulties in regional and local government, hence Christaller (1966, pp. 77–80) suggested an administrative arrangement principle in which each higher order urban area controlled a surrounding ring of six next

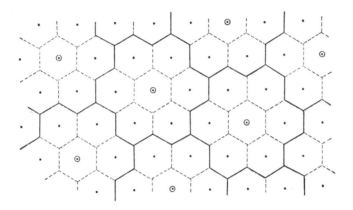

⊚ Administrative Urban Areas

Fig. 11.12. Location of urban areas according to the administrative principle.

lower order urban areas. However, as Fig. 11.12 shows, the hexagonal regularity of market areas for urban areas above the lowest order disappears.

Central place theory, as presented by Christaller, built up a hierarchy from the highest order good downwards. It required that all lower order urban areas take into account larger urban areas in deciding their location. As an alternative, Lösch (1954) starts from the other end of the scale and attempts to combine a variety of regular hexagonal patterns for individual goods and services into an aggregate picture. For each good or service, including market-oriented manufacturing, a basic network is built up in the way already described above. From the regular location pattern of lowest order urban areas, via a process of superimposition of the locational patterns of higher order urban areas, Lösch produces more complex, yet more flexible, urban space–size distributions. The size distribution of Löschian urban areas depends on how many particular goods and services of what size market area coincide at any individual central place. Spacing will also reflect the effects of such coincidence. Urban areas of the same size do not necessarily produce or supply the same order goods and services as in the Christaller model. Hence, higher order centres do not provide all the functions typical of lower order urban areas and urban areas which perform the same number of functions do not necessarily perform the same kind of functions. However, large urban areas will logically have the greatest variety of functions, especially manufacturing. The vertical organization of central places is, therefore, far less rigid, and the horizontal arrangement more complex. Where activities benefit from scale economies at different market sizes, a rigid nesting of lower and higher order urban areas would occur only where the threshold or entry zone of an activity was an exact multiple of the thresholds and entry zones of all other activities. This is unlikely, and the greater the differences between activities the more valid the Löschian system. In addition, complementary linkages may draw different activities together in different urban areas where production arrangements are flexible and allow ease of material substitution. The random coincidence of activities in space with no definite likeness or linkage is a further element allowed for in the Löschian system.

The superimposition of all possible nets to give the maximum coincidence of urban locations, gives the largest urban area or metropolis. By rotating the nets about the metropolis, Lösch produces a spatial pattern of six sectors with many and six sectors with few urban areas (Fig. 11.13). This arrangement, Lösch claims, brings the greatest coincidence of activity locations and, although it produces the fewest urban areas, the aggregate distance between all urban areas is minimized and the maximum number of goods are supplied locally. It is thus an economically efficient spatial system. It is, however, difficult to reconcile this pattern with the initial assumption of evenly distributed consumers and also, as Isard (1956, p. 271) has pointed out, the spacing of urban areas should be increasingly fine as the metropolis is approached. The latter requirement makes it impossible to retain regular-sized hexagonal market areas as Fig. 11.14 shows.

Market-oriented manufacturing can be reconciled with central place theory but, in both cases, the operation of transport factors can distort the regularity. Where major transport routes are limited central places

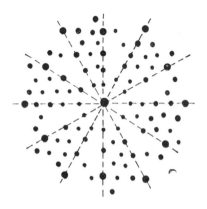

Fɪɢ. 11.13. A Löschian urban spatial system centred on a metropolis.

are strung out linearly along the route and their market areas are elongated at right angles to the route. Where urban areas owe their economic rationale to being transport foci and break-of-bulk points, they can be supported by market areas remote in distance from the actual urban location. Essentially the effect of transport is to impart linearity into the spatial pattern of urban areas.

However, the most important distortions of central place regularity arise from industrial concentration. Where manufacturing represents the economic base of urban areas, then it will follow that some urban areas will specialize in certain manufacturing industries and other urban areas of similar, or even larger, size, at varying distances away will form part of the market area for the goods of that urban area's industry. Specialization in manufacturing can be carried much further than specialization in most activities catering for distribution to a spatially dispersed population, which is the basis of the Christaller model. Specialist manufacturing urban areas can occur singly or in clusters.

No correlation should be expected between specialized urban areas of a given size or between such areas and urban areas of similar size performing central place functions. In spite of distortions wrought by industrial specialization (and transport), there are sufficient goods manufactured within central places to conform to a hierarchy, although the smaller the urban area the greater the distortion due to the presence of manufacturing. Clustered or single specialist urban areas must then be superimposed on the pattern.

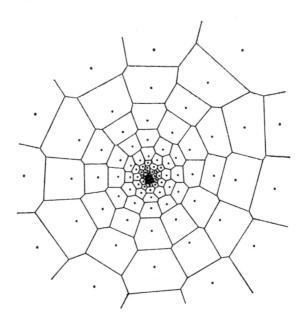

FIG. 11.14. A modified Löschian system (after Isard).

Specialist manufacturing urban areas can perform central place functions for surrounding areas, but it is argued (Berry, 1967, p. 35) that the retail and service provision supported by the residential population of such an area is less than that of a central place of similar population. Resident population is not matched by a corresponding hinterland population to that of the market centre. However, specialization in manufacturing in an urban area increases the incomes of its residents over and above *per capita* incomes in central places, and this may allow certain thresholds to be passed at lower populations than in the case of central places. Indeed, this could increase the relative attractiveness of the specialist manufacturing urban area as a retail centre for its surrounding countryside.

The problem is not so simple with clustered specialist manufacturing centres. In this case each urban area is unlikely to have a wide tributary, retail market area. Here the idea of the "dispersed city", a group of politically discrete urban areas which, although separated by tracts of agricultural land, function together as a single economic unit (Burton, 1963), has been advanced to fill the gap or "phase shift" between central places in the traditional sense and the suburban level of business centres in metropolitan areas (Berry, 1967, pp. 57–58). A "dispersed city" is essentially a cluster of urban areas whose sizes are greater than would be normally expected for urban areas so closely spaced. It therefore presupposes an economic base other than the provision of services for a surrounding area in which agriculture is the dominant activity. Manufacturing centres or the urban clusters characteristic of coalfield areas are examples. Such urban areas are not arranged in a hierarchical pattern for retail and service activities, possibly because their very proximity has served to encourage specialization rather than the dominance of any one of them. This interdependence is most strongly reflected in the case of shopping goods. In a sense such clusters resemble truncated hierarchies in which the functions of the missing regional centre are in part taken over by the next lower order group of centres. But the distortion is thus fully recognized, and the spatial occurrence of such clusters is more random than regular.

Functional specialization of urban areas, even if only in manufacturing, creates some necessity for a hierarchy of control from financial, technological, informational, and administrative points of view. In practice many control institutions are connected with political and social administration. In other cases the control activities are top hierarchical, one-of-a-kind functions which cannot pyramid in numerous cities (Ullman, 1962). The capital of a country is likely to develop in the most accessible location relative to major transport routes because national administration is cheaper from that location than any other, since such administration is largely a matter of communication between the capital and areas administered (Lean and Goodall, 1966, p. 219). This inhibits growth of national administrative activities elsewhere. Such administrative activities are important for the urban economic base since they attract other more normal commercial and manufacturing activities. The same reasoning holds true for regional and local capitals. Political and other control functions are, therefore, important in determining the vertical structure of the urban hierarchy. Specialist or central place urban areas, which by favourable location or historical accident become places where control units locate, tend to be larger than urban areas performing only similar production or retail functions. The control hierarchy introduces some order into the size distribution of urban areas but does not necessarily have the same effect on their spatial distribution.

### Correlates of Urban Size-spacing

Besides a political control hierarchy which may be effectively integrated with and, indeed may be a causative factor in, the spatial and size hierarchy of urban areas, other correlations are to be expected. These could provide alternative means of studying the urban size–space system. Foremost among expected correlations is one which examines flows within the national urban economic system. The size–space distribution discussed concentrated analysis on the nodes in the space system, but these nodes are linked by a transport network designed to facilitate inter-urban exchange. Given a statistically regular hierarchy of urban areas performing central place functions, there must be an associated hierarchy of commodity flows which exhibits similar statistically regular characteristics in terms of both average length and volume of flow (Isard, 1960, p. 227). Therefore, the import–export relationships of urban areas at the different levels in the hierarchy must differ in volume and length.

Urban areas which are specialist manufacturing or transport-oriented centres are likely to exhibit a greater volume and longer average length of journey for their associated commodity flows than a central place urban area of similar population size. The difference will be most marked if exports alone are considered because the spatial extent of the market for the specialist urban area is nowhere near as restricted as for the central place urban area.

The order an urban area occupies in the hierarchy dictates the functions it performs and these functions, and similarly those performed by specialist, non-central place urban areas, have repercussions for the internal structure of these urban areas. Thus a high degree of similarity would be expected in the extent of specialization of land use in urban areas of similar size performing the same functions.

## Changes in the Urban Space System

The urban size–space system is not static; it incorporates a dynamic process. The underlying conditions upon which a particular size–space distribution of urban areas is based do not remain unchanged for ever: natural increase of population expands available markets, and technological improvements in production and transport affect activities and urban areas differentially. Changes in underlying conditions, particularly transport improvements, alter the relative spatial positions of urban areas. In what ways will the size–space hierarchy be altered?

A competitive process is at work whereby such changes in underlying conditions increase the spatial range within which a given urban area finds itself competing with other urban areas. Thus, for a time at any rate, each urban area finds the spatial range over which it exercises a fair degree of monopolistic control reduced. The urban areas which survive or grow are those occupying locations of maximum accessibility within the transport network and which are, thus, best able to satisfy such rules as profit-maximization and market-orientation. If all urban areas are similarly affected, the magnitude of changes in the relative ordering of the urban system will be smaller than where changes differentiate between existing urban areas.

Take the effect of transport improvements on the space system of urban areas as an example. Transport improvements work to increase the competitive advantage of the larger urban areas, no matter whether they are of central place or specialist manufacturing origin. Transport improvements bring a reduction in overall costs of transport for society, and activities' responses can be viewed in substitution terms. How far will transport inputs be substituted for some other inputs of the activities concerned? Lower transport costs usually favour the growth of firms which already have the largest markets based on advantages of lower marginal costs of production. Such a firm already uses more transport inputs than its smaller competitors and, therefore, has its total costs of transport reduced more by any lowering of transport costs than any of its competitors. Such large firms also have an opportunity to tap previously unrealized scale economies. The threshold for entry to some industries is, therefore, raised by transport improvements by increasing the minimum optimal scales of operation. From this it follows that the growth of already efficient producing firms and urban areas is favoured over the growth of inefficient firms and non-producing areas. Transport improvements, therefore, also allow large manufacturers and urban manufacturing clusters with low marginal outlays per unit of product to partially or totally usurp the potential raw material consumption of such inefficient firms and non-producing centres (Pred, 1966). Reduced transport costs have, therefore, tended over the long run (1) to transform a scattered and ubiquitous pattern of production into an increasingly concentrated one, and (2) to effect a progressive differentiation and selection between urban areas with superior and inferior resources and access advantages (North, 1955).

Improved production methods also work to the advantage of large firms and existing producing urban areas and extended the market more than would have been the case with transport improvements alone. Urban areas with the greatest accessibility advantages once more benefited most from any lowering of per unit production costs.

Transport improvements similarly allowed urban areas performing central place functions with superior centrality to extend their market areas by capturing the trade areas of surrounding smaller urban areas. Likewise changes in agricultural production techniques, accompanied by a loss of rural population, leads to a decline in the functions performed by urban areas at the lower order levels of the central place hierarchy. Such small centres are the more likely to suffer decline the closer they are to a large urban area. Thus the axiate spiderweb pattern of urban locations laid down in the era of rail transport has not been materially altered by motor transport except that the latter has increased the dependence of smaller urban areas on larger urban areas.

## The Evolution of the Metropolitan Region

The relative rise and decline of urban areas as a consequence of the localization of industry and services is becoming a minor issue at the national level (Lasuen, 1969) as the urban space system becomes more and more organized in terms of metropolitan regions. Bigger, tighter-knit industrial complexes imply larger and fewer manufacturing centres. Developments in transport and communications technology make centralized control of management functions at one point in space possible and make major urban areas more attractive than smaller ones (Meyer *et al.*, 1966, ch. 2). The classical hierarchy of central place theory is also disappearing in the evolution of the metropolitan region (Berry, 1967, pp. 123–4) and is being replaced by specialized, complementary, rather than competitive, business centres. Within the metropolitan region, distance no longer provides protection, and business centres reduce competition by "product differentiation" amongst their activities. This, basically, takes the form of increasing specialization, associated with scale economies, and is thus a form of protection against competition. Within a metropolitan region urban places may also, therefore, appear more complementary than competitive (Lean and Goodall, 1966, pp. 220–1). For example, some urban areas may serve as day-trip resort centres, others as dormitory settlements for manufacturing urban areas elsewhere in that region.

At the national level, the urban space system thus appears to be tending towards a series of metropolitan regions of at least 500,000 minimum population and within 2 hours' travel time of each other. Competition between urban areas within metropolitan regions is minimized and even the metropolitan regions themselves exhibit a tendency towards complementarity rather than a hierarchical structure based on competition.

## The Influence of Government on the Size and Spacing of Urban Areas

Although the following chapter is wholly devoted to Government and the urban system, brief mention should be made here of government influence on the urban space system. In Chapter 10 it was recognized that government actions influence the relative competitive position of urban areas. Over time this must reflect in changes in urban size–space characteristics. Such changes may be brought about not only by government actions affecting the fortunes of existing urban areas but also by planners creating new urban areas.

Studies of the response of the urban space system to changing economic conditions will indicate both areas of growth and of stagnation. This is important, not only as an indicator of need, but also because a pound of government investment will generate different multiplier effects according to the location chosen for the investment. The most effective locations for such investment within the urban system must be determined. Where local government is restructured so as to concentrate administration in fewer urban centres, opportunities will be diminished for urban areas which lose their administrative functions and enhanced for the urban areas chosen as administrative centres. Similarly, investment in improvements to the transport network will improve interconnectivity between certain parts of the urban system more than between other parts. The relative advantage of the urban areas which benefit most will, therefore, be increased.

The existing urban system is slow to adapt to changing conditions. Therefore, if the trend is towards a metropolitan reorientation of the urban system, government action may be necessary to encourage the efficient transformation of the system. For example, in dealing with overspill and natural growth, planners must decide how and where it is best to accommodate the persons and activities involved. New urban areas may be one alternative, but these have to be slotted into the existing urban space system where location, function and size of urban areas are interrelated.

The economic base of the new urban area will largely determine its dependence on or independence of neighbouring urban areas. The greater the reliance of the new urban area on a specialist manufacturing base the easier it is to accommodate it into the existing spatial system. Positive proof is given by the success of the first generation of British new towns, catering largely for London's overspill, which were initially planned with a manufacturing bias to their employment structure. The difficulty of creating a new town with a central place service base was illustrated in the discussion of the possible functions for the proposed new town in mid-Wales (Welsh Office, 1966, p. 40). Retailing, administration, and public services could contribute little to the employment opportunities and service activities such as tourism, relying on wide spatial markets, appeared, alongside manufacturing, to offer the best prospects. Similar reasoning can be applied to the planned expansion of existing urban areas, as under the 1952 Town Development Act.

With increasing metropolitan polarization, ideas concerning the scale of new and expanded urban areas have undergone considerable change. They are now planned to be of a size to provide effective competition, if not counter-magnets, to existing metropolitan centres. In this sense their location within the urban system needs to be related to poles of growth. Injection of new urban centres, together with measures to stem the growth of the largest existing urban areas and to prop up stagnating urban areas, suggests that, today, changes in the urban system are largely dependent on government actions.

# CHAPTER 12

# Government and the Urban System

## The Economic Efficiency of the Urban System

The emergence of urban areas, the increasing importance of an urban way of life at the global level, and the continuing evolution of the urban system confirm the viability of urban areas and the urban system as an effective economic mechanism for transforming inputs into outputs. But urbanization is not a goal in its own right; it is no more than a means to an end. It has been argued in earlier chapters that urban organization represents an economically rational solution to society's efforts to seek an answer to the production, distribution, and consumption problems. It was also admitted that the urban system was something more than an economic mechanism and that the urban system may or may not fulfil its non-economic ends to the same degree. However, it has also been pointed out that, even on the basis of economic criteria, the urban system does not always function perfectly: adjustments in the system to changing circumstances are slow and often painful. Economic actions may be constrained by non-economic factors and forces which form part of the framework within which the economic forces operate. Moreover, purely economic actions, based on the self-seeking of individuals and organizations and representing uncoordinated decisions, do not lead to the optimum level of economic welfare because the free working of the price mechanism can lead to conflict between individual and community interests. As a response to competition, activities attempt to create protected spheres where the efficiency incentive of competition is denied and where, because prices no longer reflect true opportunity costs, resources are misallocated. Barriers within the working of the economic mechanism are, therefore, not insignificant.

The question from society's point of view is how to harness the undeniable economic benefits of urbanization without detraction (1) by the malfunctionings of the price mechanism itself, or (2) by hindrances created by non-economic factors which distort economic operations. Economic efficiency is an accepted social goal; thus all actions leading to a better use of resources and hence a fuller satisfaction of society's wants are to be approved. A clear-cut case may be made for aiding the price mechanism and, in parts, for the replacement of the price system, as a means of allocating factor inputs and final outputs. Economic criteria and economic forces cannot be ignored, even where non-economic ends are uppermost, since neglect of the economic aspects may have repercussions which make the attainment of non-economic objectives more difficult. Collective action, reflecting the public interest or community rooted values, modifies purely economic actions. The Government, as representative of the electorate in a democratic society, must, therefore, play the roles of referee, judge, initiator, teacher, and provider.

Government action, including that of urban governments, is thus very necessary, and government influence today in a mixed economy is likely to be all-pervasive. Such government action will influence the allocation of resources amongst uses and the resultant distribution of income within society. Whether or not a society, via its government, plans its future economic course, it still faces the same basic economic problem of allocating its scarce resources, each with alternative uses, amongst competing ends to achieve the fullest satisfaction of society's material wants. Certain government aims are undeniably economic in that they seek a better use of resources and hence lead to a fuller satisfaction of society's wants than would occur in the absence of such government planning. Such actions can, in practice, just as easily be undertaken by local government bodies and *ad hoc* statutory bodies. Central government may be in a position to influence the general economic efficiency of the whole urban system. Urban governments can do much to increase the economic efficiency of operation of their particular urban areas. National economic aims—of full employment, stability, and growth, etc.—demand the planned use of resources. Similar justifications can be made for the aims of regional and urban governments, especially in respect to the solution of their structural problems.

Furthermore, government actions ntroduced to achieve non-economic ends will form part of the framework within which private economic decisions are made and hence, may have consequences for the use of resources, i.e. economic repercussions.

The Government's pursuit of the objective of economic efficiency may appear most obvious in the case of economic planning, but it applies equally to other fields, such as spatial or land-use planning. The various levels and types of government action interact and interconnect. For example, economic planning must necessarily be concerned with the national level and rate of growth of economic activity. However, unless these economic measures are successful in attaining buoyant economic conditions, lower hierarchy government bodies will find it more difficult to bring about needed adjustments to solve their structural problems, such as the replacement of job opportunities following the decline of specialized and geographically concentrated industry. Action by an urban government to encourage new private investment in such a case will have a greater probability of success the more successful is national policy in achieving its objectives. A cumulative and circular causation process is at work. Government actions at various levels and of different types should therefore be viewed as complementary. However, it may be admitted that the harmonization and integration of the whole spectrum of government policies may, in any society, be far from complete.

Economic growth, as witnessed in one dimension via the differential growth of urban systems between countries and the differential growth of urban areas within nations, is not a spontaneous, nor a homogeneous, nor a harmonized phenomenon. Government measures perform a very significant priming action in initiating and maintaining economic growth: an initiative which rests squarely with the government in a mixed economy situation. The range of necessary government actions will have both direct and indirect consequences for the urban system. Expenditure of governments will influence the use of resources directly. Moreover, as much of this expenditure is on public services catering to the needs of the private sector, indirect or secondary effects will follow. For instance, a large part of the social infrastructure of the urban system, which creates external economy opportunities, has been built or established by government bodies using public funds. The timing and location of such public investment will do much to influence the growth and pattern of development within a nation's urban system. Government bodies rely on various sources of revenue, dependence changing with level in the governmental hierarchy. Since this represents a redistribution of spending power in favour of the public sector, it is equivalent to a diversion of resources to ends chosen by Government. In addition much government action takes the form of direct controls to ensure that negative externalities of any private decision are included in the project evaluation. Other legal enactments may improve the knowledge available to private decision-takers and hence increase the efficiency of operation of the price system.

Government bodies also abide by certain rules of conduct, and a criterion of economic efficiency can equally be applied to their operations. From the community view it is essential that government decisions on economic matters reflect the true opportunity costs involved. On occasions such optimization within the realm of government action may be open to question, For example, an urban government, in deciding upon a particular strategy for urban renewal within its transition zone, may choose to encourage those land uses which would make the greatest contributions to and the smallest demands on local rate income. Fiscal productivity would then be conditioning their action (Bloom, 1962) and not economic efficiency. The level and growth stability of *per capita* incomes in that urban area might well be better promoted by alternative types of land use which, although making greater demands on local rate funds, raise local incomes to a level which more than offset any increase in the rate burden of other land-users in the area.

The Government may often work through the price system, as when government contracts for supplying various goods and services are put out to tender. It may use values established within the price system as with compensation at market value where land is compulsorily acquired by local authorities. Alternatively, the Government may provide a framework which replaces the price system as when planners zone land for certain primary uses or conscription is used to ensure the armed forces obtain their supply of labour. It is important to realize that in a mixed economy prices will continue to exercise a role, albeit limited by government action, in the allocation of resources. This allocational role is intimately related to the efficient use of resources, and hence government actions will influence the efficiency with which resources are used in respect of the urban system. Will this be for better or for worse?

## The Need for Government Action in Relation to the Urban System

Prices yield a socially efficient utilization of resources only where they reflect, in opportunity cost terms, the principal social costs and benefits involved. Whilst the free-market system does bring a fair measure of order and a degree of rationality to decision making, the situation—viewed as a whole—also exhibits inefficiencies and conflicts. Such inefficiencies and conflicts are frequently most apparent and most serious in urban areas. Thus there are cogent reasons why the market cannot resolve the urban economic problems of location and resource use.

First and most important is the existence of externalities, i.e. indirect costs and benefits of a private decision which are borne by or accrue to persons other than the decision-taker. Such externalities are not taken into account by the decision-taker in arriving at the decision as to his best course of action, for he evaluates, in determining his profit or utility maximizing course of action, only those private costs he incurs and those private benefits he receives. For society, however, the true economic costs of that action, namely the social costs, comprise the decision-taker's private costs plus any indirect costs of his action. Similarly, the economic benefit to society, namely social benefits, comprises the decision-taker's private benefits plus any indirect benefits his action confers on other members of the community. The most desirable course of action from society's view is the one which maximizes net social benefit (or minimizes net social cost), and this will diverge from what is best for the individual decision-taker where externalities are sizeable. High private costs and negligible private benefits attaching to certain courses of action will not encourage private provision of facilities. Hence there is the need for government action in providing non-profit land uses in urban areas which yield high levels of indirect benefits. Prices or values established under the market structure are, therefore, only a guide. A larger unit than the private one is necessary if externalities are to be given their due weight. Government action, in particular urban and regional planning, thus forms a system which is carefully designed to improve the economic rationality of decisions in terms of the major goals of the entire community.

Secondly, it is accepted that the price system is exceptionally slow in bringing about adjustments to changing conditions. Indeed, it may take centuries for the consequences of a locational mistake to be rectified (Clark, 1968, ch. 8). It was seen that, in urban areas, demand for accommodation changed more quickly than supply and that this had consequences for the operational efficiency of urban areas since many activities had to make do with unsuitable premises. In certain circumstances, this could lead to a shortening of the economic lives of buildings, leading to more resources having to be devoted to replacement capital purposes than might otherwise have been the case. Secular stagnation or decline of particular urban areas within the urban system is another instance where the price mechanism's slowness in bringing adjustments can mean a waste of resources. The essential market concept is trial and error, so again there is a case for supplementing the workings of the market. However, in the absence of perfect foresight even planners may make mistakes, and a collective error by planners could be of considerable magnitude.

Thirdly, indeterminacy situations may occur which the market cannot resolve. As a result the pattern of resource use thrown up by the market is less than optimal. The existence of zones of mixed land use, as in the transition zone, where proximity of relatively incompatible uses depreciates the value of the location from the point of view of all users, is a reflection of this. Similarly, the interdependence trap which ensnarls property-owners in the same area prevents improvement and redevelopment of existing real properties. Such situations are all associated with high levels of uncertainty. In the face of such uncertainty the natural assumption is that the present situation will continue and this leads to a wasteful use of resources. What is impossible for the individual may be feasible for a group. Therefore, urban planning is required because the best location for one activity depends on where other activities will locate at some future date.

Furthermore, however well the market may work in allocating resources for maximum production to satisfy demands, the result may not accord with wise social policy. Whether the market solution is entirely acceptable will depend on the pattern of income distribution that is established. That pattern is automatically and simultaneously determined in the market in the solution of the resource allocation problem. Arguments against judging a situation superior allocationally but independent of distributional effects may, indeed, be strong (Margolis, 1968).  ˙

However, where belief is in freedom of individual choice the market can and must make a positive contribution to the achievement of society's goals. It must not be thought, therefore, that all the failures and sub-optimal conditions of the present urban system are due to the inadequacies of the market mechanism. Indeed, it has been argued that many so-called urban problems arise out of the fact that behaviour is not subject to any disciplinary force such as price (Thompson, 1965a, Introduction).

### Decision-taking in a Framework

The market system has never operated in a vacuum. Although there are wide limits to individual initiative and choice, private decisions have always been constrained to some extent by the economic, geographical, and institutional framework within which the decision-taker operates and has accumulated his experience. The market works to bring resources to their optimum or highest and best use within the framework which bounds the decision-takers. In practice, because of the existence of externalities, etc., the market allocation, although the most efficient in the circumstances, is, in fact, a sub-optimal position. The nature of the framework within which decisions are taken must have a bearing on the relative optimality of the solution.

There are three aspects to this framework (Goodall, 1970). Firstly, economic considerations are particularly concerned with the motivations of individuals and organizations. From an individual viewpoint, actions are guided by the profit or utility they are expected to yield, and such motivations are emphasized under the free working of a price system. However, viewed from a community point, such actions should be guided by aggregate welfare objectives. In both cases the application of economic principles, such as opportunity costs, comparative advantage, diminishing returns, and returns to scale, condition the optimal solution within the given framework.

Secondly, recognition of the spatial dimension implies cognizcance of geographical factors. These account for the heterogeneity of natural resource endowment and influence interaction between various locations of differing attributes. Locational and resource endowment differences will, in economic terms, influence the comparative advantage/disadvantage of locations for the performance of all possible activities and hence contribute to increasing spatial differentiation, one manifestation of which is the urban system itself.

Thirdly, institutional considerations are especially important in conditioning the framework since all societies enact rules and regulations, implicit as well as explicit, whose purpose is to govern the actions of members. The more economically developed the nation, the greater is the range of and the more sophisticated are the cultural, social, and legal controls present. Many such controls stem from private organizations and are designed to further the interests of a particular subgroup, as with the various co-operative market structures which producers erect under conditions of oligopolistic competition in order to curtail the area in which they are in direct price competition. The institutional framework owes most to the actions of Government, for many private decisions may be constrained and to some extent directed by public bodies. Nowhere is this more significant than in the urban system since in the development of an urban area land will automatically be divided into profit-making and non-profit-making uses (Lean and Goodall, 1966, pp. 229–32). Non-profit uses are land uses not usually provided by persons working under the profit motive and cover, in an urban area, a large part of the infrastructure such as roads, utility and welfare services, etc. Most non-profit uses are under public control, so that profit and non-profit uses correspond to public and private uses. The interdependence of the various profit uses was stressed in Chapter 4, but profit uses are dependent on the existence of non-profit uses, for, without the latter the return to profit uses would be, at least, greatly reduced. The spatial pattern of non-profit use provision is thus critical to profit-making uses, and control of non-profit use provision can be a determining factor in influencing profit-making decisions. As non-profit uses cannot compete on equal terms, for urban land with profit uses their provision must be the responsibility of the government sector.

It should, therefore, be apparent that the Government is in a specially advantageous position when it comes to influencing the efficiency with which resources are used. By changing the institutional framework and, in particular, the amount and location of non-profit land uses, the Government can make alterations to the framework which lead to a more optimal solution to the resource allocation problem. The growth and development of the urban system is therefore likely to take place as a result of a series of public and private decisions, the latter having often been guided, directed, stimulated, or even blocked at times by public controls.

## The Role of Government in a Mixed Economy

The state of the urban system today reflects a continuous stream of public decisions. Government action is both macro and micro in its scale of application. Whether or not a particular government action is designed to bring about a more efficient use of resources, it may still influence resource allocation.

Government economic policy in the United Kingdom has been dominated by two main requirements, namely the need to maintain a level of economic activity at which resources are fully employed and the need to export more goods and services in order to pay for imports and build up overseas assets and reserves. In addition the Government seeks to promote economic growth in the sense that *per capita* standards of living increase with the passage of time and to maintain the value of sterling. The Government, therefore, has to plan the use of available resources to achieve these ends, bearing in mind also the distributional effects since a desirable (i.e. acceptable to a democratic society) pattern of income and wealth is sought. A complex background framework of government measures and legislation is, therefore, necessary, and the introduction of new measures or changes in existing policies will have consequences for the urban system and individual urban areas—sometimes intentional effects and at others incidental.

At the macro- or national level, government measures may appear to have a blanket effect—as with most forms of monetary control and certain taxation policies. In this case any differential effect on the urban system or a particular urban area is unintended. For example, where a policy of credit restriction, which affects most severely those items normally financed out of borrowing—such as consumer durables, is the main explanation of the high incidence of short-time working/temporary unemployment in those urban areas where the production of consumer durables is geographically concentrated. In other cases national measures deliberately differentiate between economic sectors or geographical regions of the economy. For instance, measures taken under a distribution of industry policy to attract new manufacturing to areas of persistent unemployment will alter the relative locational advantages of the urban areas qualifying for such help. These areas should then appear more profitable locations for manufacturing industry.

At the micro-level, regional and sub-regional government action usually requires reliance on more direct controls because the amount of detail involved in analysis and decision-making increases tremendously. Thus at the local level the operation of a comprehensive system of land-use planning can make significant contributions to the economic efficiency of particular urban areas. Again this could be intended as when land-use planning facilitates the coming together of complementary economic activities in business districts or on industrial estates. Incidental effects may follow outline planning proposals which cause increased uncertainty.

Economic forces must adapt to government action of all types and at all levels because such government measures, representing part of the framework within which private decisions are made, affect factor and commodity prices, costs and revenues, and hence profit levels of private actions. The resultant adaptation may represent a more or less efficient use of resources. How economic forces adapt within the urban system or in an individual urban area following changes in government measures is, therefore, an important dimension of urban economics. The following two sections of this chapter discuss a number of examples of the possible effects of government action on the urban system and for the individual urban area.

## The Urban System

In so far as the economic growth of a nation approximates to the average rate of growth of its major urban areas, the economic efficiency of the urban system is critical to the efficient use of national resources. Although the price mechanism will, in time, bring about adjustments in the urban system, this is an extremely slow process, and problems of adjustment are much in evidence. For example, the transfer of land from profit to non-profit uses may not take place in the quantities, nor at the times, demanded for the smooth and efficient growth and development of the urban system. An efficient urban system stimulates economic advance, hence the Government, in its attempts to influence the level and course of economic activity, should be aware of the interaction between the economy and economic activities, on the one hand, and the going urban system and urban areas on the other. It could well be that the attainment of maximum rates of economic growth are possible only if the Government gives attention to the distribution of growth and potential within the urban system. Urban areas in particular locations and urban areas in certain size ranges may have more to contribute to growth than urban areas in less-favoured locations or of larger or smaller size.

Unless the Government knows which urban areas are going to grow, it can only provide for growth after that growth has taken place. A national policy is therefore required which indicates (1) that spatial pattern of urban areas, (2) that size distribution of urban areas, and (3) those rates of growth of urban areas, according to location, size, and function, that are to be preferred in the public interest. The size, spacing, and functioning of urban areas would, in the long run, under such a policy, largely be determined by government measures, although certain inertial and inherited characteristics would require many decades to alter. The economic efficiency of the urban system would then be dependent upon government action.

Certainly further evidence is required on the economic efficiency of alternative patterns of urban systems. If the central government believes that multi-million-peopled conurbations are economically inefficient, then it will seek to encourage the greatest proportion of urban economic growth in urban areas of the middle-size range. This cannot be undertaken without consideration of their spatial distribution. If the rate of economic growth demands that the growth urban areas be located in the same region as the conurbation whose further growth is being prevented, then various spatial arrangements may be possible depending on the functions of the growing urban areas. For example, the more specialist each growth urban area and the less their dependence on the conurbation the more attractive may be circuit linear patterns, such as Fig. 12.1a. Where it is thought that the conurbation has under-utilized capacity in certain economic sectors an alternative arrangement designed to take advantage of such services may represent the most efficient use of resources; hence stellar arrangements (Fig. 12.1b) or corridor/radial growth (Fig. 12.1c) may be recommended.

However, the urban space–size–function structure in a mixed economy today is largely one that has been inherited from an earlier *laissez-faire* era and only marginal adjustments have resulted from government measures. Moreover, the consequences of these measures for the urban system have not been thought out in terms of economically desirable changes in the urban system. A number of examples will illustrate this point.

## DISTRIBUTION OF INDUSTRY POLICY

Distribution of industry policy has, in the United Kingdom, for long represented an *ad hoc* plan aimed at reducing unemployment in areas where it has been persistently above the national average. As such it plays an important but subsidiary role to full employment policy. Various acts give the government powers to create the conditions necessary for an increase in job opportunities in areas of localized unemployment. The attempt was made to create conditions that would induce private manufacturing firms to choose freely locations in the aided areas. In addition a direct control, such as the industrial development certificate, could be used in a negative way to slow down or prevent growth of certain manufacturing in more prosperous areas. Distribution of industry policy will, therefore, influence the relative distribution of economic growth amongst the competing units in the urban system with those urban areas where industrial development certificates for new or expanding industry are refused suffering a decline in

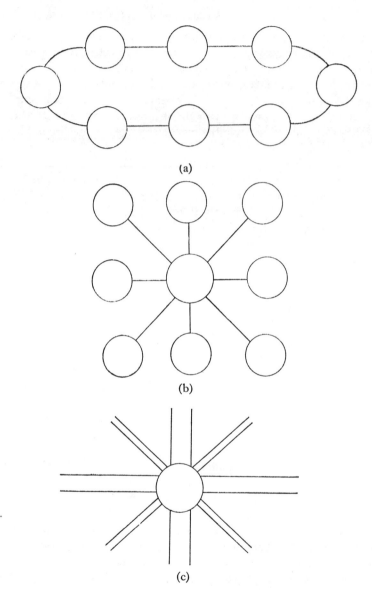

(a)

(b)

(c)

FIG. 12.1. Alternative urban arrangements. (a) Circuit linear.
(b) Stellar. (c) Radial.

their growth rate and prospects and those receiving inducements to industry an increase in their growth rate. Even urban areas outside of these two categories may find their growth rates reduced if the incentives to go to areas of unemployment are so high that some of their anticipated growth is siphoned off.

Overall the effect is (1) to bolster those parts of the urban system that have suffered a relative decline for the products of their manufacturing industries and which are unable to substitute new base industry because the relative advantages of their locations are (apparently) insufficiently attractive to new industry, and (2) to retard the growth of the fastest growing part of the urban system which appeared to offer the most favourable locational advantages for new firms. Is this desirable in the public interest? What is the cost in terms of lowering the economic efficiency of the urban system where such a policy is followed?

Such a policy contains an uncritical acceptance of the urban size–space distribution prevailing at the time of the appearance of localized unemployment. Is this acceptable?—Or is the failure of certain urban areas to adjust a function of their position in the urban system and, hence, an indicator that adjustments in the urban system itself are necessary? Certainly the urban system is dynamic and evolving, and where distribution of industry policy results in a retardation of the process of system adjustment a fuller use of labour in the short run may be achieved at the expense of the economic efficiency of the urban system and the economy as a whole in the long run.

The economic viability of certain urban areas, especially the smaller and independent manufacturing centres, is highly questionable. A policy which is directed at keeping labour in the localities where it finds itself unemployed thus promotes geographical immobility of labour, relying only on the geographical mobility of capital to achieve its ends. The policy objective might, alternatively, be summarized as seeking the locational stability of job opportunities. Local employment growth must keep pace with the local natural increase of working population if the need for involuntary migration is to be minimized. Thompson (1965a, ch. 5) suggests the latter might best be achieved by increasing the proportion of economic activities in large metropolitan areas since the latter have the greatest industrial mix, grow at average rates, and are able to substitute expanding for declining industry, hence offering the necessary changing job opportunities within a given labour market area. But distribution of industry policy has been divorced from considerations of size of urban area qualifying for aid. This is the more serious the smaller the size of individual areas that qualify, for the amount of growth taking place at any time may be too widely spread for the fullest economic benefit to be realized.

## NEW AND EXPANDED URBAN AREAS

New urban areas may be established for a variety of reasons but all, today, depend on government initiative. Where metropolitan areas are thought to be too large, their further growth can, in part, be catered for by the establishment of new urban areas. Where new urban areas accommodate persons and activities displaced from metropolitan redevelopment schemes, they aid the solution of internal problems of large urban areas. In other cases a new urban area may be created to provide better urban opportunities in an area where, for example, a dense rural population lacks certain services because the urban hierarchy has not developed fully. Indeed, with the infrastructure of existing urban areas being largely static, the most efficient way of coping with growth in the urban system could well be the expansion of chosen existing urban areas and the development of new urban areas to given sizes. This would avoid many of the problems incurred in every urban area in adjusting land in non-profit uses, etc., where growth was affecting all urban areas. In each case there is a choice between building a completely new town on a virgin site or taking an existing nucleus as the basis for large-scale expansion.

Where central governments seek to create new or expanded urban areas it must be realized that there is only a limited amount of growth to go round at any given time. New urban areas need to grow quickly in order to succeed. Thus to create too many new urban areas at one time will severely limit the chances of success for all. The same is true for the expansion of selected urban areas. Therefore planning for growth can only take place with confidence where the growth is confined to a few urban areas only.

New and expanded urban areas stemming from government policy have to be fitted into the urban system. This has repercussions. Opportunities afforded to new and expanded urban areas are opportunities denied to existing urban areas. An existing nucleus chosen as the basis for an expanded urban area already occupies a certain position in the urban system, e.g. it may be a service centre at a given level of the central place hierarchy. Expansion of such an urban area will cause a major disturbance in the urban system of that region. Higher-order urban areas will find competition is intensified, and since there is no corresponding increase in the hinterland population of the expanded urban area the region may not be able to support an additional higher order centre. Also the elevation of the selected urban area to a larger size will diminish the probable advancement in the hierarchy of any neighbouring urban area. How should new and expanded urban areas be related to the existing space–size–function distribution of urban areas? As pointed out in Chapter 11, it depends largely on the functions the urban area is to perform. A new or expanded urban area is more likely to be successful if it has a strong secondary or manufacturing base or perhaps a quaternary base of certain higher educational institutes and research organizations. In both these cases performance of central place functions is insignificant as a reason for the establishment of the new urban area. It could well be that a new manufacturing urban area grows to a size where its retail and other service activities prove a positive attraction to residents of surrounding rural areas and neighbouring smaller urban areas. In time it may thus begin to perform central place functions and occupy a relatively high order in the hierarchy. This is probably true in the case of Crawley, where the original economic base of engineering and other light industries initiated growth to a level where shopping facilities attracted, according to evidence from parking surveys, residents of neighbouring urban areas. Crawley has thus also developed to fill a gap in the urban hierarchy since there was no other urban area of over 50,000 within 10 miles—only a ring of smaller towns which lacked the sub-regional focus which Crawley now provides (Goodall and Lean, 1965).

Function also influences the size of new or expanded urban areas. Since there is no single optimum size of urban area the planned size of a new or expanded urban area will depend on such factors as its functions, its location relative to other urban areas, the relative sizes of these other urban areas, the pattern of transport routes, and the available modes of transport. In planning new or expanded urban areas such factors and relationships must be considered in relation to the economic efficiency of the planned urban area and the urban system as a whole. These factors will be of differing importance in different locations. A new urban area planned in conjunction with major improvements to the national transport network would soon develop into a regional centre performing various administrative, retail, educational, and other services for surrounding urban areas as well as developing a manufacturing base serving distant markets. In such a case the new or expanded urban area should be planned for a population of at least 250,000. Where it is thought that the expansion of manufacturing activity is dependent upon access to complementary business activities in a metropolis a new or expanded urban area of under 50,000 may be optimal for that location.

If governments, in order to retain the economic efficiency of urban areas with existing infrastructures, plan to cater for a large proportion of urban growth in the form of new or expanded urban areas, considerable changes in the urban space–size distribution will result.

OTHER NATIONAL MEASURES

National measures will determine the timing and type of much investment which is critical to the economic functioning of the urban system. In particular, expenditure by central government on infra-structural items, i.e. public investment, may have far-reaching consequences. Decisions regarding the location of new public investment such as motorways, international airports, new seaport developments, etc., are often made on the basis of what is best for the project concerned without always considering whether such a location is optimal from the national view. Although the first generation of new towns in the United Kingdom were planned without considering their place and role in the urban system there are indications that certain government actions are now taken with the whole urban system in mind. For example, proposals for counter-magnets to balance the attractions of a multi-million metropolis are planned for a size and in locations where they have a chance to achieve their objectives. There is, of course, at present little economic evidence to suggest that counter-magnets are a preferred course of action since the relative economic efficiencies of alternative urban space–size distributions have yet to be analysed in full. Until then marginal adjustments to the urban system must take place within the framework of limited knowledge available.

Adjustments to the urban system take place more readily when national economic conditions are buoyant. They are the more difficult in times of national economic hardship. Thus adjustments to the urban system do not take place regularly over time, nor do they take place uniformly in space. Adjustments take place to a greater extent under favourable conditions, the latter depending entirely on government action.

## The Individual Urban Area

There is a greater range of government participation at the level of the individual urban area since, besides national measures, consideration must also be given to actions of regional and local government authorities and any *ad hoc* statutory bodies such as river authorities and area electricity boards. At this level government action should, in economic terms, seek to improve the efficiency of an urban area as an economic mechanism. This is largely a matter of how activities can be arranged to make the most effective utilization of urban space and resources since, as was shown in Chapter 10, the type and amount of economic activities present in any urban area depend on exogenous factors. It would appear that the efficient functioning of an urban area will be facilitated by encouraging specialization and complementarity of land uses, not only of private uses but also of non-profit uses. Very often the planning of non-profit uses can bring the desired patterns of profit uses into being. However, the degree of specialization and complementarity depends on the size of the market and the level of technology. It could be a reflection on the state of urban technology that diseconomies set in after a certain level of specialization has been achieved. For example, too great a specialization of land use may throw excessive burdens on the urban transport system which shows this in the form of increased congestion.

Government at the urban level is not without its problems, for the urban authority may be viewed as a multi-product firm dispensing a highly interrelated set of local public goods as well as controlling private actions. However, the level of local government which is the optimum size to perform a given set of public functions may not be optimal for financing those same functions. Moreover, if local government boundaries are stable over time there is the likelihood that, with urban growth, the local tax base will be divorced from public service needs because the urban area is subdivided amongst several local authorities.

## ROLES OF ECONOMIC AND PHYSICAL PLANNING

The economic fate of an urban area rests only partially in its own hands since national government policies influence the course of events and the relative advantages of and the actions taken by other urban areas are outside its control. Economic planning by urban government should facilitate adjustment to changes in the external situation as well as catering for internal changes. In this sense one role of urban economic planning is to achieve an integration of urban economic activities with national and regional objectives. There are severe limits to urban government action in the field of economic planning since the urban economy is far more open than the national one. Thus urban governments are not able to influence with the same leverage the level of demand within their own area that a national government can exert on the whole economy. This is because urban governments cannot undertake deficit financing and much of the benefit of increased local government spending would be dissipated beyond the urban boundary—the multiplier effect is likely to be significantly less than one. Thus certain aspects, e.g. stabilization objectives in respect of employment, should be left to the national government and should not play a major part in decisions on spending and financing of urban public services. National governments may, of course, use urban governments as agents in their policy and thus influence local public service spending via specific grants-in-aid. Although cyclical fluctuations in economic activity levels are a national responsibility, overcoming structural problems, which usually manifest themselves locally, is an area where positive economic planning on the part of urban government can make a substantial contribution to economic welfare. In this respect the urban labour market subsumes great importance since, of the set of markets which form the urban economic mechanism, this market is spatially the most independent. Therefore the urban labour market provides an opportunity for urban governments to participate in economic planning, e.g. by promoting the retraining of labour in an attempt to overcome structural unemployment. Another critical area is the location and timing of public investment, since such expenditures are almost irrevocably committed over very long amortization periods. Therefore an understanding of the urban growth process is very necessary if the best use of resources is to be achieved. The planning of the location of such public investment also points to the need to integrate economic and land-use planning at this urban level.

Whilst an urban government may not have much control over the total amount of economic growth taking place in its area, it does have much more control over the spatial pattern of that growth. Physical or land-use planning is therefore essential if urban resources are to be used in the most efficient way since public values (reflecting externalities) will require modifications in private actions, hence, in private land uses. In many cases this can be achieved by planning the location of fixed investments (especially public ones) and their spatial relationships.

One way in which physical planning can increase the economic efficiency of urban areas is to encourage the application in land-use planning of the economic principle of specialization (Lean and Goodall, 1966, p. 260). How far can this principle be applied? As pointed out above, this depends on demand and technology. The degree of specialization of land uses, access space, and activities will be very much smaller in an urban area of 15,000 performing agricultural marketing functions for the surrounding countryside than in a regional centre of 250,000 persons. In the former case, on-street parking may be compatible with the use of a main road as a traffic artery, whereas in the latter case such parking would so interfere with traffic circulation that the economic efficiency of urban operation is diminished, and consequently off-street specialist parking facilities are provided. In the case of the small market centre the social benefits of carrying specialization to the same extent would be outweighed by the social costs of such a scheme and would not, therefore, be economically worth while. The level of minimum demand should, therefore, determine the degree of specialization the planner attempts to introduce.

Specialization in one aspect of urban activity may cause problems elsewhere if there is a disequilibrium between various contributing technologies. For example, land-use planning which leads to intense specialization of land use can also lead to extreme peaking of demand for the use of roads, parking, and other transport facilities. In these circumstances additional investment in transport facilities may, in fact, sharpen the peak demand and lower the load factor. A compromise may be necessary and a more efficient use of given existing facilities achieved by the introduction of a pricing system which takes into account at least some of the social costs of the traffic system. A number of more particular examples will illustrate how government action at the urban level may influence economic efficiency.

## GREEN BELTS

Whatever the reason for the introduction of a green belt in a particular case it cannot prevent the urban area from growing in an economic sense. What the green belt will do is to bring about a spatial rearrangement because economic adjustments will be made to the new framework which includes the green belt (Goodall, 1970). Land now within the green belt will be retained in its existing agricultural or recreational use and protected from urban development. Thus land which might have been developed for housing or industry in the absence of the green belt will suffer a fall in value because of the loss of development potential when the green belt is imposed. Where much of the green belt is recreational land, then the social benefits of such action could be high because recreational facilities are being maintained within easy access of the urban population.

With continued economic growth of the urban area, activities which would have developed sites within the green belt must seek alternative locations. In respect of that urban area the alternatives are in the existing built-up area encollared by the green belt or in the area beyond the green belt. However, for some manufacturing firms the next best location may be in another urban area, in which case the growth prospects of the encollared urban area would be lowered. Where demand for accommodation turns to the existing built-up area it will find a stock of buildings, a certain proportion of which is offered for sale at any time. This supply is likely to be inelastic and price will be bid up, with the prices of the most accessible sites rising most. Certain lower order uses will be squeezed out and need to seek alternative accommodation beyond the green belt or even in another urban area. A proportion of existing buildings will be taken over by higher order uses and in many cases this could delay redevelopment because the building's economic life is extended (see Chapter 8). Redevelopment will certainly be more expensive, but equally it may be more profitable. The amount of slum clearance may be reduced because the costs of acquiring existing interests in properties required for local authority comprehensive re-development schemes are likely to have increased. Moreover, possibilities on redevelopment depend on what planners will allow and where permitted, use on redevelopment is of a lower intensity than that which exists, redevelopment will certainly be delayed.

The existing built-up area will not be able to accommodate all these demands, and certain demands—plus any displacement of lower-order uses—will have to be satisfied in the area beyond the green belt. Such uses substitute sites previously regarded as sub-optimal which now represent the best possible location within the new framework. The more accessible areas beyond the green belt will now come under pressure for development: land of lower value is being substituted for increased transport costs. A more dispersed pattern of urban uses may, therefore, result. Where the new development beyond the green belt is economically tied to the urban area, e.g. residents and employment opportunities, transport facilities may become congested and require additional investment. More resources may be devoted to transport inputs than if some alternative form of containment and expansion plan had been adopted. To encollar an expanding area by means of a green belt could thus bring increased costs of urban operation without commensurate increases in the level of benefits.

ZONING AND DENSITY CONTROLS

By zoning land for permitted uses planners can encourage land use specialization. Zoning is usually accompanied by some control over the intensity of development, expressed in terms of gross densities in the case of residences and plot ratios for business uses. For uses permitted in the zone the effect is to reduce the competition for available land, leaving the price mechanism to allocate, e.g. in the case of land zoned for residential use, the sites amongst competing speculative residential builders. In so far as demand is reduced and/or supply is increased, the price of residential land will be lower than otherwise. This could encourage greater residential building and/or the use of larger plots, depending on demand conditions.

Where zoning is accompanied by use, intensity controls development potential will be shifted where the permitted intensity of use is below that to which the free market would develop. Those zones which would have been developed more intensively suffer a fall in value. However, the imposition of low densities on such zones will require more land to accommodate a given number of persons and activities than if higher densities were permitted. Additional sites, as determined by planning allocation, acquire development potential in excess of what would have settled on them in the absence of such controls.

Urban development is, therefore, spread over more land. This may bring social benefits because more land has been made available as open space and buildings are not crowded on top of each other. It may also raise social costs since more resources have to be devoted to the construction and operation of transport facilities, public utility services, and the like. Activities forced to seek alternative locations will attempt to substitute sites which most closely approximate conditions at the sites denied them, but the closest substitutes may suffer comparative access disadvantages, especially where complementary linkages are required. If such density controls are justified, then net social benefits should be maximized, but if the same level of benefit can be achieved at a lower social cost for an alternative density/zoning arrangement, the latter is to be preferred.

Again private activities have adapted their actions to the framework created. In certain cases, private activities may be worse off, but additional social benefits should accrue to others to offset this if the community is to benefit as a whole.

CONTROL OF LOCAL INDUSTRIAL DEVELOPMENT

Urban government is not always able to harness economic forces to help meet its goals. Where economic pressures build up within an urban area as a result of planners' actions, private activities will still adapt to changing circumstances as well as bringing pressure to bear to get the plans altered. If planning creates conditions which make an urban area a particularly favourable location for manufacturing, so that job opportunities are greater than the working population, this will lead to net commuting in from the surrounding countryside and urban areas. Wage rates will be driven up as firms compete for labour. Over-crowding of residential accommodation may follow as the flow of in-migrants increases. Pressures build up to increase residential accommodation which in turn may require alterations to urban plans in respect of traffic systems, provision of non-profit uses, location of neighbourhood business centres, etc. (Lean and Goodall, 1966, pp. 267–8).

If manufacturers are prevented from expanding in that urban area in such circumstances, what adjustments will they contemplate? Manufacturers may respond by using existing labour more intensively by working overtime or by relying on more part-time workers such as married women. Such expediencies tend to increase costs of production. Another possibility is to substitute capital, in the form of more automatic machinery, for labour, and the rise in wages consequent upon the shortage of labour may make this profitable. Yet another course of action is to contract activity in that urban area. This represents an absolute loss of productive potential if the manufacturers do not expand elsewhere so that the nation suffers. Where manufacturers decide to expand elsewhere there may be a loss of efficiency since such separation of their activity is forced. Transfer of activities may take two forms: the opening of branch plants elsewhere or contracting work out to other firms. Both represent a loss of job opportunities to the urban area concerned, although the sub-contracting could be temporary. Should such transfer be accompanied by idle machinery in the original factory resources are wasted because non-movable plant and machinery must be duplicated elsewhere (Goodall and Lean, 1965).

Urban government must assess the economic effects of its actions, for it is probably easier and cheaper to make any necessary alterations at the early stages of a plan than to wait until pressures have built up and the plan is fully operative. A lack of awareness of such consequences could bring more intractable problems at a later date.

RENT CONTROL

Rent control, enacted at the national level, has major repercussions at the local level. Most usually applied to residential accommodation, rent control is introduced in situations of excess demand, and involves laying down maximum rents, which lie below corresponding free market levels, and granting security of tenure to sitting tenants. What are its effects for urban areas?

Firstly, the imposition of rent control alters conditions of supply in the accommodation market and the supply of new rentable accommodation is likely to be reduced (except for certain very specialized parts such as luxury apartments and tied dwellings). Thus any increase in urban households seeking accommodation faces a limited choice with the greatest flexibility being in new owner-occupied housing. In so far as owner-occupied housing has different locational requirements from rental housing, the form of urban development could be affected. Owner-occupied housing has a wider range of locational choice because its occupants are less tied to public transport facilities than the occupants of rented accommodation. Consequently certain families who would have occupied rented accommodation, in order to obtain some form of housing, become reluctant owner-occupiers. Those families unable to afford owner-occupied housing have to double-up wherever they can, i.e. increase overcrowding in existing dwellings which may accelerate rates of depreciation and promote the formation of slums. Alternatively, they have to rely on the provision of rented accommodation by urban governments as a welfare service. Thus council estates—houses or flats depending on the size of and location within an urban area—come into being as a feature of urban land-use patterns and require a further transferance of land from profit to non-profit uses. Council housing has certain locational requirements related to the needs of the prospective occupants, but is also influenced by the availability of low-cost land. In certain cases the choice of location may be complicated by the existence of subsidies which allow building on more expensive sites than would otherwise be possible. It might also be argued that provision of below-cost council housing in relatively accessible locations represents a disguised wage-subsidy to firms employing workers residing there.

Secondly, there is the effect on the controlled dwellings themselves. The capital value of rent controlled property is likely to fall because of the disadvantages attaching to this type of investment, particularly the inability to adjust the rent upwards to meet changing circumstances and of not being able to transfer the property at will between the various sub-parts of the housing market. Capital value falls further where landlords try to maintain falling real incomes in inflationary conditions by cutting down on repairs and maintenance, so accelerating the depreciation of property. Since controlled properties tend to be of a similar age and found in the same parts of an urban area, especially transition zones, rent control may be a contributory cause of slum formation. Indeed, the question of where and how to house the lower-income groups in an urban area is still basically unresolved.

Many further examples could be explored, and it often appears that government action in one sphere necessitates government action in another sphere. Government measures do not always have clear-cut and favourable economic results, nor is there a clear-cut appreciation of the economic costs that should be shouldered in order to achieve certain non-economic ends. But society should be made aware of any economic (opportunity) costs of achieving its non-economic goals. Often the price is one that society is prepared to pay and there is no need to disguise the cost.

## Conclusion

The economic advantages of an urban way of life have made the paramount contribution to the present level of development of society, especially to the material standards of living presently enjoyed. However, the urban system and individual urban areas, viewed as economic mechanisms, have not and do not, function perfectly. There is a need, on occasions, to replace the price mechanism and, on others, to extend its use in order to improve urban areas as economic mechanisms. But government action, in changing the framework within which private decisions are made, can bring about a more or less efficient use of resources. Since the economic advantages of urbanization are undeniable, the onus must be on the Government, at all levels, to see that these advantages are exploited to the fullest benefit of society consistent with the attainment of other societal priorities.

The formulation by governments of public policies may be viewed as a hierarchy of policy decisions ranging from the general down to the particular (Chapin and Weiss, 1962, p. 451). At each level of this hierarchy there is a range of choices open to government decision-makers, and these decisions must be made on the basis of certain criteria. Amongst such criteria economic ones—in particular maximization of net social benefit—must loom large, although in certain cases economic motives may be overridden by non-economic considerations. In the latter case the additional economic cost or loss of benefit should be assessed. The urban system requires improvement, and the Government may set high standards regarding urban building and urban form. These standards would dictate the total resource expenditure needed on the urban system. To set standards too high in this direction will mean that something else must suffer, e.g. the education or medical services, and this is a choice that the Government must make on behalf of the electorate. The Government thus also works within limitations.

In any society which emphasizes the virtues of economic competition there will always be a tendency for the actions of private individuals and businesses to be motivated according to the principle of profit or utility maximization. Governments may achieve much by using the market mechanism as fully as possible, but if the greatest net social benefit is to be realized for society then the Government must take positive and forceful steps to see that externalities, for example, are given due weight. Only if the Government is successful in this respect will the urban system and individual urban areas make their maximum contribution to the economic well-being of society.

# Bibliography

ALONSO, W. (1964) The historic and structural theories of urban form: their implications for urban renewal, *Land Economics* **40** (2), May.

ALONSO, W. (1965) *Location and Land Use*, Harvard University, Cambridge, Mass.

ANDERSON, T. R. (1962) Social and economic factors affecting the location of residential neighborhoods, *Regional Science Association Papers* **9**, 161–70.

ANDREWS, R. B. (1955) Mechanics of the urban economic base: the concept of base ratios, *Land Economics* **31** (1), February.

APPLEBAUM, W. and COHEN, S. (1961) The dynamics of store trading areas and market equilibrium, *Annals Association of American Geographers* **51** (1), March.

BABCOCK, F. M. (1932) *The Valuation of Real Estate*, McGraw-Hill, New York.

BAKER, C. A. (1910) Population and costs in relation to city management, *Journal Royal Statistical Society* **83**, 73–79.

BARNETT HOUSE SURVEY COMMITTEE, OXFORD UNIVERSITY (1938) *A Survey of the Social Services in the Oxford District*, Vol. 1, *Economics and Government of a Changing Area*, Oxford Univ. Press, London.

BECKMANN, M. (1968) *Location Theory*, Random House, New York.

BERRY, B. J. L. (1960) *An Inductive Approach to the Regionalization of Economic Development*, Univ. of Chicago, Dept. of Geography, Research Paper 62.

BERRY, B. J. L. (1961) City size distributions and economic development, *Economic Development and Cultural Change* **9** (4), 573–88.

BERRY, B. J. L. (1967) *Geography of Market Centres and Retail Distribution*, Prentice-Hall, Englewood Cliffs, NJ.

BLOOM, M. (1962) Fiscal productivity and the pure theory of urban renewal, *Land Economics* **38** (2), May.

BLUMENFELD, H. (1955) The economic base of the metropolis, *Journal American Institute of Planners* **21**, Fall.

BOS, H. C. (1965) *Spatial Dispersion of Economic Activity*, Univ. Press of Rotterdam, Rotterdam.

BOUDEVILLE, J. R. (1966) *Problems of Regional Economic Planning*, Univ. Press, Edinburgh.

BOULDING, K. E. (1963) The death of the city: a frightened look at post-civilization, in Handlin, O. and Burchard, J. (eds.), *The Historian and the City*, MIT, Cambridge, Mass.

BOURNE, L. S. (1967) *Private Redevelopment of the Central City*, Univ. of Chicago, Dept. of Geography Research Paper No. 112.

BREGER, G. E. (1967) The concept and causes of urban blight, *Land Economics* **43** (4), November.

BRIGHAM, E. F. (1965) The determinants of residential land values, *Land Economics* **41** (4), November.

BURBY, R. J. (1967) *Lake-oriented Subdivisions in North Carolina: Decision Factors and Policy Implications for Urban Growth Patterns*, Center for Urban and Regional Studies, Institute for Research in Social Science, Univ. of North Carolina, Chapel Hill.

BURGESS, E. W. (1925) The growth of the city: an introduction to a research project, chapter 2 in Park, R. E., Burgess, E. W., and McKenzie, R. D., *The City*, Univ. of Chicago Press, Chicago.

BURTON, I. (1963) A restatement of the dispersed city hypothesis, *Annals Association of American Geographers* **53** (3), September.

CAMPBELL, A. K. and BURKHEAD, J. (1968) Public policy for urban America, pp. 577–640 in Perloff, H. S. and Wingo, L., Jr. (eds.), *Issues in Urban Economics*, Johns Hopkins, Baltimore.

CHAMBERLAIN, E. (1933) *The Theory of Monopolistic Competition*, Harvard Univ. Press, Cambridge, Mass.

CHAPIN, F. S., Jr. (1965) *Urban Land Use Planning*, 2nd edn., Univ. of Illinois, Urbana.

CHAPIN, F. S., Jr., and WEISS, S. F. (eds.) (1962) *Urban Growth Dynamics*, Wiley, New York.

CHRISTALLER W. (1933) *Die zentralen Orte in Süddeutschland*, Fischer, Jena.

CHRISTALLER, W. (1966) *Central Places in Southern Germany*, trans. by Baskin, C., Prentice-Hall, Englewood Cliffs, NJ.

CLARK, C. (1945) Economic functions of a city in relation to its size, *Econometrica* **15** (2), 139–48.

CLARK, C. (1951) Urban population densities, *Journal Royal Statistical Society*, Series A, **114,** 490–6.

CLARK, C. (1968) *Population Growth and Land Use*, Macmillan, London.

CLAWSON, M. (1962) Urban sprawl and speculation in suburban land, *Land Economics* **38** (2), May.

COHEN, S. B. and LEWIS, G. K. (1967) Form and function in the geography of retailing, *Economic Geography* **43** (1), January.

COKE, J. G. and LIEBMAN, C S. (1961) Political values and population density control, *Land Economics* **38** (4), November.

CRAVEN, E. (1969) Private residential expansion in Kent, 1956–64: a study of pattern and process in urban growth, *Urban Studies* **6** (1), February.

CROSSON, P. R. (1960) Further comment on economic base theory, *Land Economics* **36** (2), May.

CULLINGWORTH, J. B. (1961) Housing and the private landlord, *Guardian*, 24 March.

CZAMANSKI, S. (1965)   Industrial location and urban growth, *Town Planning Review* **36** (3), October.

DALY, M. T. (1967)   Land value determinants, Newcastle, New South Wales, *Australian Geographical Studies* **5** (1), April.

DAVIS, O. A. (1960)   A pure theory of urban renewal, *Land Economics* **36** (2), May.

DENMAN, D. (1964)   *Land in the Market*, Hobart Paper, 30, Institute of Economic Affairs, London.

DEPARTMENT OF THE ENVIRONMENT (1971)   *New Out-of-town and Other Shopping Centres*, Draft of Development Control Policy Note (May), London.

DICKINSON, R. E. (1951)   Regional relations of the city, pp. 260–73 in Hatt, P. K. and Reiss, A. J. (eds.), *Cities and Society*, Free Press, Glencoe.

DONNISON, D. V., COCKBURN, C., and CORLETT, T. (1961)   *Housing since the Rent Act*, Occasional Papers on Social Administration, No. 3.

DUNCAN, B. (1964)   Variables in urban morphology, pp. 17–30 in Burgess, E. W. and Bogue, D. J. (eds.), *Contributions to Urban Sociology*, Univ. of Chicago, Chicago.

DUNCAN, O. D. (1951)   Optimum size of cities, pp. 759–72, in Hatt, P. K. and Reiss, A. J. (eds.), *Cities and Society*, Free Press, Glencoe.

DUNN, E. S. (1954)   *The Location of Agricultural Production*, Univ. of Florida Press, Gainsville.

DUNNING, J. H. (1969)   The City of London, a case study in urban economics, *Town Planning Review* **40** (3).

DZIEWONSKI, K. (1966)   A new approach to the theory and empirical analysis of location, *Regional Science Association Papers*, vol. 16.

ECONOMIC COMMISSION FOR EUROPE (1966)   *Major Long-term Problems of Government Housing and Related Policies*, 2 vols., United Nations, ST/ECE/HOU/20, New York.

FERGUSON, C. E. (1960)   Statics, dynamics, and the economic base, chapter 15 in Pfouts, R. W. (ed.), *Techniques of Urban Economic Analysis*, Chandler-Davis, West Trenton, NJ.

FIREY, W. (1947)   *Land use in Central Boston*, Greenwood, New York.

FIREY, W. (1951)   Ecological considerations in planning for rurban fringes, pp. 791–804, in Hatt, P. K. and Reiss, A. J. (eds.), *Cities and Society*, Free Press, Glencoe.

FLORENCE, P. S. (1955)   Economic efficiency in the metropolis, in Fisher, R. M. (ed.) *The Metropolis in Modern Life*, Doubleday, New York.

FLORENCE, P. S. (1964)   *Economics and Sociology of Industry*, Watts, London.

GARNER, B. J. (1966)   *The Internal Structure of Shopping Centres*, North-Western Univ. Studies in Geography, 12.

GARRISON, W. L., BERRY, B. J. L., MARBLE, D. F., NYSTUEN, J. D., and

MORRILL, R. L. (1959) *Studies of Highway Development and Geographic Changes*, Univ. of Washington Press, Seattle.

GILLIES, J. and GRIGSBY, W. (1956) Classification errors in base-ratio analysis, *Journal American Institute of Planners* **22**, Winter.

GOODALL, B. (1969) *The Location of a New Church*, Report to Kings' Road and Wycliffe Baptist Churches, Reading.

GOODALL, B. (1970) Some effects of legislation on land values, *Regional Studies* **4** (1).

GOODALL, B. and LEAN, W. (1965) Economic pressures for further growth in Crawley, *Journal Town Planning Institute* **51** (8), September/October.

GOTTMANN, J. (1961) *Megalopolis*, The Twentieth Century Fund, New York.

GREGORY, D. (1970) *Green Belts and Development Control*, University of Birmingham, Centre for Urban and Regional Studies, Occasional Paper, No. 12.

GREVE, J. (1961) *The Housing Problem*, Fabian Research Series No. 224.

GRIFFIN, D. W. and PRESTON, R. E. (1966) A restatement of the transition zone concept, *Annals Association of American Geographers* **56** (2), June.

HAIG, R. M. (1926) Toward an understanding of the metropolis, *Quarterly Journal of Economics* **40**, February, Part I, Some speculations regarding the economic basis of urban concentration; May, Part II, The assignment of activities to areas in urban regions.

HAMILTON, F. E. I. (1967) Models of industrial location, pp. 361–424, in Chorley, R. J. and Haggett, P. (eds.), *Models in Geography*, Methuen, London.

HANDLIN, O. (1959) *The Newcomers*, Harvard Univ., Cambridge, Mass.

HARRIS, B. (1967) The city of the future: the problem of optimal design, *Regional Science Association Papers* **19**, 185–95.

HARRIS, B. (1968) Quantitative models of urban development: their role in metropolitan policy-making, pp. 363–412, in Perloff, H. S. and Wingo, L., Jr. (eds.), *Issues in Urban Economics*, Johns Hopkins, Baltimore.

HARRIS, C. D. and ULLMAN, E. L. (1945) The nature of cities, *Annals American Academy of Political and Social Science* **242**, 7–17.

HAUSER, P. M. and SCHNORE, L. F. (eds.) (1965) *The Study of Urbanization*, Wiley, New York.

HARVEY, R. O. and CLARK, W. A. V. (1965) The nature and economics of urban sprawl, *Land Economics* **41** (1), February.

HAYES, C. R. (1957) Suburban residential land values along the C. B. and Q. railroad, *Land Economics* **33** (2), May.

HOLTON, R. H. (1957) Price discrimination at retail: the supermarket case, *Journal of Industrial Economics* **6** (1), 13–32, October.

HOOVER, E. M. (1937) *Location Theory and the Shoe and Leather Industries*, Harvard Univ. Press, Cambridge, Mass.

HOOVER, E. M. (1948) *The Location of Economic Activity*, McGraw-Hill, New York.

HOOVER, E. M. (1968)  The evolving form and organization of the metropolis, pp. 237–84, in Perloff, H. S. and Wingo, L., Jr. (eds.), *Issues in Urban Economics*, Johns Hopkins, Baltimore.

HOOVER, E. M. and VERNON, R. (1959)  *Anatomy of a Metropolis*, Harvard Univ., Cambridge, Mass.

HORWOOD, E. and BOYCE, R. (1959)  *Studies of the Central Business District and Urban Freeway Development*, Univ. of Washington, Seattle.

HOTELLING, H. (1929)  Stability in economic competition, *Economic Journal* **39** (153), 41–57, March.

HOWARD, E. (1898)  *Garden Cities of Tomorrow* (reprinted 1960), Faber & Faber, London.

HOYT, H. (1933)  *One Hundred Years of Land Values in Chicago*, Univ. of Chicago, Chicago.

HOYT, H. (1939)  *The Structure and Growth of Residential Neighborhoods in American Cities*, US Federal Housing Administration, US Gov. Printing Office, Washington, DC.

HOYT, H. (1961)  The utility of the economic base method in calculating urban growth, *Land Economics* **37** (1), February.

HUFF, D. L. (1962)  A note on the limitations of intra-urban gravity models, *Land Economics* **38** (1), February.

HUGHES, J. T. and KOZLOWSKI, J. (1968)  Threshold analysis—an economic tool for town and regional planning, *Urban Studies* **5** (2), June.

ISARD, W. (1956)  *Location and Space Economy*, MIT, Cambridge, Mass.

ISARD, W. *et al.* (1960)  *Methods of Regional Analysis: An Introduction to Regional Science*, MIT, Cambridge, Mass.

JOHNSTON, R. J. (1969)  Some tests of a model of intra-urban population mobility: Melbourne, Australia, *Urban Studies* **6** (1), February.

KAIN, J. F. (1962)  The journey to work as a determinant of residential location, *Regional Science Association Papers* **9**, 137–60.

KAISER, E. J. (1968)  Locational decision factors in a producer model of residential development, *Land Economics* **44** (3), August.

KARIEL, H. G. (1963)  Selected factors areally associated with population growth due to net migration, *Annals Association of American Geographers* **53** (2), June.

KEEBLE, D. E. (1965)  Industrial migration from north-west London, 1940–64, *Urban Studies* **2** (1), 15–32, May.

KEYNES, J. M. (1936)  *General Theory of Employment, Interest and Money*, Macmillan, London.

KING, L. J. (1961)  A multivariate analysis of the spacing of urban settlements in the United States, *Annals Association of American Geographers* **51** (2), 222–33, June.

KNOS, D. (1962)  *Distribution of Land Values in Topeka, Kansas*, Univ. of Kansas, Lawrence, Kansas.

KOZLOWSKI, J. and HUGHES, J T. (1967)   Urban threshold theory and analysis, *Journal Town Planning Institute* **53** (2), February.

LAMPARD, E. E. (1955)   The history of cities in the economically advanced areas, *Economic Development and Cultural Change* **3**, 81–136, January.

LAMPARD, E. E. (1968)   The evolving system of cities in the United States: urbanization and economic development, in Perloff, H. S. and Wingo, L., Jr. (eds.), *Issues in Urban Economics*, Johns Hopkins, Baltimore.

LANE, T. (1966)   The urban base multiplier: an evaluation of the state of the art, *Land Economics* **42** (3), August.

LASUEN, J. R. (1969)   On growth poles, *Urban Studies* **6** (2), June.

LEAN, W. (1969)   *Economics of Land Use Planning: Urban and Regional*, Estates Gazette, London.

LEAN, W. and GOODALL, B. (1966)   *Aspects of Land Economics*, Estates Gazette, London.

LE CORBUSIER (pseud: Jeanneret-Gris, C.E ) (1947)   *City of Tomorrow and its Planning*, translated from 8th French edn. by F. Etchell, Architectural Press, London.

LESSINGER, J. (1962)   The case for scatteration, *Journal American Institute of Planners* **28**, August.

LILLIBRIDGE, R. M. (1952)   Urban size: an assessment, *Land Economics* **28** (4), November.

LOEWENSTEIN, L. K. (1963)   The location of urban land uses, *Land Economics* **39** (4), November.

LOGAN, M. I. (1966)   Locational behaviour of manufacturing firms in urban areas, *Annals Association of American Geographers* **56** (3), September.

LÖSCH, A. (1954)   *The Economics of Location*, translated by Woglom, W. H., Yale Univ., New Haven.

LOWRY, I. S. (1960)   Filtering and housing standards: a conceptual analysis, *Land Economics* **36** (4), November.

LUTTRELL, W. F. (1962)   *Factory Location and Industrial Movement*, 2 vols., National Institute of Social and Economic Research, London.

McDONALD, I. J. (1969)   The leasehold system: towards a balanced land tenure for urban development, *Urban Studies* **6** (2), June.

McMILLAN, T. E., JR. (1965)   Why manufacturers choose plant locations versus the determinants of plant locations, *Land Economics* **41** (3), August.

MADDEN, C. H. (1956)   On some indications of stability in the growth of cities in the United States, *Economic Development and Cultural Change* **4**, April.

MALISZ, B. (1969)   Implications of threshold theory for urban and regional planning, *Journal Town Planning Institute* **55** (3), March.

MANN, P. H. (1965)   *An Approach to Urban Sociology*, Routledge & Kegan Paul, London.

MARGOLIS, J. (1968)   The demand for urban public services, pp. 527–66 in Perloff, H. S. and Wingo, L., Jr. (eds.), *Issues in Urban Economics*, Johns Hopkins, Baltimore.

MARTIN, J. E. (1964)   The industrial geography of Greater London, pp. 111–42, in Clayton, R. (ed.), *The Geography of Greater London*, George Philip, London.

MARTIN, J. E. (1966)   *Greater London: An Industrial Geography*, Bell, London.

MATTILA, J. M. and THOMPSON, W. R. (1968)   Toward an econometric model of urban economic development, pp. 63–80, in Perloff, H. S. and Wingo, L., Jr. (eds.), *Issues in Urban Economics*, Johns Hopkins, Baltimore.

MAYER, H. M. (1965)   A survey of urban geography, pp. 81–113, in Hauser, P. M. and Schnore, L. F. (eds.), *The Study of Urbanization*, Wiley, New York.

MEIER, R. L. (1962)   *A Communications Theory of Urban Growth*, MIT, Cambridge, Mass.

MEYER, C. W. (1962)   Urban growth patterns and the cost of telephone service, *Land Economics* **38** (3), August.

MEYER, J. R. (1963)   Regional economics: a survey, *American Economic Review* **53**, 19–54.

MEYER, J. R., KAIN, J. F., and WOHL, M. (1966)   *The Urban Transportation Problem*, Harvard Univ., Cambridge, Mass.

MONSEN, J. (1961)   Who owns the city? *Land Economics* **38** (2), May.

MORRILL, R. L. (1965)   Expansion of the urban fringe: a simulation experiment, *Regional Science Association Papers* **15**, 185–99.

MOSER, C. A. and SCOTT, W. (1961)   *British Towns: A Statistical Study of the Social and Economic Differences*, Oliver & Boyd, Edinburgh.

MURDOCK, J. C. (1962)   Homer Hoyt and the dilemma of urban economic base analysis: a reply, *Land Economics* **38** (1), February.

MURRAY, J. C. (1970)   The central business district of Widnes: a study of location and movement, *Reading Geographer* **1**, 14–23, June.

MUTH, R. F. (1961)   The spatial structure of the housing market, *Regional Science Association Papers* **7**, 191–205.

MUTH, R. F. (1965)   The variation of population density and its components in South Chicago, *Regional Science Association Papers* **15**, 173–83.

MUTH, R. F. (1968)   Urban residential land and housing markets, pp. 285–334, in Perloff, H. S. and Wingo, L., Jr. (eds.), *Issues in Urban Economics*, Johns Hopkins, Baltimore.

MYRDAL, G. M. (1956)   *Development and Underdevelopment*, National Bank of Egypt, Cairo.

MYRDAL, G. M. (1957a)   *Rich Lands and Poor: The Road to World Prosperity*, Harper Brothers, World Perspectives, vol. 16, New York.

MYRDAL, G. M. (1957b)   *Economic Theory and Under-developed Regions*, Duckworth, London.

NEUTZE, G. M. (1965)   *Economic Policy and the Size of Cities*, Australian Nat. Univ., Canberra.

NORTH, D. C. (1955) Location theory and regional economic growth, *Journal of Political Economy* **63** (3), 243–58, June.

NOURSE, H. O. (1963) The effect of public housing on property values in St. Louis, *Land Economics* **39** (4), November.

NOURSE, H. O. (1966) The economics of urban renewal, *Land Economics* **42** (1), February.

OGBURN, W. F. and DUNCAN, O. D. (1964) City size as a sociological variable, in Burgess, E. W. and Bogue, D. J. (eds.), *Contributions to Urban Sociology*, Univ. of Chicago, Chicago.

PARKER, W. N. and DAVIES, D. G. (1962) The agricultural adjustment to urban growth, chapter 5 in Chapin, F. S., Jr., and Weiss, S. F. (eds.), *Urban Growth Dynamics*, Wiley, New York.

PENNANCE, F. G. and GRAY, H. (1968) *Choice of Housing*, Institute of Economic Affairs, London.

PERLOFF, H. S. and WINGO, L., JR. (eds.) (1968) *Issues in Urban Economics*, Johns Hopkins, Baltimore.

PHILBRICK, A. (1957) Areal functional organization in regional human geography, *Regional Science Association Papers and Proceedings* **3**.

PHILLIPS, H. S. (1942) Municipal efficiency and town size, *Journal Town Planning Institute* **28** (5), May/June.

PRED, A. R. (1966) *The Spatial Dynamics of U.S. Urban-Industrial Growth: 1800–1914*, MIT, Cambridge, Mass.

RANNELLS, J. (1956) *The Core of the City*, Columbia Univ. Press, New York.

RATCLIFFE, R. U. (1949) *Urban Land Economics*, McGraw-Hill, New York.

ROBBINS, S. M. and TERLECKYJ, N. E. (1960) *Money Metropolis*, Harvard Univ., Cambridge, Mass.

SCHECHTER, H. B. (1961) Cost-push of urban growth, *Land Economics* **37** (1), February.

SCHEITINGER, E. F. (1964) Racial succession and changing property values in residential Chicago, pp. 86–99, in Burgess, E. W. and Bogue, D. J. (eds.), *Contributions to Urban Sociology*, Univ. of Chicago, Chicago.

SCHILLER, R. (1971) Location trends of specialist services, *Regional Studies* **5** (1), 1–10, April.

SCHUMPETER, J. A. (1939) *Business Cycles: A Theoretical, Historical and Statistical Analysis of the Capitalist Process*, McGraw-Hill, New York.

SEGAL, M. (1960) *Wages in the Metropolis*, Harvard Univ., Cambridge, Mass.

SENIOR, D. (ed.) (1966) *The Regional City*, Longmans, London.

SEYFRIED, W. R. (1963) The centrality of urban land values, *Land Economics* **39** (3), August.

SHINDMAN, B. (1955) The optimum size of cities, *Canadian Geographer* **5**, 85–88.

SIMON, H. A. (1955) On a class of skew distribution functions, *Biometrika* **42**, 425–40.

SMITH, R. D. P. (1968) The changing urban hierarchy, *Regional Studies* **2** (1).

STANBACK, T. M., JR., and KNIGHT, R. V. (1970)   *The Metropolitan Economy*, Columbia, New York.

STEFANIAK, N. W. (1963)   A refinement of Haig's theory, *Land Economics* **39** (4), November.

STEWART, C. T., JR. (1958)   The size and spacing of cities, *Geographical Review* **48** (2), 222–45, April.

STOKES, C. J. (1962)   A theory of slums, *Land Economics* **38** (3), August.

STOUFFER, S. A. (1940)   Intervening opportunities: a theory relating mobility and distance, *American Sociological Review* **5** (6), December.

THOMPSON, W. R. (1965a)   *A Preface to Urban Economics*, Johns Hopkins, Baltimore.

THOMPSON, W. R. (1965b)   Urban economic growth and development in a national system of cities, pp. 431–78, in Hauser, P. M. and Schnore, L. F. (eds.), *The Study of Urbanization*, Wiley, New York.

THOMPSON, W. R. (1968)   Internal and external factors in the development of urban economics, pp. 43–62, in Perloff, H. S. and Wingo, L., Jr. (eds.), *Issues in Urban Economics*, Johns Hopkins, Baltimore.

THÜNEN, J. H. VON (1875)   *Der isolierte Staat in Beziehung auf Landwirtschaft und Nationalökonomie*, Hempel & Parey, Berlin.

TIEBOUT, C. M. (1956a)   A pure theory of local expenditures, *Journal of Political Economy* **64** (5), October.

TIEBOUT, C. M. (1956b)   The urban economic base reconsidered, *Land Economics* **32** (1), February.

TIEBOUT, C. M. (1956c)   Exports and regional economic growth, *Journal of Political Economy* **64** (2), April.

TSURU, S. (1963)   The economic significance of cities, pp. 44–55, in Handlin, O. and Burchard, J. (eds.), *The Historian and the City*, MIT, Cambridge, Mass.

TUNNARD, C. and PUSHKAREV, B. (1963)   *Man-made America: Chaos or Control*, Yale Univ. Press, New Haven.

TURVEY, R. (1957)   *The Economics of Real Property*, Allen & Unwin, London.

ULLMAN, E. L. (1958)   Regional development and the geography of concentration, *Regional Science Association Papers and Proceedings* **4**, 179–200.

ULLMAN, E. L. (1962)   The nature of cities reconsidered, *Regional Science Association Papers* **9**, 7–23.

VERNON, R. (1962)   *Metropolis 1985*, Harvard Univ., Cambridge, Mass.

WEBER, A. (1909)   *Über den Standort der Industrien, I: Reine Theorie des Standorts*, Mohr, Tübingen.

WEISS, S. F., SMITH, J. E., KAISER, E. J., and KENNEY, J. B. (1966)   *Residential Developer Decisions. A Focused View of the Urban Growth Process*, Center for Urban and Regional Studies, Institute for Research in Social Science, Univ. of North Carolina, Chapel Hill.

WELSH OFFICE (1966)   *A New Town in Mid-Wales: Consultants' Proposals*, HMSO, London.

WENDT, P. F. (1956)   *Real Estate Appraisal*, Henry Holt, New York.

WIBBERLEY, G. (1959)   *Agriculture and Urban Growth*, Michael Joseph, London.

WINGO, L., JR. (1961)   *Transportation and Urban Land*, Resources for the Future, Washington, DC.

WINGO, L., JR. (1966)   Urban renewal: objectives, analyses and information systems, pp. 1–29, in Hirsch, W. Z. (ed.), *Regional Accounts for Policy Decisions*, Johns Hopkins, Baltimore.

YEATES, M. H. (1965)   Some factors affecting the spatial distribution of Chicago land values, 1910–1960, *Economic Geography* **41** (1), January.

YEOMANS, K. A. (1968)   *Applied Statistics*, Penguin, Harmondsworth.

ZIMMER, B. G. and HAWLEY, A. H. (1961)   Suburbanization and some of its consequences, *Land Economics* **37** (1), February.

ZIPF, G. K. (1949)   *Human Behaviour and the Principle of Least Effort*, Addison-Wesley, Cambridge, Mass.

# Author Index

Alonso, W.   149, 155, 161–7, 180, 203, 230, 347
Anderson, T. R.   160, 347
Andrews, R. B.   239, 347
Applebaum, W.   114, 347

Babcock, F. M.   76, 111, 347
Baker, C. A.   296, 347
Barnett House Survey Committee   296, 347
Beckmann, M.   273, 303, 347
Berry, B. J. L.   24, 95, 134, 141, 221,293,306,312,313,317,347,349
Bloom, M.   323, 347
Blumenfeld, H.   244, 347
Bos, H. C.   304, 347
Boudeville, J. R.   259, 347
Boulding, K. E.   24, 347
Bourne, L. S.   78, 180, 213, 225, 226, 348
Boyce, R.   103, 351
Breger, G. E.   222, 348
Brigham, E. F.   103, 157, 348
Burby, R. J.   106, 171, 195, 196, 348
Burgess, E. W.   109, 111, 348
Burkhead, J.   180, 348
Burton, I.   313, 348

Campbell, A. K.   180, 348

Chamberlain, E.   120, 348
Chapin, F. S. Jr.   41, 194, 199, 220, 346, 348
Christaller, W.   305, 309, 310, 311, 348
Clark, C.   105, 155, 284, 297, 325, 348
Clark, W. A. V.   186, 188, 350
Clawson, M.   186, 188, 199, 348
Cockburn, C.   149, 170, 349
Cohen, S. B.   114, 144, 347, 348
Coke, J. G.   189, 348
Corlett, T.   149, 170, 349
Craven, E.   195, 348
Crosson, P. R.   236, 348
Cullingworth, J. B.   222, 348
Czamanski, S.   122, 234, 275, 349

Daly, M. T.   103, 349
Davies, D. G.   102, 354
Davis, O. A.   223, 349
Denman, D.   199, 349
Department of the Environment   145, 349
Dickinson, R. E.   186, 349
Donnison, D. V.   149, 170, 349
Duncan, B.   158, 349
Duncan, O. D.   32, 296, 349, 354
Dunn, E. S.   114, 349
Dunning, J. H.   99, 147, 349

# Subject Index

Indivisible factor units 31, 36, 96,
119, 138, 180, 191, 288
*see also* Factors of production
Induction 4
Industrial complex analysis 116
Industrial complexes 25, 119, 129,
290, 317
Industrial Development Certificate
132, 331, 333
Industrial estates 108, 129, 133,
145, 202, 329
Industrial location policy 132, 329,
331, 333–4
Industrial mix 12, 26, 37, 333
and urban growth 46, 265–6
Industrial Revolution 24, 25
Industrialization and urbanization
2, 19, 25–26
Industry *see* Manufacturing
Inertia 26, 107, 121, 130
Infilling 181, 198, 199, 201
Initial advantage 37, 121, 130
related to urban growth 25, 263,
267, 272, 279, 282
Innovation 2, 26, 33, 34, 36, 38,
120, 143, 213, 235, 263, 269,
277, 283, 289
and circular and cumulative causation 178, 270–2
determination of amount in any
location 40, 43, 237, 266,
268
environmental 196
Input–output analysis 237, 250–4,
275
calculation of production (inter-
industry) coefficients 252,
253
construction of tables 250–2
sectoralization of urban economy
250
use of iterative procedure in
prediction 252–4
Institutional factors 188
as framework within which econo-

mic forces operate 105, 107,
326–8
Integration, vertical *see* Vertical
integration
Interdependence 1, 17, 31, 243,
313, 327
and location 89, 129
Interdependence trap 325
and urban blight 223
Interest rates 50–51, 68, 79, 175
discounting and 53, 61, 207–8
in development 71, 74
Interests in real property *see* Real
property
Intermediate locations 116, 118–19
Internal economies of scale *see*
Economies of scale
Internal functions of activities 52,
84, 131, 143, 181
*see also* Contacts, nature of
Internal reorganization of land uses,
an adaptation process 105,
181–5, 205–32
Intervening opportunities 261
Intra-urban location decisions 80–
102, 114–47, 148–69
*see also* Households; Manufacturing; Retailing
Invasion-succession 100, 220, 224,
226
Invention 2, 26, 36, 40, 235, 237, 263
effects for urban growth 43,
178, 266, 268, 270, 277, 283
Investment 12, 44, 52, 53, 180,
206, 225, 266, 273
alternatives to real property 51
locational decisions and 115, 268,
274, 275–7
multiplier effect of 3, 235, 238
planning and 16, 322, 336–7, 339
Investors in real property, motivation of 50–52, 53

Job access and choice of residence
152, 156–9, 161

Job opportunities in urban areas
29, 40–41, 88, 149, 157, 178,
322, 331, 333, 343
Joint-stock organization 43, 267,
282
Journey to work, length of 132,
156, 157–8, 169, 232, 272,
295

Labour 37
elasticity of supply of 38, 333
specialization and 30
supply of 30, 35, 37, 38, 118, 126,
128–9, 148, 266, 270, 271,
323
Labour market, urban 2, 21, 158,
338–9
elasticity of 274
skill availability in 128
supply in 28, 146
Land
as factor of production 38
characteristics of 9–10, 85
economic concept of 75–76
legal concept of 76
Land market, urban 18, 21, 48–49
functions of 177
Land-use patterns, urban 3, 13,
80–113, 183
determination of 92–93, 179
differences in, between areas
105–7
generalized pattern of 95–102
locational choice and 82–83
principles underlying 94–95, 105
rationality of 80
similarity between areas 93
specialization in 80–81, 96–102,
229
theory and 114, 203–4
Land-use planning 107–9, 176,
338
interaction with other forms of
planning 108, 322

objectives of 227–8
spatial effects of 108, 133, 203–
4, 329
specialization and 108–9, 339–
40
types of control and coverage
200–1
Land values
aggregate
maximum 95
minimum 94–95
amenity and residential 89, 103
building values and 75, 78, 95
changing patterns of 228–30
distance from central business
district and 103, 155
effect of industry on residential
103
land use and 102–4
peak urban 97
radial roads and effect on 103
residential 103, 155, 168, 175
suburban railways and 103
urban, patterns 102–4
Landlord and Tenant Act, 1927 69
Landlord and Tenant Act, 1954 69
Landlord–tenant bargaining under
leasehold arrangements 61
Lateral expansion of urban areas
181, 201
Leasehold enfranchisement 69
Leaseholds
building 61
occupation 60
Legal factors
in urban land-use patterns 65,
105, 107
in urban change 184
Light industry *see* Manufacturing
Linear programming 254–8
graphical solution 255–8
optimum resource use and 254–
5
Linear urban areas 106, 331
*see also* Urban shape

Linkages   25, 35, 129
  *see also* Complementary linkage;
    Diagonal linkage; Horizontal
    linkage; Vertical linkage
Local accessibility   86, 101, 103,
    104, 136, 138, 139, 225, 229
Local authority-developer partner-
    ship in redevelopment   228
Local Employment Act, 1960   44
Local government, boundary prob-
    lems   194, 231, 298, 338
  economic effects of its fragment-
    ation   2, 3, 21, 47, 107, 123,
    160, 232
  reorganization of   196, 232, 282
Localization economies   29
  *see also* Economies of scale, exter-
    nal
Location
  costs of production and   84–85
  in practice   114
  investment and   115
  prestige value in   85
  relative advantage of   80–81
  sales turnover and   85
  user requirements and   84–85
Location criteria   83–84, 114–15
  *see also* Profit-maximization; Soc-
    ial costs and benefits
Location rent   156–7
Location theory
  agricultural   114
  general equilibrium and   120–1
  industrial   114
  nature of traditional   12–14, 116–
    22
  residential land use and   148–51
  urban system and   272–5
Locational analysis   114–22
Locational change   121–2
  disinvestment costs and   121
Locational choice, intra-urban as a
    business decision   114–47
Locational mobility   13, 28, 122
  relocation and   122

Locational stability   13, 121, 333
London   18, 35, 101, 318
  City of   35, 98
  shopping areas of   137

Macro-economics   11–12, 234–5
Maintenance of real property   49,
    171, 173, 174, 207, 213, 221,
    222, 223, 345
Major urban areas
  of England   37
  of U.S.A.   37
Managerial factor in urban size   46,
    282, 298
Manufacturing   122–33, 292, 335
  adjustment to controls on ex-
    pansion   343
  availability of urban labour for
    128–9
  central area   100
  central place theory and   311–13
  changing urban, patterns   130–2
  choice of intra-urban location by
    116, 123–9
  core-periphery contrasts in
    126–7
  decentralization of   122, 131–2,
    181, 187, 224
  distribution of industry policy and
    331, 333–4
  effects of government action at
    intra-urban level   132–3,
    342–3
  heavy and light   100, 122, 125–6,
    128
  location of large and small firms   180
  location theory and   13
  market factor and   124–5, 300–4
  peripheral location of heavy   124,
    126
  size of plant   28, 127–8
  suburban   102, 126
  thresholds and   125, 316

transport factor at intra-urban
 level and 102, 125
urban attraction for 25, 122–3
zone of transition as nursery for
 100, 131
Market mechanism *see* Price
 mechanism
Market-oriented locations 116,
 117, 119, 315
Market price *see* Price determination
Marketing principle of urban spacing
 307–8
Markets
 cost of production and extent of
 286–90
 determination of hexagonal, net
 300–7
 factor use thresholds and 288
 overlapping, in retailing 135,
 137, 142
 specialization and extent of 286–8
 structure of 118–19
 urban size and extent of 286–92
Massing of reserves 36
Material-oriented locations 116, 117
Megalopolis 203
Merchant banks 35, 98
Metropolitan region 28, 41, 143,
 144, 263, 282, 333
 evolution of 19, 280, 284, 292,
 310, 317
 new and expanded urban areas in
 201, 319, 334–5, 336
Micro-economics 5–7
Migration 38, 148
 inter-urban 27, 178
 rural to urban 27, 178
 suburban 27, 171
Minimum costs of friction hypothesis 86, 94
Monetary policy 328–9
Monopolies Commission 69
Monopolistic competition 120,
 134, 150, 315

Monopoly 9–10, 66, 94, 95, 135,
 273–4
Mortgages 61, 68
 *see also* Option mortgage scheme
Motivation
 of investors 50–52
 of property users 50–52
Multiple nuclei theory
 criticism of 113
 outline of 109
Multipliers 3, 235, 245, 249, 254
 and effects 12, 240–2, 244,
 270–1, 275, 279, 338


National government, role of 12,
 17
Natural endowment, economic importance of 85, 327
Neighbourhood characteristics and
 residence 152, 159, 160,
 174, 207, 213
Neighbourhood effects 159
 in redevelopment 227
 need for planning intervention
 and 227–8
 on changes in building use 184,
 219–23
 *see also* Externalities
Neighbourhood evolution, cycle of
 220–2
Neighbourhood obsolescence 211
Neighbourhood prestige, for residence 101
Neighbourhood shopping centres
 101, 202
 *see also* Shopping centres
New towns 108, 201, 318, 336
New York 203
Non-economic factors
 interaction with economic forces
 2, 19, 23, 42–45, 321, 322
 role in urbanization 19, 23, 346
 urban growth and 46, 112, 178,
 275, 320

John Rassato

HME 0634    84 888 1

[ Teppr Archer ]